MAC PROGRAMMING FOR DUMMIES™

Dan Parks Sydow

IDG Books Worldwide, Inc.
An International Data Group Company

San Mateo, California ♦ Indianapolis, Indiana ♦ Boston, Massachusetts

Mac Programming For Dummies

Published by
IDG Books Worldwide, Inc.
An International Data Group Company
155 Bovet Road, Suite 310
San Mateo, CA 94402

Library of Congress Catalog Card No.: 94-76644

ISBN: 1-56884-173-6

Printed in the United States of America

10 9 8 7 6 5 4 3 2 1

1D/QX/SX/ZU

First Printing, July 1994

 is a registered trademark of IDG Books Worldwide, Inc.

About IDG Books Worldwide

Welcome to the world of IDG Books Worldwide.

IDG Books Worldwide, Inc., is a subsidiary of International Data Group, the world's largest publisher of business and computer-related information and the leading global provider of information services on information technology. IDG was founded more than 25 years ago and now employs more than 5,700 people worldwide. IDG publishes more than 200 computer publications in 63 countries. Forty million people read one or more IDG publication each month.

Launched in 1990, IDG Books is today the fastest-growing publisher of computer and business books in the United States. We are proud to have received 3 awards from the Computer Press Association in recognition of editorial excellence, and our best-selling ...*For Dummies* series has more than 7 million copies in print with translations in more than 20 languages. IDG Books, through a recent joint venture with IDG's Hi-Tech Beijing, became the first U.S. publisher to publish a computer book in the People's Republic of China. In record time, IDG Books has become the first choice for millions of readers around the world who want to learn how to better manage their businesses.

Our mission is simple: Every IDG book is designed to bring extra value and skill-building instructions to the reader. Our books are written by experts who understand and care about our readers. The knowledge base of our editorial staff comes from years of experience in publishing, education, and journalism — experience which we use to produce books for the '90s. In short, we care about books, so we attract the best people. We devote special attention to details such as audience, interior design, use of icons, and illustrations. And because we use an efficient process of authoring, editing, and desktop publishing our books electronically, we can spend more time ensuring superior content and spend less time on the technicalities of making books.

You can count on our commitment to deliver high-quality books at competitive prices on topics customers want to read about. At IDG, we value quality, and we have been delivering quality for more than 25 years. You'll find no better book on a subject than an IDG book.

John Kilcullen
President and CEO
IDG Books Worldwide, Inc.

For More Information...

For general information on IDG Books in the U.S., including information on discounts and premiums, contact IDG Books at 800-434-3422 or 415-312-0650.

For information on where to purchase IDG books outside the U.S., contact Christina Turner at 415-312-0633.

For information on translations, contact Marc Jeffrey Mikulich, Foreign Rights Manager, at IDG Books Worldwide; FAX number: 415-358-1260.

For sales inquires and special prices for bulk quantities, contact Tony Real at 415-312-0644.

The ...*For Dummies* books series is distributed in the United States by IDG Books Worldwide, Inc. It is distributed in Canada by Macmillan of Canada, a Division of Canada Publishing Corporation; by Computer and Technical Books in Miami, Florida, for South America and the Caribbean; by Longman Singapore in Singapore, Malaysia, Thailand, and Korea; by Toppan Co. Ltd. in Japan; by Asia Computerworld in Hong Kong; by Woodslane Pty. Ltd. in Australia and New Zealand; and by Transword Publishers Ltd. in the U.K. and Europe.

IDG Books Worldwide, Inc. is a subsidiary of International Data Group. The officers are Patrick J. McGovern, Founder and Board Chairman; Walter Boyd, President. International Data Group's publications include: **ARGENTINA'S** Computerworld Argentina, Infoworld Argentina; **AUSTRALIA'S** Computerworld Australia, Australian PC World, Australian Macworld, Network World, Mobile Business Australia, Reseller, IDG Sources; **AUSTRIA'S** Computerwelt Oesterreich, PC Test; **BRAZIL'S** Computerworld, Gamepro, Game Power, Mundo IBM, Mundo Unix, PC World, Super Game; **BELGIUM'S** Data News (CW) **BULGARIA'S** Computerworld Bulgaria, Ediworld, PC & Mac World Bulgaria, Network World Bulgaria; **CANADA'S** CIO Canada, Computerworld Canada, Graduate Computerworld, InfoCanada, Network World Canada; **CHILE'S** Computerworld Chile, Informatica; **COLOMBIA'S** Computerworld Colombia, PC World; **CZECH REPUBLIC'S** Computerworld, Elektronika, PC World; **DENMARK'S** Communications World, Computerworld Danmark, Macintosh Produktkatalog, Macworld Danmark, PC World Danmark, PC World Produktguide, Tech World, Windows World; **ECUADOR'S** PC World Ecuador; **EGYPT'S** Computerworld (CW) Middle East, PC World Middle East; **FINLAND'S** MikroPC, Tietoviikko, Tietoverkko; **FRANCE'S** Distributique, GOLDEN MAC, InfoPC, Languages & Systems, Le Guide du Monde Informatique, Le Monde Informatique, Telecoms & Reseaux; **GERMANY'S** Computerwoche, Computerwoche Focus, Computerwoche Extra, Computerwoche Karriere, Information Management, Macwelt, Netzwelt, PC Welt, PC Woche, Publish, Unit; **GREECE'S** Infoworld, PC Games; **HUNGARY'S** Computerworld SZT, PC World; **HONG KONG'S** Computerworld Hong Kong, PC World Hong Kong; **INDIA'S** Computers & Communications; **IRELAND'S** ComputerScope; **ISRAEL'S** Computerworld Israel, PC World Israel; **ITALY'S** Computerworld Italia, Lotus Magazine, Macworld Italia, Networking Italia, PC Shopping, PC World Italia; **JAPAN'S** Computerworld Today, Information Systems World, Macworld Japan, Nikkei Personal Computing, SunWorld Japan, Windows World; **KENYA'S** East African Computer News; **KOREA'S** Computerworld Korea, Macworld Korea, PC World Korea; **MEXICO'S** Compu Edicion, Compu Manufactura, Computacion/Punto de Venta, Computerworld Mexico, MacWorld, Mundo Unix, PC World, Windows; **THE NETHERLANDS'** Computer! Totaal, Computable (CW), LAN Magazine, MacWorld, Totaal "Windows"; **NEW ZEALAND'S** Computer Listings, Computerworld New Zealand, New Zealand PC World, Network World; **NIGERIA'S** PC World Africa; **NORWAY'S** Computerworld Norge, C/World, Lotusworld Norge, Macworld Norge, Networld, PC World Ekspress, PC World Norge, PC World's Produktguide, Publish& Multimedia World, Student Data, Unix World, Windowsworld; IDG Direct Response; **PAKISTAN'S** PC World Pakistan; **PANAMA'S** PC World Panama; **PERU'S** Computerworld Peru, PC World; **PEOPLE'S REPUBLIC OF CHINA'S** China Computerworld, China Infoworld, Electronics Today/Multimedia World, Electronics International, Electronic Product World, China Network World, PC and Communications Magazine, PC World China, Software World Magazine, Telecom Product World; IDG HIGH TECH BEIJING'S New Product World; IDG SHENZHEN'S Computer News Digest; **PHILIPPINES'** Computerworld Philippines, PC Digest (PCW); **POLAND'S** Computerworld Poland, PC World/Komputer; **PORTUGAL'S** Cerebro/PC World, Correio Informatico/Computerworld, Informatica & Comunicacoes Catalogo, MacIn, Nacional de Produtos; **ROMANIA'S** Computerworld, PC World; **RUSSIA'S** Computerworld-Moscow, Mir - PC, Sety; **SINGAPORE'S** Computerworld Southeast Asia, PC World Singapore; **SLOVENIA'S** Monitor Magazine; **SOUTH AFRICA'S** Computer Mail (CIO), Computing S.A., Network World S.A., Software World; **SPAIN'S** Advanced Systems, Amiga World, Computerworld Espana, Communicaciones World, Macworld Espana, NeXTWORLD, Super Juegos Magazine (GamePro), PC World Espana, Publish; **SWEDEN'S** Attack, ComputerSweden, Corporate Computing, Natverk & Kommunikation, Macworld, Mikrodatorn, PC World, Publishing & Design (CAP), Datalngenjoren, Maxi Data, Windows World; **SWITZERLAND'S** Computerworld Schweiz, Macworld Schweiz, PC Tip; **TAIWAN'S** Computerworld Taiwan, PC World Taiwan; **THAILAND'S** Thai Computerworld; **TURKEY'S** Computerworld Monitor, Macworld Turkiye, PC World Turkiye; **UKRAINE'S** Computerworld; **UNITED KINGDOM'S** Computing /Computerworld, Connexion/Network World, Lotus Magazine, Macworld, Open Computing/Sunworld; **UNITED STATES'** Advanced Systems, AmigaWorld, Cable in the Classroom, CD Review, CIO, Computerworld, Digital Video, DOS Resource Guide, Electronic Entertainment Magazine, Federal Computer Week, Federal Integrator, GamePro, IDG Books, Infoworld, Infoworld Direct, Laser Event, Macworld, Multimedia World, Network World, PC Letter, PC World, PlayRight, Power PC World, Publish, SWATPro, Video Event; **VENEZUELA'S** Computerworld Venezuela, PC World; **VIETNAM'S** PC World Vietnam.

About the Author

Dan Parks Sydow is a graduate of Milwaukee School of Engineering, with a degree in Computer Engineering. He has worked on software in several diverse areas, including the display of images of the heart for medical purposes. Since Dan can't stand the sight of blood — even electronic blood — he quit his nine-to-five job as a software engineer to become a freelance writer.

Dan got hooked on Macintosh programming ten years ago when the Macintosh was first introduced. Since then he has spared no effort in avoiding all other types of computer. He enjoys shedding light on topics that people have been led to believe were beyond their reach, and has written several computer programming books, all dealing with the Macintosh.

Credits

Vice President and Publisher
Chris Williams

Editorial Director
Trudy Neuhaus

Brand Manager
Amorette Pederson

Manuscript Editor
Julie Stillman

Technical Reviewer
Tim Monroe

Production Director
Beth Jenkins

Assoc. Production Coordinator
Valery Bourke

Production Staff
Kent Gish
Adam P. Harrison
Drew R. Moore
Tricia R. Reynolds
Gina Scott

Production Quality Control
Steve Peake

Proofreader
Deborah Kaufmann

Book Design
University Graphics

Cover Design
Kavish + Kavish

Dedication

To my wife, Nadine.

Acknowledgments

Many thanks to Chris Williams, Trudy Neuhaus, and Amy Pedersen for making this book happen; to Julie Stillman and Tim Monroe for so nicely cleaning up my text with their edits and reviews; to Carole McClendon for introducing me to IDG Books; to Rustle Laidman for a much-appreciated last-minute technical assist; and, last but not least, to Mike Doyle for testing the software.

(The publisher would like to give special thanks to Patrick J. McGovern, without whom this book would not have been possible.)

Contents at a Glance

Cartoons at a Glance
by Rich Tennant

Table of Contents

• •

The 5th Wave

By Rich Tennant

Introduction

● ●

*M*acintosh computers are easy and fun to use. Even people who have never used a computer before find that within just a couple of hours they feel comfortable using a Mac to type a letter or draw a simple picture. But what about programming a Macintosh — is that also easy and fun? Not always. Don't worry though — it doesn't have to be nearly as painful as you may have been led to believe.

You've picked up this book for one of several reasons. You've programmed a computer, but not a Macintosh. Or you've never programmed, but are curious enough to try your hand at it. Or, you just happen to be the type that enjoys pain. Now, now — let's end that fallacy right here. Contrary to popular belief, no ordinance or law exists that states that the words "programming" and "fate-worse-than-death" must always appear together.

Why *is* programming thought of as aggravating, time-consuming, detail-oriented, and difficult? Because it can be — as practiced by professional software engineers. What about people who — instead of aspiring to become professional programmers — just happen to enjoy a good challenge? For you, there's good news. And this book is it.

Programming can be fun, interesting, and rewarding. It doesn't have to be difficult. Just learning the very basics of Macintosh programming is enough to enable you to write a program that uses windows, menus, and graphics. You don't need a degree in computer engineering or a technical reference book the size of the New York City telephone directory. Instead, you need a book that skips the technical details and theory. You need a book that presents you with just the essentials necessary to write a program that will run on a Macintosh. You need a book with a bright yellow cover, and a title along the lines of *Mac Programming For Dummies*.

About This Book

Many books about computers are reference books. Only when you need help with a problem, do you refer to the book. As such, that type of book isn't meant to be read from cover to cover. This isn't one of those books.

You may have read computer books that teach you how to use an existing program on your computer. Books like that show you how to do certain things with a certain program. An example might be learning how to format text using WordPerfect. This isn't one of those books.

Very good — now you know what this book isn't. What then, is this book? It's a book that teaches you how to actually write a brand-new, never-before-seen-by-another-person, Macintosh program. If you've never written a computer program, this may sound like an insurmountable task. If you have programmed, but not on a Macintosh, this may sound like an insurmountable task. It isn't.

Now, I know that on the bookstore shelf, just inches away from where this book was sitting, were Macintosh programming books that were twice as thick as this one. Books with enough techno mumbo-jumbo and four-syllable words to make a rocket scientist scratch his head in wonderment. How then can I make the claim that anyone can learn — with minimal effort — to write a Macintosh program? Here's how. I:

- ✔ Spare you the unnecessary technical details.
- ✔ Make no attempt to interest advanced Mac programmers.
- ✔ Spare you the unnecessary technical details.
- ✔ Make no attempt to cover every facet of Macintosh programming.
- ✔ Spare you the unnecessary technical details.
- ✔ Avoid assumptions about what you already know about programming.

If you want to delve into the deepest, darkest, inner workings of a computer — don't buy this book. If you want to learn the basics of programming the Macintosh — do buy this book. If you want to learn the fundamental concepts that will allow you to create a Macintosh program that will open a window, draw and write to that window, and display menus — do buy this book.

Because the concern of this book is with writing programs, not using them, it's important that you know just how to use this book. Which leads to the very next topic . . .

How to Use This Book

The very fact that you've bought, or are considering buying, a programming book with the word "Dummies" in the title tells me that you're probably new to programming. Or at least new to programming the Macintosh. Learning to program is an incremental process. And you should learn each increment, or step, in a specific order. As your experience in writing Macintosh programs grows, you'll be able to take liberties and try out ideas of your own. But for now, I strongly recommend that you start, as they say, at the beginning. I won't give any exotic examples, or pull any fast ones, but the programming examples will build on material presented in previous chapters. So do read the book from cover to cover — front cover to back cover, that is!

Who Are You?

You probably picked up this book for one of three reasons:

   ✔ You've never programmed a computer before.

   ✔ You've programmed a computer, but never a Macintosh.

   ✔ You've tried programming a Mac, but were frustrated in your attempts.

If you fall into any one of the above three categories, this book is for you. If you have prior programming experience, that's great. But this book never assumes you do. The explanations and programming examples make no assumptions about your programming knowledge — everything starts at step one.

Speaking of programming examples . . . you will need a Macintosh if you want to create a Macintosh program. Sure, you can read this book and think you've learned what to do. To really be sure, however, you have to try out the examples given in the book.

If you don't own a Mac, find someone who does. Use it as often as you can (I'm assuming, of course, that you know this person). With this book firmly in hand, sit down at that person's Mac and test your newly learned programming skills.

What kind of Macintosh do you need? Just about any model will do. The Classic, MacII, LC, Centris, Quadra — even the PowerBook — are all suitable.

Along with a Macintosh you'll need a program called a compiler. A compiler turns words that are readable by you, the person, into ones readable by a Macintosh, the computer. If you don't have a compiler, buy the THINK C compiler from Symantec Corporation. It's available in several versions, such as THINK C 6.0, THINK C 7.0, Symantec C++ 6.0, and Symantec C++ 7.0. All the examples in this book work with any of these versions.

How This Book Is Organized

This book contains six major parts. Each part is composed of three or more chapters — that makes the material easy to digest. But please remember to chew thirty times before swallowing.

Just a bit earlier I recommended reading this book in order, without skipping material. Let me elaborate just a little. I don't want to scare you into thinking you must read at a snail's pace, avoiding at all cost the skipping of even a single word. Before and after I list any source code — that stuff that lets the computer understand what you want it to do — I'll quickly review the concepts the source code covers.

If you've programmed before, but not on a Macintosh, I hereby grant you permission to skim — and perhaps even skip — a chapter or two that pertain to the most basic of programming concepts. In particular, you may be familar with the material in chapters 13, 14, and 15. For the rest of you, don't skip — you'll be quizzed at the end!

Part I   Introducing the Macintosh (the Basics)

What makes the Macintosh different from other computers? What makes programming the Mac different from programming other computers? I give up, what? Just kidding. Here, you'll see why you need a book that devotes itself to just the Macintosh. You'll also become convinced that programming need not be such a scary endeavor — honest!

Part II   Resources: This Is Programming?

Text is boring. Windows, menus, icons, and pictures are neat. The Macintosh is fun because programs that run on it contain some or all of these neat elements. That makes Mac programming fun to look at and fun to work with. All this talk about fun is fine, but what about adding all of these cool items to a program you're creating? Is that process fun, too? As a matter of fact, it is! And one of the reasons is resources. Resources are the means of creating things such as windows and menus with — hold on to your hat — absolutely no programming on your part! In this part of the book you'll learn exactly what resources are and how you can easily create them.

Part III   Using a Compiler

To write a program, you type in a series of commands — commonly referred to as *source code*. A computer can't, however, understand the words you type into it. The words have to be translated into numbers — something a computer loves. Turning words into numbers sounds like a tedious and ugly task. Fortunately, you'll never know for sure — because you'll never have to do it. Instead, you just run a program that does the work for you. The program that performs this translation is a *compiler*. In Part III I talk about what a compiler is and how to use one. In particular I'll talk about Symantec's THINK C compiler — the most popular Macintosh compiler on the market.

Part IV   Learning the C Language

While it would make things easy if you could type in English language statements like, "Place a window on the screen and draw in it," things haven't quite progressed to that point — yet. Instead, you need to be a little more formal in the ways you tell the Mac to do something. That's what a computer language is for. When you write a computer program, you do so in a computer language. There are several languages to choose from. This book gives all examples in the C language — the most popular programming language. This part of the book describes computer languages in general, and the C language in particular.

Part V   The Moment of Truth: Writing a Program!

With the preliminaries out of the way, it's time to create a Macintosh program — a real one. A program with a window and a menu. You provide a little flair to the program by adding animation to it. This section describes a very simple technique that allows you to bring your program to life. And isn't that what the Macintosh is all about?

Part VI   The Part of Tens

Ten things to do in order to make a program, and ten things you don't want to do. And, ten indispensible functions — aids that will make writing a program with menus and windows easy.

Part VII   Appendices

You won't remember everything that you read in this book. So I've provided a few appendices for those occasions when you get stuck: Appendix A is a reference for the C language; Appendix B is a reference for the Toolbox; Appendix C will help you solve your compiling dilemmas; and, Appendix D is the glossary.

Icons Used in This Book

Optional reading — while not technically intense, these explanations may not be suitable for small children! ■

Don't worry, you can't wreck your Mac. But you can wreck the work you're doing on it — I'll point out the areas where this could happen. ■

Programmers are crazy about optimizing their efforts — just about *everything* has a shortcut. I'll note the more worthwhile ones. ■

Programming is shrouded in secrecy. Knowing a little Mac psychology goes a long way to understanding why some seemingly obscure terminology needn't be. ■

What's Next?

Why, reading the book — of course. The introduction is over and it's time to program. And, dare I say it . . . to actually have a little fun!

Part I
Introducing the Macintosh (the Basics)

In this part . . .

Line a few different types of computers in a row and, by looking at the screens of each, pick out the Macintosh. It's not to hard to do, right? That's because the Mac has a look all its own. The Macintosh seems to stand out — even when compared to other systems that use menus, windows, and icons. Because the Mac is different from other computers, it probably won't come as much of a surprise to learn that the way in which the Mac is programmed is a little different, too.

"Different" is often equated with "difficult." Well, that's not always the case. And programming the Mac is one example. To prove it, this part presents the code for an actual, honest-to-goodness Macintosh program — code that takes up less than a single page in this book!

Chapter 1

Windows, Menus, and a Mouse — That's the Mac

• •

In This Chapter

▶ What a graphical user interface is

▶ The parts of the interface

▶ The parts that you, the programmer, need to work with

• •

During the telecast of the Super Bowl in January of 1984 a commercial — one that would be aired only a single time — told of the emergence of a new computer. This computer, it seemed, would change the way people thought of computing. The computer was, of course, the Macintosh. While it may not have revolutionized computing overnight, in the last ten years the Mac has lived up to its promise of changing how people would interact with computers.

The Graphical User Interface

What was it about the Macintosh that, a decade ago, set it apart from all other personal computers? It was its *graphical user interface*. The graphical user interface, or GUI (pronounced "gooey"), is made up of icons, menus, and windows. "Graphical user interface" is a mouthful, and GUI is just too darned ugly a word — so from here on I'll usually just refer to it as the "interface."

A decade ago, most computers didn't have an interface like the Mac. The interface computers had was *DOS* (Disk Operating System). Anyone working on a DOS computer will probably see a lot of words on their screen — not pictures. They tend to type keyboard commands to get things done — they generally don't use a mouse.

Macintosh programmers don't care much for DOS programmers. It's nothing personal, though. It's just that Mac programmers feel they're riding the wave into the 21st century, and other programmers are still floundering about in the Stone Age. ∎

Here's what a user of a typical DOS computer might see on the screen:

```
C:\> CD \MYDATA
C:\MYDATA > DIR
Directory of C:\MYDATA
NOTES.WP   1412  12-28-93  13:26p
  1 file(s)      1412 bytes
```

Pretty exciting stuff, huh? Compare the DOS screen with a look at a Macintosh screen, with its windows, menus, and icons:

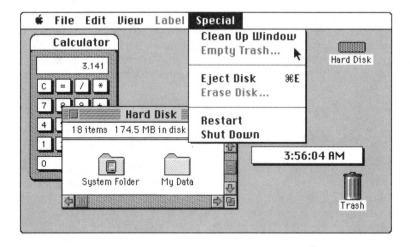

Looking at these two figures, it's quite apparent why many people prefer to do their work on a Macintosh computer. The screen of a Mac provides a much friendlier *environment*, or atmosphere, to work in.

By the way... "DOS" is pronounced "doss," not "dooze" or "dose." You may already know that, but I just wanted to be sure. That's to prevent you from being on the receiving end of a scornful look or comment from an established Mac programmer. That brings us to another bit of Mac psychology (really, computer programmer psychology in general). Some programmers like to make themselves look better by making others look worse. Jumping all over someone who incorrectly pronounces a computer-related term is a favorite tactic of this type of programmer. I'll help you weather this storm by providing the pronunciation of words whose pronunciation isn't intuitive. ▪

The Macintosh computer isn't the only one with a graphical user interface. IBM and IBM-compatible computers can run Microsoft Windows. Most would agree that the Macintosh, however, is the standard by which other graphical user interfaces are judged. Microsoft Windows evolved from DOS — so most programmers who write Windows programs are very familiar with DOS. Many "think DOS" when they program. That's not true about Mac programmers. The Mac's graphical user interface didn't evolve from a text-based system like DOS. Right from its introduction in 1984, the Mac had a graphical interface.

Interface Parts

Users of Macintosh programs become familiar with the various parts of the graphical user interface — such as menus and icons — so that they can make better use of the computer. As a soon-to-be Macintosh programmer, you'll become familiar with these same interface components — but from a different perspective.

Using the Mouse

The mouse is used to make menu choices, move windows, and double-click on icons. In general, the mouse is the user's means of interacting with the computer. Or, if you want to go toe-to-toe with Mac programmers, you can say that the mouse is the standard input device for communicating with the Macintosh.

Working at Your Desk

The interface begins at the ever-present background screen. Apple calls it the *desktop* — that gray area that covers most of your Macintosh monitor. The analogy is, of course, that you organize electronic files and folders on the desktop as you would real ones on a real desk. Just what a trash can is actually doing on *top* of your desk is anyone's guess. Oh well, no analogy is perfect. Still, the desktop is a catchy name, and one that is deeply embedded in the history of the Macintosh.

Itty-Bitty Pictures

An *icon* is a picture. Not just any picture, though. It is a small graphic symbol that is a representation of something. If an icon is well designed, its representation will be obvious. Icons are small — about a half-inch square or less. Here are a few of the icons you'll find on the Macintosh desktop:

Ordering from the Menu

Most computers perform an action in response to a command the user types in. On a Macintosh, you don't have to type orders. Instead, you order from a *menu* — sometimes referred to as a *pull-down menu*. To issue a command, you click the mouse on a menu name and then make a selection from the list of commands that drop down. Since a menu does in fact drop down, rather than pull down, you might think that a better name would be drop-down menu. That may be true, but it's a little late in the game to make a change in terminology.

Menus are one of the most powerful features of the Macintosh interface. Having all the available commands spelled out before you as menu *items* means you don't have to memorize or look up the names of commands. And even if a command is easy to remember, most people find selecting a menu item quicker than typing in a command. Below is a figure that shows how to duplicate a file in DOS and on a Mac:

C:\> COPY DOC1.WP DOC2.WP

File	
New Folder	⌘N
Open	⌘O
Print	⌘P
Close Window	⌘W
Get Info	⌘I
Sharing...	
Duplicate	⌘D
Make Alias	
Put Away	⌘Y
Find...	⌘F
Find Again	⌘G
Page Setup...	
Print Window...	

Windows Give

Windows are an important part of any graphical user interface. Windows are so important that Microsoft has named its own GUI for IBM computers after them. For users of IBM computers (and clones), Microsoft Windows is all but replacing DOS. That gives you a hint at how much people enjoy working with a graphical user interface.

Unlike a DOS program that writes text directly to the screen, a program designed for a computer with a graphical user interface writes text to a window. The same applies to graphics. Because just about everything on a Mac is done in a window, the creation of a window will be one of the first programming tasks you'll learn.

Dialogs Get

Windows generally *display* information. How does a program *receive* information from the user? Often it's through a *dialog box*. Here's a couple of dialog boxes:

You can see that a dialog box may or may not look a lot like a window. And, it may or may not behave like one. How can you tell the difference between a window and a dialog box? If you are the programmer who designed the program, you'll know. If you're just someone using a program, you might not. Here's a scientific, highly technical test you can apply to determine if the thing you're looking at on the screen is a window or a dialog box: if it has a bunch of stuff in it that you can click on, it's probably a dialog box.

Speaking of stuff in a dialog box — let's take a look the definition of most of the different types of items you might find in a dialog box:

- ✔ *Push button:* A mouse click on one of these causes some immediate action to take place. The OK or Done button found in just about every dialog box is the prime example.

- ✔ *Radio buttons:* These allow you to select from a number of options. This type of button travels in packs — never alone. Only one member of the group is ever selected at any given time.

✔ *Check box:* Some options can be turned on or off. A check box lets you do that.

✔ *Text box:* If you've ever typed a number or word into a rectangle, you've worked with a text box. If a program needs information — whether it be your bowling score or your date of birth — this item allows you to type it in for the Mac to use. A text box is also called an *edit box* sometimes, just to confuse you.

Here's a figure that contains an example of each of the dialog items mentioned above:

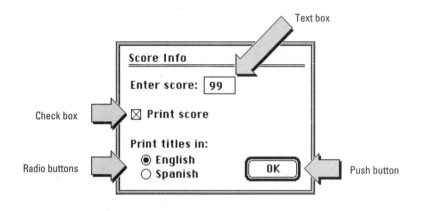

Wrapping It Up

That's just about it for the interface — except for one more figure. I created the following figure for two purposes. First, I wanted to summarize many of the parts of the Mac's graphical user interface in one figure. Second, I wanted to test the capabilities of IDG Books' layout department — could they accurately reduce the size of my figure?

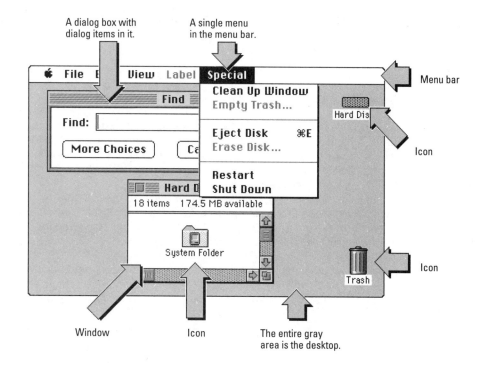

A dialog box with dialog items in it.

A single menu in the menu bar.

Menu bar

Icon

Icon

Window   Icon   The entire gray area is the desktop.

The Parts You Need

The list of things that a programmer can do with the parts of the interface is just about endless. So I obviously can't produce it in its entirety. But here are a few common tasks Mac programmers can perform:

- ✔ Build a functioning, pull-down menu into a program.
- ✔ Add a movable window to display graphics, text, or animation.
- ✔ Create a dialog box with radio buttons, check boxes, text boxes, and push buttons.
- ✔ Allow a program to open, save, and print files.
- ✔ Design a unique icon.

The list goes on and on. This wealth of programming options really gets a seasoned programmer excited. It also can scare the living daylights out of someone who hasn't programmed! While many programmers may follow the philosophy of "the more the merrier," you should keep one very important point in mind:

You don't *have* to include everything from the above list for a program to run on a Macintosh. In fact, in this book I'll concentrate only on the first two items in the list — menus and windows.

Menus and Windows Will Do It

Once you know how to create a program that uses windows and menus, you then know many of the basic techniques of programming for the Mac's graphical user interface. What can you do with just menus and windows? Let's look at menus first.

Want to give a user of your program the ability to open a window? Add a menu item called Open that does just that. Want to let the user draw a circle? Create a menu item called Draw Circle. Any option you want to provide for the user can be added by creating a menu item in your program.

What about displaying text or graphics? A window can contain either words or drawings, or both. What if you want to create an animated effect — a moving picture? Because a window can hold graphics, it can also hold moving graphics.

The figure below summarizes why a program with but a single menu and a single window allows you to write a true Macintosh program.

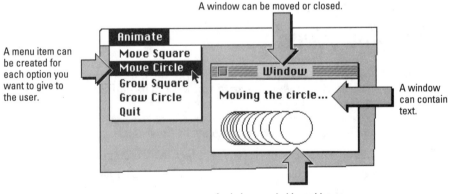

A window can be moved or closed.

A menu item can be created for each option you want to give to the user.

A window can contain text.

A window can hold graphics or even moving graphics—animation.

So, You Think You're Getting Shortchanged, Huh?

As I just said, a program with a menu and a window allows you to write a program that will do just about anything you want it to do. Menus and windows — that's it? That's it as far as what the user of one of your programs will see. You, the programmer, will have become wiser about far more than that. In covering these two parts of the interface, you'll pick up knowledge and experience in all of the following programming areas:

- Menus: how to make, display, and work with them.
- Windows: how to display, move, and draw in them.
- Text: how to write words — in different sizes and styles — to a window.
- Graphics: how to draw lines and shapes to create pictures.
- Animation: how to make graphics that appear to move.
- Events: how to see just what the user is doing.

That last point sounds particularly interesting — and possibly illegal! Macintosh programs — more than many other types of programs — are interactive. A user does something, and the program responds. That implies that the program must somehow know what the user is doing. Macintosh users enjoy the resulting feeling of control. And Macintosh programmers enjoy creating programs that satisfy users. ■

After you read this book, and following the examples given in it, I'm willing to bet that you'll be hooked on Macintosh programming. What do you do after that? Remember those other programming books you saw in the bookstore — the ones on the shelf right by this one? Those very fat, wordy, intimidating ones? They won't look so intimidating anymore. Once you've mastered the techniques presented in this book, you'll be ready to move on to any one of the host of intermediate-level programming books on the market.

Chapter 2

What Makes Macintosh Programming So Different?

● ●

In This Chapter

▶ Why the interface presents special programming challenges

▶ How programs start out as source code

▶ Why DOS programs aren't better — even though they're easier to write

▶ How information is transferred to and from a program

▶ Why menus and windows are interesting and fun to use and program

● ●

The programming skills and techniques needed to write a program that runs on a Macintosh are different from those necessary to write a program designed to run on other computers. In this chapter I'll cover those differences — but in only the most basic sense. I won't discuss any of the details of writing a program. There's plenty of time — or should I say pages — left for that.

The Interface — That's the Difference

Why are Mac programs easy to use? Because the programmer puts extra effort into things to make it that way. For a computer that has a graphical user interface, there are more things that you, the programmer, are responsible for. So it's the interface that's the key difference between programming a Macintosh and programming other computers. With that said, should I wrap up this chapter right here and now? Sorry, you don't get off the hook quite that easily . I'll use the rest of this chapter to elaborate on the differences between Mac programming and non-Macintosh programming.

Programmers who write programs for DOS computers just write lines of text to the screen. They don't have to worry about how to display a window or create a pull-down menu, and all that other fun stuff — like programmers who write programs for Windows or Macintosh do. If you haven't done much programming — or any programming for that matter — you may actually have an advantage over programmers with years of experience on DOS computers. No, I'm not just saying that to make you feel better! It's true. Those programmers have to "unlearn" many of their old ways of doing things. You get to start with a fresh, clean slate. By the way, if you find a slate, let me know. I haven't seen one around for years!

Before explaining the differences between Macintosh programming and other types of programming, I'll digress a bit. Programming — any programming — relies on *source code*. That's the stuff that lets you tell a computer just what to do. Since you'll be reading quite a bit about source code in the rest of this book, I'll define it here and now.

Secret Agents Aren't the Only Ones Using Code!

A *programmer* creates a program — a *user* simply uses that program. The programmer writes *source code* to create the program — the user doesn't know or doesn't give a hoot about source code. Before this book is over, you — the programmer — will have become very intimate with this thing called source code.

Like a relationship with a person, your relationship with source code will be both very satisfying and very frustrating. Just when you think you have things all figured out, along comes a new twist or turn that throws you completely off course.

I know many of the pitfalls that most new Mac programmers encounter — so I can help you bypass them. I've programmed the Mac for a decade, so I can aid you in your relationship with source code — I'm an expert at relationships. Of course, my six ex-wives might not agree… ■

Learning the Language

Computers, while exceedingly powerful, lack one important capability that people possess — the ability to interpret. For example, you and I know the difference between two uses of a word such as "lead." If I were to say, "You can lead a horse to water," or, "Lead is a heavy, soft, malleable metal," you could recognize these two very different uses of the word. From the words that surround a word — that is, by the context in which it is used — people can interpret its meaning. That's a skill that a computer doesn't have.

How do you then get a computer, which has no interpretive power, to understand and do what you want it to do? By issuing it commands. But not just any old commands. You use only commands that are defined by a rigid set of rules. That way, nothing is left open to interpretation. That's what a *computer language* is all about.

Like a spoken language — such as English or Spanish — a computer language has a limited vocabulary. Fortunately, the number of words a computer language allows you to use is very limited. That means learning a computer language is much easier than learning a spoken language.

Different Languages

Just as there are different spoken languages, there are different computer languages. Wouldn't just one be enough? Again, like spoken languages, one would be enough — if you could get everyone in the world to agree to the same one! Over time, different people, different universities, and different companies have all created what they felt was the best computer language. And over time, as computers changed, computer languages have changed.

BASIC, Pascal, C, and C++ are the names of four common computer languages. In this book I use the C language for all of the programming examples. What criteria did I use to make this choice? I studied, experimented, and worked with each. Then I accepted the $100 bribe Dennis Ritchie, the creator of the C language, offered me. Seriously though, I selected the C language because it is currently the language of choice of Macintosh programmers.

Computer programmers battle ceaselessly about which language is the best one to use. Like debates about politics or religion, no one ever wins one of these arguments. Should you be in the vicinity of one of these "discussions," my best advice is to head for cover! ■

I devote the five chapters of Part IV to the C language — so I won't make an attempt to explain the details of it here.

All Programs Were Once Source Code

The rough draft of this book, whether I wrote it in English, Spanish, or Sanskrit, is called a manuscript. The same can be said of computer languages — regardless of which you use, you get the same result: *source code*. No matter which computer language a programmer uses to write a program, the result is a page — or perhaps tens or hundreds of pages — of commands. The culmination of the programmer's efforts is called source code, whether the programming language was BASIC, Pascal, or C.

How does source code differ from the program itself — the program that the user double-clicks on to run? The source code is transformed into the actual program by something called a compiler. A compiler performs this feat in just a couple of seconds. I discuss compilers in Part III. ▪

Source code — simply called *code* by most programmers — can be thought of as the interior of a program. It's something the user of a program doesn't see or work with. What the user does see — menus, windows, graphics — can be thought of as the exterior of a program.

If you've seen programs that run on a Macintosh and programs that run on other types of computers, you may have noticed that they don't closely resemble one another. Their exteriors are different. Does that mean that their interiors — the source code from which the programs evolved — also look different? Clever you — indeed it does! I won't show you any source code in this chapter. I will, however, explain in general terms how the different look of two programs means that there was a different programming effort put into each. In fact, I'll go into that right now...

Programs — Inside and Outside

A program that runs on a Macintosh computer is easier to use than a DOS program. A Mac program is easier to use because its exterior — what the user sees — contains useful features such as windows and menus. What about its interior — its source code? Is the code for a Macintosh program easier to write than the code for a DOS program? Instead of answering that question directly, I now present an analogy that provides the answer. Sure, it's annoying not to get a quick answer — but this short story will be helpful.

Imagine a car built in the 1970s. On a cold day you'd start the car by pumping the gas pedal several times, and perhaps then holding the pedal to the floor as you turned the ignition over. To stop the car on a wet or icy road you'd pump the brake pedal. What about a car of the 1990s? With fuel injection you simply turn the key and start the car — regardless of the temperature outside. With anti-lock brakes you simply press down on the brake pedal — regardless of road conditions. The car of the 90s is easier to use and works better than a car built in the 70s. But which would you rather repair yourself?

In order to improve the parts of the car that the driver uses, the parts on the inside became more complicated. That's true with many things that are affected by technology. A smooth, sleek, easy-to-use exterior masks a complex, highly refined interior.

This isn't Chilton's Auto Guide, this is a book on programming the Mac. So how does all of the above pertain to programming? A Macintosh program is like the car of the 90s, while its DOS counterpart is the car of the 70s. So while the user of the Mac version finds it is easier to use and more intuitive than the DOS version, the programmer who writes the Macintosh version sees things from a different perspective. The programmer of the Mac version of a program is responsible for more things than the programmer of the DOS version.

What about that other graphical user interface — Windows? Is the Mac programmer responsible for more, or different, things than a Windows programmer? More, no. Different, yes. While there are similarities between how a Mac program and a Windows program look, the programmers responsible for writing the source code for each do things in a different way.

DOS Programs — Easier Doesn't Mean Better

I just stated that it's easier for a programmer to write a DOS program because the programmer is responsible for less. Just what is meant by "responsible for"? Let's take a look. As you read, refer to the following figure. It shows part of a screen displaying a DOS program that acts as a very simple calculator:

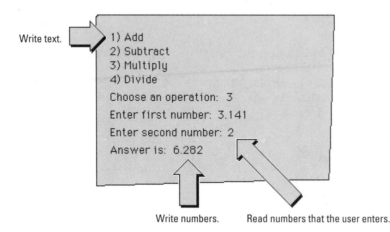

Write text.

1) Add
2) Subtract
3) Multiply
4) Divide

Choose an operation: 3

Enter first number: 3.141

Enter second number: 2

Answer is: 6.282

Write numbers.   Read numbers that the user enters.

What is the person who programmed this calculator responsible for? Writing text to the screen. The menu that lets a user select an arithmetic operation is one example. The programmer also wrote code that lets the program read numbers typed in by the user. Finally, the programmer wrote code that performs a calculation and then displays, or *writes*, a number to the screen.

Data is a general term for letters, words, or numbers.

When a computer program displays words or numbers on the screen for the user to view, it is *writing* data to the screen.

When a computer program receives words or numbers from the user, it is *reading* data. The most common means of entering data for the program to read is by typing on the keyboard. There is another means, but it is usually not available in DOS programs. Macintosh programs sometimes allow you to use the mouse to enter data. ■

The number of things that the DOS programmer is responsible for doesn't sound overwhelming — and it's not. Because a DOS program doesn't contain windows, icons, or menus, a DOS program is easier to write than a Macintosh program.

To someone who hasn't programmed before, or has programmed very little, easier surely sounds better than harder. But there is a price one pays to write a simple program — you end up with a simple program! A simple program, like the calculator pictured a couple of pages back, doesn't look very interesting and doesn't do a whole heck of a lot.

Macintosh Programs — Interesting, Fun, Exciting!

Why has the Macintosh become so popular over the last several years? Mac programs are easy to use, fun to work with, and interesting to look at. Remember how the DOS calculator program looked? The figure below shows a Macintosh calculator program. It is a free program that Apple includes with all Macintosh computers.

In the previous section I discussed the things a DOS programmer would be responsible for should he decide to write a calculator program. Now let's look at what a Macintosh programmer would be responsible for if he were to write a spiffy calculator program like the one pictured:

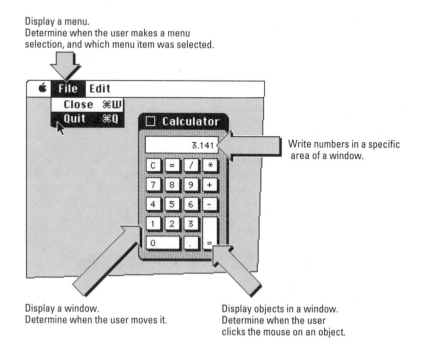

Display a menu.
Determine when the user makes a menu
selection, and which menu item was selected.

Write numbers in a specific
area of a window.

Display a window.
Determine when the user moves it.

Display objects in a window.
Determine when the user
clicks the mouse on an object.

As I discuss the responsibilities of the Mac programmer, I'll also point out how they differ from those of the DOS programmer. Heck, I've got to tie this conversation to the chapter title at some point!

Giving Information

The preceding example shows that the Mac programmer, like the DOS programmer, writes data and reads data. But the Mac programmer does both a little differently. Let's look at writing data first. Remember where the calculated result was written to in the DOS calculator? In a DOS program, data is written at the current location of the cursor:

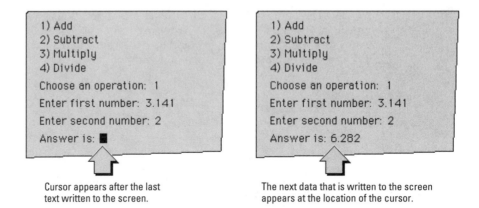

Cursor appears after the last
text written to the screen.

The next data that is written to the screen
appears at the location of the cursor.

In a Mac program, data can be written *anywhere* in a window. In the Macintosh
calculator program, the user clicks the mouse on a number or symbol button
and the corresponding number or symbol is written in the white box at the top
of the calculator. As a digit is entered, it always appears at the far right of the
white box. Here the "3", ".", and the "1" are entered one after another:

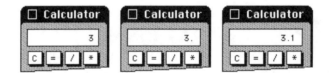

Not only can text and numbers be written anywhere in a Macintosh window,
they can even be made to overlap other text. And the *style* — the appearance —
of data can be altered:

Macintosh text
        Macintosh text

The ability to control the appearance and placement of data is an important
feature that separates the Macintosh from many other computers. Another
difference is how the user of a program enters data into the Mac.

Getting Information

Programs written for DOS computers read data by pausing and waiting for the user to type in words or numbers. Pressing the Enter or Return key signals the program to read the typed value and then continue on. Once again, the calculator example:

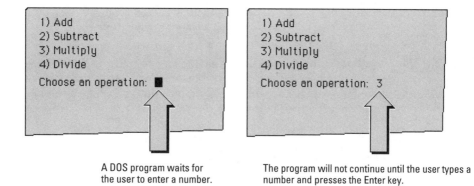

A DOS program waits for the user to enter a number.	The program will not continue until the user types a number and presses the Enter key.

Ready for one of the most central of all Macintosh programming themes? Ready or not, here it is: *The user is the boss*. People like using the Macintosh because they feel as if they are in control. A good Macintosh program seldom freezes the screen and forces the user to do something before continuing on. Where have you seen this type of unfriendly behavior? In the preceding example of the DOS calculator program that won't continue until the user enters a number. ■

A Macintosh program can read data in a variety of ways. Like DOS programs, a Mac program can be designed so that a user types in a number:

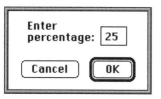

Note in the preceding example the presence of both a Cancel button and an OK button in the dialog box. That gives the user the option of changing his or her mind. And that agrees with the Macintosh philosophy of making the user the boss. ■

If a Mac programmer wants to let the user make use of the mouse rather than the keyboard, the programmer can use radio buttons or a scale with a slider to read in a value. Here are examples of each of these methods:

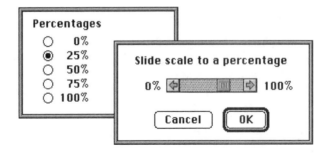

Writing text to the screen and reading data from the user are the two primary responsibilities of a non-Mac programmer. You — the challenge-loving individual that you are — will have additional duties. Adding a window to your program will be one of them.

Working with Windows

Programs written for a DOS computer simply display text and numbers on the screen. On a Mac, everything is displayed in a window. A program that uses a window gives you, the programmer, the following responsibilities:

- ✔ The opening, or displaying, of the window.
- ✔ Drawing or writing to the window.
- ✔ Providing the means to let the window be moved about the screen.
- ✔ The closing of the window.

Is this myriad of options the Macintosh provides the user starting to give you the impression that there might be just too much for a Mac programmer to learn? Are you getting nervous about all of this talk about responsibility? You aren't? Good. Then skip the rest of this note. But for those of you considering giving up, I'll let the cat out of the bag and mention a topic that I had hoped to save for a future chapter — the Toolbox.

If you've programmed before, you might be familiar with *functions*. A function is code that is written to perform a single task. Apple has written thousands of them, and tucked them all safely inside your Macintosh. Yes, you read that right — *thousands* of them. What kind of tasks do the functions do? They simplify such things as creating and moving windows, and creating and displaying menus. Since these functions are used by programmers as tools to build Mac programs, Apple got cute and named the entire collection of them the Toolbox.

I cover functions in general, and the Toolbox functions in particular, in Chapter 14. ■

Opening a window and writing text to it is a simple process. I know, I know —
you've heard claims like this before. But in Chapter 4 I'll prove it. There you'll
see the code for a Mac program that uses a window. And best of all, the code
for the program fits on less than half a page!

Menus Mean Choices

Another major difference between Macintosh programs and those written for
other computers is the idea of pull-down menus. I've stressed that Mac users
like to feel that they are in control of a program, rather than at the mercy of
what a program allows or forces them to do. Macintosh menus enhance that
feeling of control. A program that doesn't have pull-down menus may still offer
a form of a menu — but it's not the same. The menu choices will be listed on
the screen, and the user *must* select one before the program will continue:

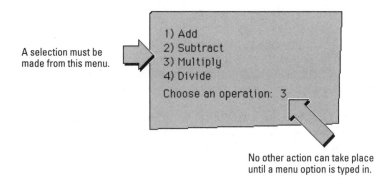

A selection must be
made from this menu.

1) Add
2) Subtract
3) Multiply
4) Divide

Choose an operation: 3

No other action can take place
until a menu option is typed in.

The above example is in stark contrast to the "Macintosh way" of doing things.
With Macintosh menus, the user has a choice of making several — perhaps
dozens — of choices. And if the user decides not to make a selection from one
particular menu, he can still perform other actions. The screen doesn't freeze
up and force the user to make a decision. A different menu can be selected, or a
window can be moved:

Other menus can be used.

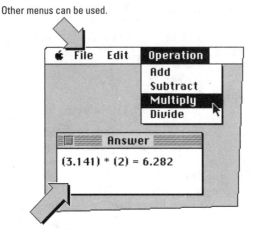

Windows can be moved.

When compared to the DOS brand of menus, Macintosh pull-down menus offer a seemingly infinite variety of choices to the user. With this vast improvement you might think that there is a comparable increase in work for the Mac programmer. Think again! Macintosh menus are easy to implement, and involve only a minor amount of extra work for the programmer.

Menus and windows are two of the most distinguishing features of a Macintosh program. They are also the two topics I'll spend the most time on. By the time you complete this book you'll be able to include menus and windows in each and every Macintosh program you write.

Chapter 3

Removing the Fear, Part I: Don't Let Mac Programmers Scare You!

● ●

In This Chapter

▶ How source code is used to create a program

▶ Why you need to know the rules of the C language

▶ The terminology associated with source code

▶ How compiling turns source code into a program

● ●

Many Macintosh programmers — the majority, in fact — are helpful and considerate when they recognize a newcomer in their midst. Others, well... let's just say they aren't quite as friendly. You're the new kid on the block, and they're going to make sure you know it.

Many programmers enjoy the almost god-like status they hold over mere mortals — those lowly nonprogrammers like yourself. Why wouldn't they want to keep that power? Using a vocabulary that is incredibly complex is one method of locking the door that separates them from you. In this chapter a few of the barriers are broken. I'll define some programming terms — in words that everyone can relate to. Words like source code and compiler, and a few others. Removing the pomp from these words should put you at ease, and keep your knees from shaking every time you hear a Mac programmer begin to talk.

Source Code

In the previous chapter you were introduced to *source code*. Source code is a general term for one or more commands in a computer language — any language. Since I'll be mentioning source code throughout this book, I'll take the time here to demystify this treacherous-sounding term.

The most intimidating thing about source code may be the last half of its name — code. Codes generally imply secrets, symbols, top-level intelligence officials, charges of treason, and your subsequent execution. So why *wouldn't* the name intimidate you? To lessen the fear of this word, try thinking about it more along the lines of the definition given in *Webster's New World Dictionary*. Webster says a code is a system of symbols in which letters, figures, etc. are given certain meanings. Now that's not so bad, is it?

Up to this point I've talked about source code in general terms. Now, to give you something to grab onto, I'll go into specifics. Since this book uses the C language, I'll give an example in that language.

In the field of mathematics, the numbers used in counting are called whole numbers. These are numbers such as 0, 1, 2, 3, and so on. Whole numbers never have a decimal point. You may already be aware of the fact that whole numbers can also be called *integers*.

Many people — programmers in particular — prefer "integer" to the words "whole number." Now, the word "integer" isn't a terribly long word, is it? So you might think that there is no need to abbreviate it. Wrong. While programmers eventually become pretty good typists, they'd rather spend their time doing other things. Like thinking about what to type next. So in the programming world, abbreviations are everywhere. As it turns out, the word "integer" is shortened to the word "int."

While the use of "int" for "integer" might seem like nothing more than an abbreviation to you, it can be thought of as something else. The word "int" now stands for something — it *symbolizes* the word "integer." Now recall Mr. Webster's words regarding the definition of the word "code." A code is a system of symbols in which letters are given certain meaning. So there you pretty much have it — source code is a set of abbreviations. There's nothing sneaky or devious about it.

The Rules of the Game

Only one of the following four sentences is grammatically correct. See if you can guess which one it is:

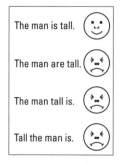

The first one — very good! And without a hint, yet! Now, why *aren't* the other three sentences correct? Because the English language has a set of rules that guides us on how we can create sentences — and the last three sentences violate one or more of these rules. You might not remember all the rules regarding the use of subjects, verbs, and prepositional phrases, but they do exist.

A computer language is similar to a spoken and written language like English in that it too has rules. It has fixed rules that regulate how you can piece together the symbols that make up the language. Take the C language symbol "int" that you learned about in the previous section. When writing source code, you can't just take the word "int" and haphazardly scatter it about. It is used only in certain well-defined instances. Of course, I'll cover those instances in future chapters when I discuss the C language in detail.

Let's dig into this business about rules just a little more. The English language has plenty of rules. To get the following example I first waited until my family was asleep. Then I peeked at my son's eighth-grade grammar book and found this:

The company offers a comprehensive medical plan.

Why did I wait until everyone was asleep? So I'd be spared the embarrassment of getting grilled about why I even needed to look in an eighth-grader's book to find an example! That's right — I don't remember the rules of grammar! The book said that the above example has something to do with subject-verb agreement, in case you're wondering.

The C language, like the English language, has several rules. Once again we'll move away from theory and on to a real example.

Besides providing you with some symbols — like "int — the C language allows you to make up your own symbols. Let's say you're writing a program for a car dealership. One of the things the dealer wants to keep track of is the number of trucks he has on the lot. You'll create a symbol that will help your program keep track of the number of trucks. What will you call the symbol? Perhaps simply "trucks." Not incredibly clever, but it does the trick.

Now, let's further suppose that the dealership has five trucks. You want to somehow relate the number five to the symbol "trucks." Using a format similar to our English grammar example, you'd do so using the following rule:

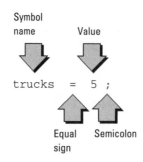

The above figure tells you that to give a symbol a value, you first list the symbol's name, followed by the equal sign. After that you give the value that is to be associated with the symbol. Finally, end it all with a semicolon.

To further the comparison between rules of the English language and rules of a programming language, I offer another figure. Remember the figure that started off this section? Here's a similar one. Which of the four bits of source code associates the number five with the symbol "trucks"?

```
trucks = 5;

trucks is 5;

trucks equals 5;

5 = trucks;
```

Whether or not the above bit of C language code makes perfect sense to you isn't the issue here. If you've ever looked at a computer programming book, with its pages and pages of source code, you've probably felt overwhelmed. Try as you might, you couldn't understand a bit of it. Stop and think for a moment. Were your expectations realistic? Just because many of the individual words in the source code looked English-like, did you really think you should be able understand it? Especially when you didn't know any of the rules?

Once you know the rules of the game, the game becomes much easier to play. Do I feel strongly about that statement? You be the judge:

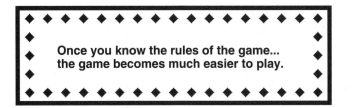

> ◆ ◆ ◆ ◆ ◆ ◆ ◆ ◆ ◆ ◆ ◆ ◆ ◆ ◆ ◆ ◆ ◆
>
> **Once you know the rules of the game...**
> **the game becomes much easier to play.**
>
> ◆ ◆ ◆ ◆ ◆ ◆ ◆ ◆ ◆ ◆ ◆ ◆ ◆ ◆ ◆ ◆ ◆

Right now, you don't know all — or perhaps any — of the rules. The chapters in Part IV lay out all of the rules for you — by examining and explaining the C language. If you have read and understood the words on this page, you are fully capable of understanding how to write source code. Stop doubting yourself!

Source Code Terminology

While I'm on the subject of source code, I'll tie together some of the many words used to describe it.

The following little gem of C language code is from the previous section:

```
trucks = 5;
```

The above line contains a single command — it tells the program to assign the number five to the symbol named "trucks". In programming, a single command such as this is called an *instruction*, or *statement*. You can use the two terms interchangeably.

Each single instruction usually appears on a single *line*. But they don't have to. It's done this way for clarity. Placing two instructions on two separate lines makes it clear that two separate commands are taking place.

Though source code may look about as organized as the contents of a bowl of alphabet soup, this isn't the case. Instructions are written to carry out specific tasks. An example might be the instructions necessary to display a window on the screen. Rather than scatter these instructions all about, the programmer will place them together. When a number of instructions that perform a single task are grouped together, the result is called a *routine*. Because a routine has a single function, it is sometimes called just that — a *function*. Routines, or functions, keep source code looking nice and tidy — to the eyes of the programmer, anyway! The following figure — while sparing you the details of the code itself — gives you an idea of how source code might be divided into a few functions:

Function to display
a window

Function to write
a message in the
window

Function to close
the window

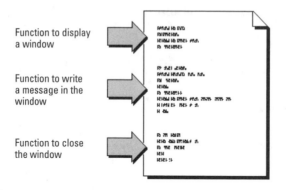

When several functions are grouped together, the result is a *program*. A program can consist of just a few functions, or hundreds. Don't worry — the programs in this book will contain just a single function.

Let's summarize all of the above code-related terms:

- A single command is called an *instruction* or *statement*.
- For clarity, each instruction usually appears on its own *line*.
- Any instruction, or group of instructions, is called *source code*, or simply *code*.
- Several lines of code that are devoted to a single task are collectively called a *routine*, or *function*.
- A *program* is a collection of several functions.

Compiling Your Code

After source code, the next subject that might send a shiver down the spine of anyone new to programming is *compiling*. As is often the case, the word itself is much scarier than the process of doing it.

Source Code Is Nothing But Text

In the previous section you saw that you type several commands — or instructions — to create source code. What I didn't mention was that you can save your work exactly as you save anything else you type — by saving it to a file. The type of file it will be saved as is a text file. If "text file" sounds familar, it should. This is the same type of file that all word processors can create. Word

processors, like Microsoft Word, provide a menu of file formats. Part of that
menu is shown here:

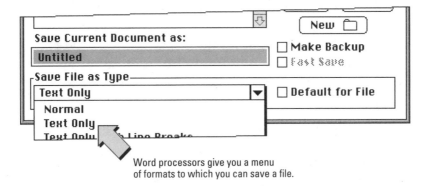

Word processors give you a menu
of formats to which you can save a file.

Normally, a word processor saves a file in its own special format. That allows it
to save all of the text along with all of the special formatting — such as italics,
or multiple fonts — that you've added:

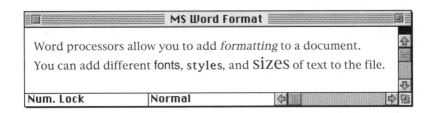

When you save a document as a text file, only the text itself will be saved. If
you've underlined words, or made any other style changes, this information
is lost.

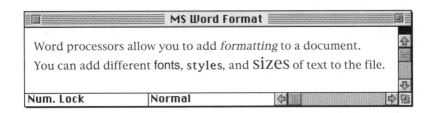

Now you know exactly what a text file is, and that word processors can create
them. You also know that source code is saved as a text file. This tells you that
you can create a source code file using a word processor. Let's say you created

a source code file using Apple's popular TeachText program — a text editor that Apple distributes freely. When you quit TeachText, you'd see the icon for TeachText and any other programs you have visible on your desktop, and a brand-new icon for the source code file. Your desktop might look a little like this:

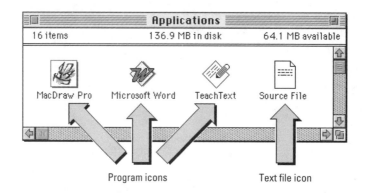

Program icons   Text file icon

Every program has an icon — it's what you double-click on to run the program. Every file — such as a text file — has an icon too. Double-clicking on a program icon runs that program. Double-clicking on a text file runs the word processor that created the text file. So what happens when you double-click on the source code file? The word processor that created it will run, and a window containing the contents of the source code file will open. If you were hoping that the code you typed would run — like a program runs — you'll be disappointed. Don't get too downhearted, though. The solution is just around the corner...

Completing the Picture — Compiling

Your source code file is nothing more than a text file with words in it. Even though it contains source code written in a programming language, the Macintosh views it as nothing more than a normal text file. You want your source code to become a program — so something is obviously missing:

So how do you get your typed-in source code — saved in a text file — to become an actual program? After creating the source code you need to *compile* it. A compiler is a software program that turns the source code words into numbers. Words mean nothing to your Mac, but numbers it loves. The hundreds, thousands, or in some cases even millions of numbers that the compiler generates are what make up a program. Before going any further, let's complete the picture:

Now, how on earth does the compiler know what numbers to create? Who cares! Whether it's using complex mathematical formulas or voodoo, it's obviously doing something very right. Why question it? What you *will* need to know is how to go about compiling your source code.

If you've programmed before, you might be familiar with *linking*. On some computers there are two steps involved in converting source code into a program. First, you compile the source code, then you link it. It's that way on a Macintosh, too. But Mac compilers combine these steps so the part about linking seems invisible to you. ■

Different software companies make different C language compilers. Apple makes one called MPW — Macintosh Programmers Workshop. But well over 80% of the Macintosh C language compilers sold today are made by Symantec Corporation. Theirs is called THINK C. Because THINK C is very popular, relatively inexpensive, and easy to use, it's the compiler I use for the examples in this book. I cover it in detail in Part III. For now, I'll continue demystifying the process of compiling by giving you a very quick look at the THINK C compiler.

After source code is typed in it gets compiled using the Compile menu item from the Source menu of THINK C. That's all there is to it. Here's a look at the THINK C Source menu:

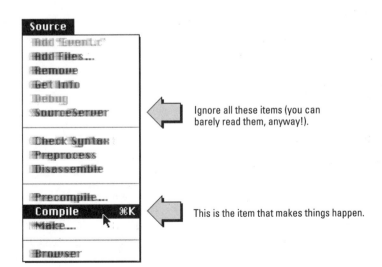

Sorry about blurring that figure, but I did it because I don't want you to get worried about the host of other items in the menu. It's just as well if you don't even know what they are. The Source menu contains several items, but Compile is far and away the item you'll use the most. In fact, even when I cover the THINK C compiler in depth in Part III, I only mention one other item in this menu.

The Compile menu item compiles a source code file, but it doesn't create a program out of it. So why do it? To make sure your source code is all correct. You and I never make mistakes, of course, but some people do. When the compiler encounters a line of source code that it doesn't think is right, it lets you know. After the offending bit of code is corrected, the file is again compiled. Once everything is OK, it's time to make a program out of it.

A software program is often called an *application*. If you're making your own program, or application, you might say that you're building it. In fact, that's exactly what you'll say. THINK C provides a menu item called Build Application. It's found in the Project menu. Like the Compile item in the Source menu, the Build Application item is about the only menu item you'll use from the Project menu. I won't repeat my cheap theatrical stunt of blurring the menu here. Instead, I'll trust that you won't become engrossed in, or intimidated by, the other menu items in the Project menu:

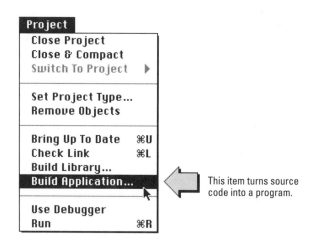

This item turns source code into a program.

The Build Application item sneaks a little code of its own into your code. It does this so that when you quit the compiler, a brand-new icon — representing your program — will appear on the desktop. If you haven't yet compiled your source code file, selecting Build Application will first complete that task. If you have compiled your source code, Build Application will jump right to the part about adding its own code.

Each of the two menus I've just shown has about a dozen items in it. I said that you'll only use one or two items from each menu. That, of course, begs the question, "What are all those other menu items *doing* there?" Remember, I didn't say *no one* would ever use these items. I just said that *you* don't need to use them. More experienced programmers will take advantage of some or all of the features these items provide.

One last point about compilers — and this is a really neat point. Built right into the compiler is a *text editor*. A text editor is like a word processor, except that it can only produce text files. It can't make a file that has words with fancy formatting, like underlining or boldfacing. That's fine with you, because the compiler only compiles text files. What's so neat about having a built-in text editor? It makes creating a program that much easier. Here are the steps you'll need to perform to create a Mac program:

1. Run the compiler program.

2. Type in your source code using the built-in text editor.

3. Select Build Application from the Project menu.

4. Quit the compiler program.

5. Brag to all your friends that you've just created a Macintosh program.

Well, maybe it won't go *quite* that smoothly, but that's a pretty darned good assessment.

Chapter 4

Removing the Fear, Part II: The One-Minute Program

1 n the previous chapter you saw a little code — very little. In this chapter you'll see just a little more — about a dozen lines, or instructions. Source code can be intimidating because when you see it, you usually see pages and pages of it. Would it help remove some of the fear if I told you that the few lines of code that appear in this chapter comprise an entire Macintosh program? It's true. As you can well imagine, Macintosh programs can get much larger. But isn't it nice to know that the first one you'll be exposed to practically fits in the palm of your hand?

It's Time to Establish Some Conventions

From this point on, you'll find source code scattered about the pages of each chapter. To help you quickly identify what is source code and what is regular text, all code that is mixed in with text will appear in italics:

Code words within a sentence will be in italics.

Earlier you saw that variable *trucks* is an *int*, or integer.

Other times you'll see a block of code. Some examples work best when you view several lines of code listed together. In those cases each line will be listed in a font that differs from that used for normal text:

```
int   trucks;
int   cars;

trucks = 5;
cars = 12;
```

Entire section will be in the code font.

A block of code, like the one above, is called a *code snippet*. That's because it isn't an entire program — it's just a part snipped from a complete program. ■

That's It? That's a Mac Program?

I can write a Mac program in a dozen lines of code or less. Sounds kind of like "Name That Tune," doesn't it? It's true, though — as you'll see in a moment. I won't explain all of the code in detail — exactly how it works isn't important here. What is important is that you realize these few unimposing lines of text are capable of opening a window and writing words into it. It runs on a Mac, it opens a window, it uses the window. Why, I believe that qualifies as a Macintosh program! Granted, it's a simple program. Still, it should do much to eliminate any anxiety you might have about writing source code.

The Unveiling of the Program

Here, in its entirety, is the source code for the much-heralded example:

```
main()
{
    WindowPtr   TheWindow;

    InitGraf( &thePort );
    InitFonts();
    InitWindows();

    TheWindow = GetNewWindow( 128, 0L, (WindowPtr)-1L );
    SetPort( TheWindow );
    MoveTo( 30, 50 );
    DrawString( "\pHello, World!" );
    while ( !Button() )
        ;
}
```

What incredible things does the above program do? First, of course, you must compile the above code — you have to build an application. If you don't understand that last sentence, slow down — you've been reading too fast! I just covered compiling and building applications in the previous chapter!

Again, what incredible things does the program do? It displays a window, then writes the words "Hello, World!" in it. When the mouse is clicked, the window disappears and the program ends. Here's what a user would see after running the program:

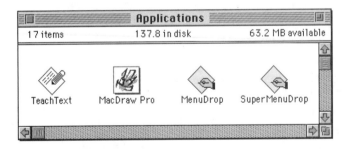

You'll notice that it appears our program has no name. That's because a Mac program is named *after* it has been compiled. In fact, you can even change the name of a program after it's all done and sitting on your desktop. Simply click on the program's name and type in a new one. For example, I made a copy of one of my own programs — MenuDrop — and then renamed it SuperMenuDrop. The result is shown here:

Software companies see very little humor in users copying and renaming their programs. After all, they spent a great deal of time and money to develop their software programs. And companies would see even less humor in such antics if attempts were then made to distribute these newly named programs. If you tried this, not only would you have the dreaded Software Police after you, you'd probably have federal authorities knocking on your door. ■

As I discuss my example program in the remainder of this chapter I'd rather not have to keep referring to it as "my example program shown near the start of this chapter." So I'll give it a name now. Macintosh programmers take a lot of pride in their work and thus put a lot of time and effort into thinking of catchy, original, names for their programs. With that in mind, I'll call my program ExampleOne.

Examining the Code — But Not Too Closely

In Chapter 16 I'll rip the preceding program — ExampleOne — apart. Not literally, of course. Rather, I'll remove each line of code from the program and examine and explain it in detail. I'll wait until Chapter 16 because by that point you'll have read all about the C language. In this chapter I'll cover some of the instructions in the ExampleOne program, but only at a superficial level.

Since I know you're not familiar with the C language I won't mention too many specifics of the program in this chapter. But even without a knowledge of the particulars of C, you can still get a lot out of ExampleOne. Here's what you can learn from a brief look at a very short program:

- ✔ Source code really does have structure and organization.
- ✔ At first glance source code appears to be quite cryptic — it isn't.
- ✔ Just about anyone is capable of writing at least a minimal Mac program.

Get as much as you can out of this discussion about source code. But don't dwell on every word, and don't expect to understand every programming concept behind every bit of code you see here. This is not a tutorial on the C language or on source code. That comes in Part IV of this book. This material is an overview — treat it as such. ∎

Get Ready, 'Cause Here I Come

When you write a Mac program, some of the commands you write — the instructions — will be very short and very simple. Yet they will appear to be making a lot of things happen. How this happens is good news for you. When you write a Macintosh program, you won't be going it alone. Apple has written a ton of source code, and has buried it deep inside your computer. Some of the instructions you write make use of this code. I'll have more to say about how this works throughout the book — including later in this chapter.

One of the first things you do when you write a Mac program is let this Apple-written code know that you are going to make use of it. Think of it as telling the Macintosh to "get ready, 'cause here I come." This process is called *initialization*. The ExampleOne program uses three separate instructions to initialize the Mac:

```
InitGraf( &thePort );
InitFonts();
InitWindows();
```

ExampleOne writes text to a window. On a Macintosh, the typeface in which a text is written is called a font. The *InitFonts* instruction warns the Mac that this program will write to a window, and will thus use a font. The Macintosh then does some internal hocus-pocus that gets itself all prepared to write text.

From the above paragraph you can see that when a word starts with "Init," the "Init" means initialize. The second half of the word tells what gets initialized. Pretty intuitive, isn't it? *InitFonts* initializes fonts. *InitWindows* initializes windows. *InitGraf* initializes...well, maybe that's not quite so intuitive. More on *InitGraf* later.

You might think that since every Macintosh computer can be used to write programs, the Macintosh might have the ability to initialize itself. That would make sense, but it doesn't work that way. So in every Macintosh program you see you'll find at least a few of these instructions that begin with "Init."

Opening a Window

The ExampleOne program displays a window. This line of code prepares the Macintosh to do that:

```
WindowPtr  TheWindow;
```

That's a little bit like the initialization I just talked about, but not exactly. Similar, but different. Now isn't that helpful? Let me try again. This line of code lets the Mac know that a window is going to be created and displayed at some point in the program. Knowing that, the Mac will make sure there's a little space reserved somewhere to hold information about this soon-to-arrive window.

What kind of information about a window does the Mac have to keep track of? For one, the type — or look — of the window that will open. Remember, windows don't all look the same:

Now that we've got the Mac all excited about the idea of a new window coming into existence, we certainly don't want to let it down. The following line of code is the one that actually creates a window:

```
TheWindow = GetNewWindow( 128, 0L, (WindowPtr)-1L );
```

The *GetNewWindow* part of that last line sounds straightforward enough. But where is the program getting the new window from? And what's all that business between the parentheses that follow the word *GetNewWindow*? Not so fast! Remember, this is an overview — I don't have to tell you everything right here and now!

Notice the return of *The Window*. A moment ago I said that *The Window* would be used to hold information about a window. Take another look at this line of code:

```
TheWindow = GetNewWindow( 128, 0L, (WindowPtr)-1L );
```

It serves two purposes. First, it displays a new window. Second, it gives *The Window* the information it needs about the new window. Actually, this single line of code encompasses about four or five separate programming topics. So I think I'll stop right now before I get in too deep!

Writing to a Window

After displaying a window on the screen, ExampleOne writes a few words in it. The line of code that does the actual writing of the words is:

```
DrawString( "\pHello, World!" );
```

While you might not know what a string is, you certainly know what the word "draw" means. The Macintosh, being the very graphical kind of computer that it is, doesn't simply write text. No, the Mac considers writing a very dull sport. It much prefers to draw things. Not just lines and shapes, but even words.

By the way, a string is a group of characters — letters, digits, etc. Thus "dog," "Hey, you!," and "Ab123&%*" are all strings. I'll present a more formal definition in Part V.

You're probably also wondering about that funky-looking "\p" that precedes the words "Hello, World!" Those two characters always precede the text, or string, in *DrawString* — but they don't show up when the string is written in the window. As usual, more on this later. ■

What about those two lines of code that precede the *DrawString* line? Here they are:

```
SetPort( TheWindow );
MoveTo( 30, 50 );
```

Imagine that ExampleOne displayed three windows at the same time. What do you think would happen if you wrote — excuse me, drew — some words using *DrawString*? Which of the three windows would the text appear in? That's a real dilemma, and *SetPort* solves it. I won't tell you how it solves it, but I will tell you that it involves your old friend, *TheWindow*.

The idea of *which* window to draw text in brings up a second problem — where in the proper window should the text be drawn to? If you just say "draw some words," where will they end up?

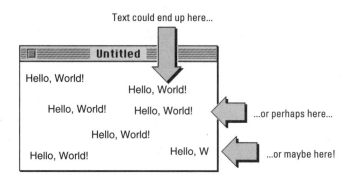

The line that contains *MoveTo* handles where text should be drawn in a window:

```
MoveTo( 30, 50 );
```

Those two numbers that follow *MoveTo* — 30 and 50 — tell the Mac exactly where in the window to draw to.

Button, Button, Who's Got the Button?

The mouse has the button — and clicking on it ends the ExampleOne program. Here are the two lines of code that take care of that task:

```
while ( !Button() )
    ;
```

In plain ol' English, here's how to read the above two lines: "While the mouse button is not clicked down, hang around." Once the mouse button is clicked, the user will find himself back at the desktop.

You know from working with other programs that a Mac program usually doesn't end when the user clicks the mouse. But I thought a simple ending would be very appropriate for this simple example.

The Function of the Program

There's only three lines of code I didn't cover yet — not to mention several blank lines. These three lines are the two braces, {}, and *main( )*.

By the way — blank lines don't count. In source code, you can stick a blank line anywhere and it won't upset things. Blank lines are also known as white space. Why insert a blank line if it doesn't do anything? To add clarity to your source code. Rather than have line after line of uninterrupted code, throw an empty line in to break things up. Notice that I used blank lines to group together related lines of code. An example is the three lines of code that handle initializations:

```
InitGraf( &thePort );
InitFonts();
InitWindows();
```

If you look back at the code for the complete program you'll see that I have a blank line before and after these three lines. ■

In the previous chapter I said that code can be grouped together in *functions*. Most programs have several functions — ExampleOne has just a single function named *main*. How can you tell where a function begins and ends? By the braces:

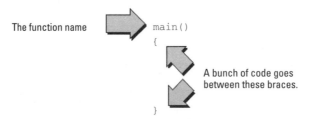

```
main()
{


}
```

The function name

A bunch of code goes between these braces.

How much code goes between the braces? What does the code here do? That all depends on what the function is supposed to do. In our example the function initializes things, opens a window, and draws some text to the window. To accomplish that, I wrote ten lines of code between the braces (not counting the empty lines). Other functions do other things, and could have more lines of code or fewer lines of code.

That's It ... Or Is It?

At this point you've seen at least a rudimentary explanation for each line of code in the ExampleOne program. So the chapter is complete, right? Come on, you know better. As long as I have the source code right in front of me, I might as well cover a couple of general topics that apply to it.

Source code and compiling are two of the most feared topics new programmers encounter. I described them in Chapter 3. Those two topics apply to any kind of programming — not just Macintosh programming. Since Mac programs are so different from programs written for other types of computers, you may have guessed that there are a couple of dreaded programming topics that pertain only to the Mac. How right you are. I'll devote the remainder of this chapter to one of the biggest and baddest of them: the Toolbox.

Using the Toolbox

Imagine this: A computer company hires top-notch, professional programmers to write thousands of small, efficient programs. Miniprograms, if you will. Each miniprogram can do something exciting, useful, or both. Like put a window on the screen. Or draw a circle in a window. Or move a window across the screen. But wait, there's more. Then this company devises a way that you, a beginning programmer, can use any one of these programs just by typing a single line of source code. Wait, one more thing. Then, they give all these miniprograms away! I'm not kidding! What Apple did was somehow stuff all these miniprograms into computer chips and solder them right inside every single Macintosh. Not only did they do all this, they came up with a clever name for this collection of miniprograms — the Toolbox.

Calling the Toolbox

The miniprograms that make up the Toolbox are the tools you'll use to build your programs. To make use of a Toolbox miniprogram you *call* it:

 **Hey, Toolbox!**

No, not like that! When I say you call a Toolbox miniprogram, I mean it a little more figuratively. Your source code is going to call on a miniprogram to perform a task.

Though you probably weren't aware of it, you've already come in contact with several *Toolbox calls*. Our infamous ExampleOne program made use of eight of them! I've repeated the source code for the program below. This time I've placed all of the Toolbox calls in **boldface** type:

```
main()
{
    WindowPtr  TheWindow;
    InitGraf( &thePort );
    InitFonts();
    InitWindows();
    TheWindow = GetNewWindow( 128, 0L, (WindowPtr)-1L );
    SetPort( TheWindow );
    MoveTo( 30, 50 );
    DrawString( "\pHello, World!" );
    while ( !Button() )
        ;
}
```

You're Not Alone!

From the above code you can surmise that the Toolbox is a very important part of Macintosh programming. In this section I've tried to answer briefly the question of what the Toolbox is. As is often the case in programming, my answer may have prompted even more questions. How can you tell what source code is a Toolbox call? How do you know when to use a Toolbox call? How do you know the names of all of the Toolbox calls? Patience my friend. I discuss the Toolbox in great length in Chapter 14.

If you aren't expected to know everything about the Toolbox from this section, what *should* you leave with? The idea that you are not alone in your programming endeavors. Apple support is right there beside you. In front of you, actually — right inside your Mac. The invisible code that Apple has tucked away in your Macintosh will do all sorts of helpful and wonderful things for you. And, best of all, you'll never have to know how it works! And not knowing about things is something that just about all of us are very good at mastering! In future chapters you'll learn a lot more about the Toolbox, but you'll never have to learn how each miniprogram works. You only have to know that they do in fact work very well.

Part II
Resources: This Is Programming?

The 5th Wave   By Rich Tennant

AT THE REAL PROGRAMMERS DATING BAR

WHOA! LOOK AT THE POCKET PROTECTORS ON THIS ONE!

In this part . . .

The Macintosh is a fun computer to use. Now, if only it were a fun computer to program. But wait . . . it is! Though writing programs for many other kinds of computers consists of typing in line after line of mind-numbing text and numbers, programming the Mac consists of working with neat pictures that represent the windows and menus that are to appear in your program. Well, yes, it also includes a *little* bit of that mind-numbing business. But don't worry about that just yet. Instead, enjoy the three chapters in this part. They deal with *resources* — the fun part of programming.

Chapter 5

What Are Resources?

● ●

In This Chapter

▶ Everything on the Mac's screen starts as a resource

▶ Resources are created without programming skills

▶ Resources are kept in a file

▶ How resources and source code interact

● ●

*I*n the previous chapter you were introduced to the Toolbox. In this chapter — and the two following it — you'll learn about another topic very important to Macintosh programming — resources.

A *resource* defines what one part of the graphical user interface looks like. What parts of the Mac interface are defined by resources? Take a look:

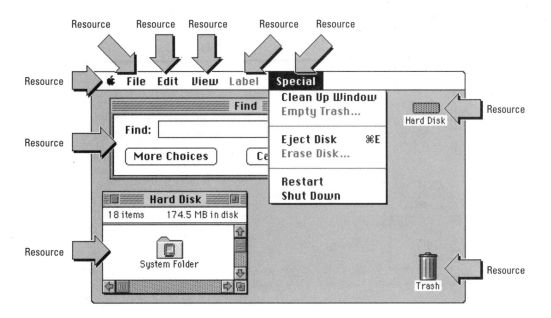

Resources are the fun part of programming. Hey, I heard that snicker! It's true though. Resources can be fun because they involve absolutely no programming. You don't use source code and you don't use a compiler to create a resource.

Okay then, what parts of the interface aren't defined by resources? Take another look:

Those last two figures should make it quite clear that resources are crucial to a Mac program. Without them, a Mac program would look much like a program written for another type of computer. It would consist of nothing more than words on the screen.

What do I mean when I say a resource defines a part of the interface? That depends on the part of the interface in question. If you were writing a Macintosh program with menus, you'd define each menu by specifying the menu's name and the names of the items that are to appear in the menu. Here's a typical Edit menu:

Edit
Undo

Cut
Copy
Paste

Using words, you'd define the above menu something like this:

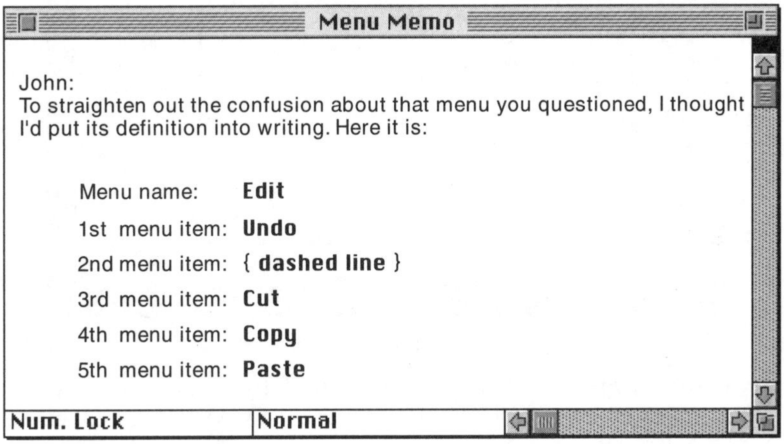

```
========================== Menu Memo ==========================
John:
To straighten out the confusion about that menu you questioned, I thought
I'd put its definition into writing. Here it is:

        Menu name:      Edit
        1st  menu item: Undo
        2nd menu item:  { dashed line }
        3rd  menu item: Cut
        4th  menu item: Copy
        5th  menu item: Paste

Num. Lock              Normal
```

With resources, though, you don't have to type in quite as many words to define a menu. And, as you create the menu you get to see exactly what it will look like.

Look Ma, No Programming!

I said that a resource defines what one part of the interface looks like. One resource might define what menu items are in a menu. A different resource could define what a certain window will look like. In any case, the act of creating the resource doesn't involve programming. Let's look at a hypothetical example.

Hypothetically Speaking...

Let's say I want to create a window. I run my graphics program and draw exactly what it should look like. Here I am in my paint program, in the middle of drawing a window:

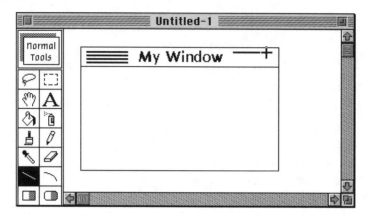

When I have my window just how I want it to look, I select Save from the File menu and then quit the graphics program. There — I've defined a window. And without a bit of programming.

What can I do with this window? I can make use of it anytime, anywhere, in my source code. Kind of like this:

```
main()
{
    Display My Window
}
```

No, that isn't really how it's done. Dirty trick? Maybe. But I did warn you beforehand that the example was going to be hypothetical. Anyway, what I'm trying to do is give you an idea of how something created without programming might be used later on with programming. While resources aren't created in a graphics program, they are created in a separate program that's as easy to use as a graphics program. And, like the above example, you then make use of your window (or whatever else you've created) from within your own source code.

Remember the line of code that displayed a window in Chapter 4's ExampleOne program? Here it is:

```
TheWindow = GetNewWindow( 128, 0L, (WindowPtr)-1L );
```

I said in Chapter 4 that *GetNewWindow* is a *Toolbox call* — a miniprogram written by Apple. The purpose of the *GetNewWindow* Toolbox call is to open and display a window. Which window? Window number 128. What exactly is 128 (besides a number, of course)? It's the number of a *resource* that defines what the window looks like.

So even if it's not quite as clearly stated as in my hypothetical example:

```
main()
{
    Display My Window
}
```

source code really does make use of resources. ■

Resource Files

I mentioned that resources don't involve programming. As you saw above, that's only partly true. Now wait a minute. Before you think that I lied about that "no programming" business, read on. Creating resources — any number of resources — involves absolutely no programming. Getting your program to recognize and make use of resources does involve programming. So you can see that I wasn't entirely dishonest with you.

Resources are created and saved in their own special file — just as source code is. Here's a folder that contains both a source code file and a resource file:

The source code file has the icon of a text file. In Chapter 6 you'll see why the resource file has the interesting icon shown above.

Having the resources for a program in their own file — separate from the source code for a program — allows you to create the resources independently from the source code. Just as I promised, creating resources does not depend on knowing or using any source code. Someone who has never programmed a line of code can create a file that holds resources.

The Resource/Source Code Connection

I said that source code is needed for a program to make use of resources. Since the source code and the resources exist in two separate files, there must be something that binds the two together:

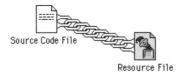

Source Code File

Resource File

That's a little dramatic, but it does give emphasis to what must take place. The contents of the resource file and the contents of the source code file do in fact get bound together to form a program:

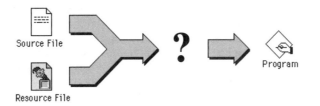

Source File

Resource File

Program

Yes, it's the return of the mysterious question mark. You first encountered it back in Chapter 3 when I mentioned that something turned source code into a program. Do you remember what that something was? Here's the answer:

Source File   Compiler   Program

That's right — the compiler. It's now time to give the faithful compiler a second round of applause. Why? Because it actually performs a second task. Its first task is to turn your human-readable source code into the numbers that are understandable to a computer. Its second task is to merge this modified source code and the resources together. The result? A Macintosh program — one that has graphical user interface components, such as menus and windows. With this new bit of knowledge we can update the previous figure to one that looks like this:

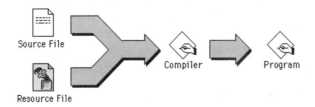

Source File

Resource File   Compiler   Program

But How Do You Create a Resource?

In this chapter I've managed to use up quite a few pages discussing resources. Yet I never said exactly how you create them. What can you conclude from this? That I get paid by the page, and I'm padding the book? A nice guess, but that's not the case. I'm trying to present an overview of what resources are, and how they fit into the grand scheme of a Mac program. That way, when you *do* see how to create a resource you'll know what it's being made for and how it will be used.

So how *do* you go about creating a resource? Why, by reading the next chapter, of course.

Chapter 6

Using ResEdit, the Resource Editor

● ●

In This Chapter

▶ How a resource is created

▶ The types of resources

▶ Using ResEdit, the resource editor

▶ Creating a resource file

▶ Creating and editing a menu resource

● ●

*E*nough talk about what resources are — let's make one! This chapter shows you how to do that. I'll take you on an in-depth tour of the process of creating a resource that can be used as a menu in any Mac program you make. Once you see how to make one resource, you'll have a pretty good idea of how to make others.

Editing — It's Not Just for Text Anymore

What does the word "edit" mean to you? *Webster's New World Dictionary* says to edit is to "revise and make ready a manuscript for publication." What does Webster know? Heck, he died over 150 years ago! In the Macintosh world, editing might have absolutely nothing to do with manuscripts, or even words.

Editor: Forget That Text!

When you first saw the word "editing" in a few of this chapter's headings, you probably got pretty excited. Finally, terms that sound familiar — edit, editing, editor. An editor is for editing text, right? *Maybe.* A *text* editor is for editing text. There are also other types of editors. For example, a sound editor shows a sound as a sound wave, and lets you edit it. That's what I'm doing right here:

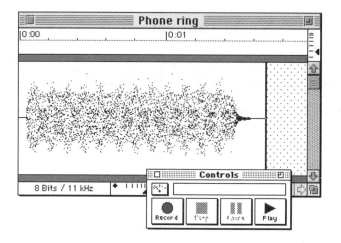

What does editing sounds have to do with resources? Absolutely nothing. But it's such a cool topic that I just had to throw it in this book somewhere. On the other hand, maybe showing a sound editor isn't so frivolous. It does demonstrate that text isn't the only thing you can edit.

ResEdit: The Resource Editor

By now you've surely surmised that, like text and sounds, resources can be edited. And — again like text and sounds — you use a software program for editing. Apple makes a *resource editor* called ResEdit that does just that. Here's its icon, along with the icons of a popular text editor and sound editor:

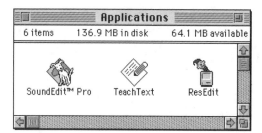

To avoid the ridicule of seasoned Mac programmers, be sure to pronounce the word ResEdit correctly: "rez-ed-it." ■

If the icon for ResEdit looks familiar, it's because you saw one very similar to it in Chapter 5. There you saw the icon for a resource file. That file was created by

ResEdit. Just as a word processor creates files that bear its likeness, so does a resource editor:

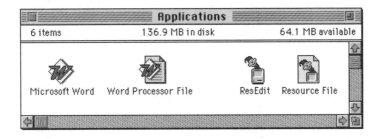

ResEdit is the resource editor I use for all the example programs in this book — but it isn't the only resource editor in existence. What criteria did I use to select it? Glad you asked:

- ✔ It's by far the most popular resource editor among Mac programmers.
- ✔ It's a straightforward, easy-to-use program.
- ✔ It comes free with almost all Macintosh compilers.

I thought you'd like that last point! When you create a Macintosh program you make resources and write source code. Then you use a compiler to turn it all into a program. That's always the scenario. Companies that make compilers know you'll need a resource editor — that's why they include a copy of ResEdit with each compiler.

What's in a Name?

Resources come in different types. One type defines a menu. Another type defines a window. Each type has a name, of course. Since the ResEdit program makes use of these names, I thought it wise to spend a moment setting the ground rules for the naming of these types before jumping right into ResEdit.

Don't Quote Me on This

By convention, most books enclose a resource type in single quotation marks. So the resource type of a window, a '*WIND*' resource, is written as you see it here in this sentence. Another commonly used resource, the resource for a menu, is written as: '*MENU*'.

For any resource type, the quotations themselves are not part of the name. Why include them, then? Two reasons. First, it makes it easy to spot a resource type when it's mentioned in a body of text. Second, a resource type is *always* four characters. But in *some* resources, the fourth character is a blank — a space. So a sound resource, which is written as the letters s, n, d, followed by a space, is written like this: 'snd '. That reminds you that a space is included as part of the name.

A 'MENU' Is Not a 'menu'

If I write the word dog as DOG, you'll still recognize it as meaning a four-legged, barking pet. You may wonder *why* I capitalized it, but you'll still understand what it means. To you, dog and DOG mean the same thing. This same freedom to capitalize or not capitalize a word does *not* apply to the naming of resources.

In the previous section I mentioned the '*MENU*' resource. Note that each of the four characters in '*MENU*' is an uppercase letter. That's important. When the Mac sees '*MENU*', it knows you're talking about a menu resource. If it sees '*menu*', it has no idea what you're referring to. If you ever see the menu resource written as '*menu*', it's the typesetter's fault — not mine!

When the proper use of uppercase and lowercase in a word is important, that word is said to be *case-sensitive*. It turns out that *all* resource names are case-sensitive — not just the '*MENU*' resource.

Can you skip the talk about case-sensitive and just remember to always use uppercase when writing the name of a resource? I'd like to say it's as easy as that, but it's not. Some resource names *do* appear in lowercase characters, such as the 'snd ' resource you saw in the previous section.

A Few Common Resources

In this book you'll be exposed (though not indecently!) to three resource types: '*WIND*', '*MENU*', and '*MBAR*'. But there are a lot more. Here's a table of a few of the more common types.

Resource Types and Their Purpose	
Resource Type	What It's For
'WIND'	Defines how a window will look
'MENU'	Lists a menu name and the items in it
'MBAR'	Lists the individual menus that will be in a menu bar
'DLOG'	Defines how a dialog box will look
'DITL'	Lists the items—such as buttons—that will be in a dialog box
'ALRT'	Defines how an alert will look
'ICON'	Defines how an icon will look
'PICT'	A picture
'snd '	A sound

Using ResEdit

The more you program the Mac, the more you'll use ResEdit. Because resources are such an important part of creating a Macintosh program, using a resource editor is important too. That makes the decision to devote the remainder of this chapter to exploring ResEdit a very practical one.

Every Macintosh program has both a resource file and a source code file. Many programmers start a new program by creating the resource file — so that's what I'll do here.

Creating a Resource File

To run ResEdit, double-click the ResEdit icon. You'll come face-to-face with the ResEdit Jack-in-the-Mac introductory screen:

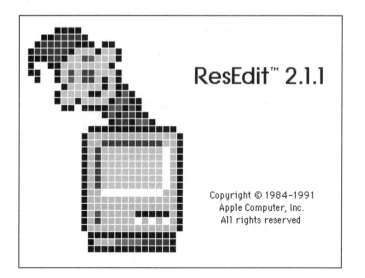

Software programs come in different versions. For ResEdit, version 2.1.1 is the most popular. If you have a copy of ResEdit with a different number, it should still work just fine.

After staring at the introductory dialog box for a while, click the mouse to continue. ResEdit provides a dialog box that gives you the option of opening an existing resource file or creating a new one. I'm giving the feature-length tour here, so I'll assume you don't have a resource file to open. Click the New button:

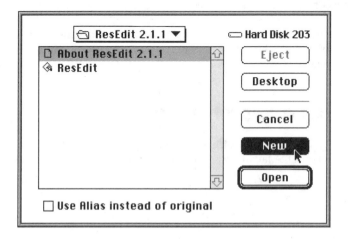

Any Mac file has a name, and a resource file is no exception. In future chapters
I'll discuss appropriate file names. For now, I'll type in something clever like My
Resource File, and then click on the New button:

```
┌─────────────────────────────────────────────┐
│   ┌──────────────────────┐    ┌─┐ Hard Disk 203│
│   │ 🗁 ResEdit 2.1.1 ▼  │                     │
│   ┌──────────────────────────┐  ┌──────────┐  │
│   │ 🗋 About ResEdit 2.1.1  ⇧│  │  Eject   │  │
│   │ 🐾 ResEdit               │  └──────────┘  │
│   │                          │  ┌──────────┐  │
│   │                          │  │ Desktop  │  │
│   │                          │  └──────────┘  │
│   │                          │  ──────────────│
│   │                          │  ┌──────────┐  │
│   │                        ⇩│  │  Cancel  │  │
│   └──────────────────────────┘  └──────────┘  │
│                                  ┌══════════┐  │
│   New File Name:                 ║   New    ║  │
│   ┌──────────────────────────┐   └══════════┘  │
│   │ My Resource File         │           ↖     │
│   └──────────────────────────┘                 │
└─────────────────────────────────────────────┘
```

After clicking the New button a brand-new, empty window will open. Note that
the window's title is the name I gave to the resource file:

```
┌═══════════════════════════════════════════════┐
│▦□▦▦▦▦▦▦  My Resource File  ▦▦▦▦▦▦▦▦▦📑│
├───────────────────────────────────────────┬───┤
│                                           │ ⇧ │
│                                           ├───┤
│                                           │   │
│                                           │   │
│                                           │   │
│                                           │   │
│                                           │   │
│                                           │   │
│                                           │   │
│                                           │   │
│                                           ├───┤
│                                           │ ⇩ │
│                                           ├───┤
│                                           │ ⬓ │
└───────────────────────────────────────────┴───┘
```

This window — called the *type picker* — will eventually hold all of the different
resources you create for this one file. Before proceeding, I'm going to digress
for a moment to explain the differences between the type picker window and

the other two kinds of windows used by ResEdit. It will also allow me to stall on my explanation of how to actually add a resource to the file — thereby building the suspense to a nearly unbearable level!

The Windows of ResEdit

The type picker doesn't display each resource in a resource file. Instead, it will display each *type* of resource in the file. Remember the different types — such as '*WIND*' and '*MENU*'? If a resource file had one '*WIND*' resource and one '*MENU*' resource, its type picker window would look like this:

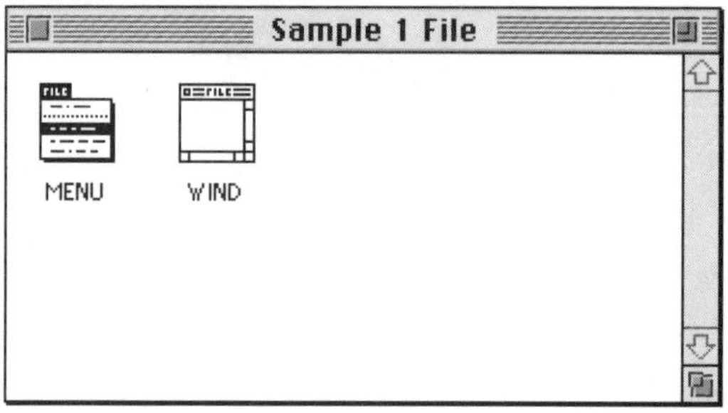

Sample 1 File

MENU   WIND

That's the type picker for a file with one '*MENU*' resource and one '*WIND*' resource. Now, let's look at the type picker for a different resource file — one that has *two* '*MENU*' resources and one '*WIND*' resource:

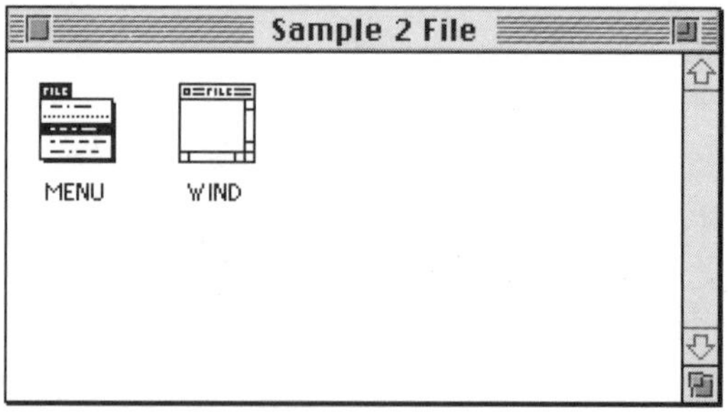

Sample 2 File

MENU   WIND

No, you didn't overlook anything, and it's not a misprint. The two type pickers look the same. That's because each of the examples has the same *types* of resources. That's all that the type picker shows — resource types. To see each *individual* resource of a single type in a file, double-click on an icon in the type picker. Here I double-clicked on the '*MENU*' icon in the first resource file — the one with one '*MENU*' resource:

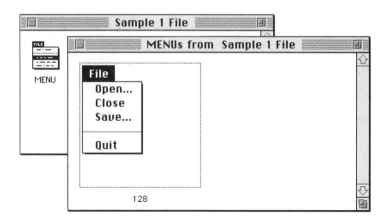

The new window that opened is a *resource picker*. It shows all of the resources of a certain resource type. Here's the resource picker for the second resource file — the one with two '*MENU*' resources:

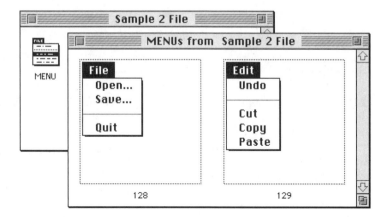

Aha! Now we're getting somewhere. This resource file has two '*MENU*' resources, and the '*MENU*' resource picker shows two menus. We're not through yet, though. So far you've seen that the type picker displays the different resource types, and the resource pickers display the different resources in each type. But ResEdit is a resource editor — so how do you edit one of these resources? Just double-click on a resource in the resource picker. I double-clicked on the dashed box that surrounds the File '*MENU*' resource in the Sample 2 File. Here's the new window I saw:

```
┌─────────────────────────────────────────────┐
│▤▤▤▤▤ Sample 2 File ▤▤▤▤▤│▤│
│┌───────────────────────────────────────────┐▤│
││▤▤▤ MENUs from  Sample 2 File ▤▤▤│▤│
│┌─────────────────────────────────────────────┐│
││▤▤▤▤ MENU ID = 128 from Sample 2 File ▤▤▤▤││
││┌──────────────────────┐  Entire Menu:        ☒ Enabled ││
│││ File                 │⇧                              ││
│││   Open...            │  Title: ◉  ┌─────────────┐││
│││   Save...            │           │ File        │││
│││  ─────────           │           └─────────────┘││
│││   Quit               │         ○  🍎 (Apple menu)  ││
│││                      │                            ││
│││                      │                   Color   ││
│││                      │          Title: ▓         ││
│││                      │ Item Text Default: ▓      ││
│││                      │⇩  Menu Background: □      ││
│└┴──────────────────────┴───────────────────────┘│
└─────────────────────────────────────────────────┘
```

MENU

This window is an *editor* — it's the third and final window type ResEdit uses. An editor is where you make changes to a single resource. There's a different editor for each type of resource. A little later in this chapter I'll cover the '*MENU*' editor.

Beware of menu overload! So far you've seen menu written as: '*MENU*', MENU, and menu. How do they differ? This might help:

'*MENU*' — refers to a menu resource. By convention, most Mac books place resource names between single quotes. This helps you quickly tell when a resource is being referred to.

MENU — also refers to a menu resource. This is the same resource as '*MENU*'. ResEdit works with nothing *but* resources, so every four-character word you see in the resource editor obviously refers to a resource. So Apple doesn't bother to surround each in quotes in its screen displays.

menu — the actual menu in a program, not the resource. Each menu in a program is defined by a '*MENU*' resource — though most program users aren't aware of this. ■

Now, let's recap the three kinds of ResEdit windows:

- ✔ *Type picker*. One per resource file. Displays the different types of resources in a resource file.

- ✔ *Resource picker*. One per resource type. Displays the individual resources for a single resource type.

- ✔ *Editor*. Every resource type has its own editor that allows changes to any resource of that type.

Words are great, but how about a picture? Coming right up:

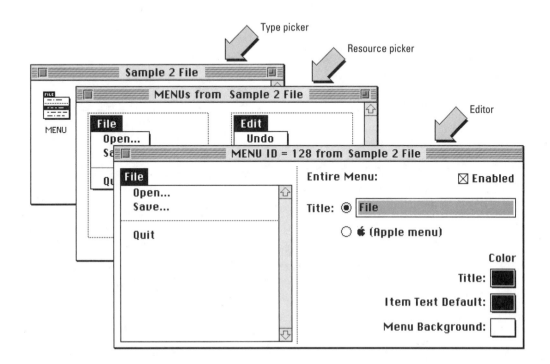

Creating Your Very First Resource

After creating a resource file — and before the discussion of ResEdit windows — we were at this point:

The above window is the type picker for the My Resource File resource file, but it doesn't have any types in it. To add a resource, select Create New Resource from the Resource menu:

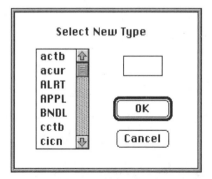

The next thing you'll see is the Select New Type dialog box, shown here:

You'll use the scrollable list in the dialog box to choose which type of resource to create. Try scrolling through this list once. Pretty imposing, huh? There are over 100 resource types listed here. That's the bad news. Don't worry, though — the good news far outweighs the bad. A lot of these types create obscure resources that you'll never have to worry about. The '*itlk*' type, for example, is defined by Apple as follows: "Remappings of certain key combinations before KeyTrans function is called for the corresponding '*KCHR*' resource." Say again? I've programmed the Mac since it first came out a decade ago, and I've yet to use that one. As a matter of fact, I've yet to even hear of anyone else using that one.

If you don't think that definition of the '*itlk*' resource sounds obscure, then you should be reading a much more advanced book — or maybe writing one! ■

Some of the other resource types aren't as obscure, but I won't focus on them in this book. Even if I only cover a few types, I think I can manage to keep you well occupied.

To create a resource, scroll through the list until you find the type you're interested in. To make a '*MENU*', scroll until the word MENU appears in the list. Next, click the resource type to highlight it. When you do, the resource type will be displayed in the previously empty edit box. With the type selected, click the OK button:

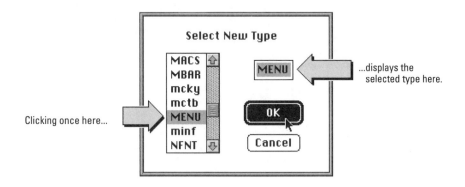

Clicking once here...

Select New Type

MACS
MBAR
mcky
mctb
MENU
minf
NFNT

MENU

...displays the selected type here.

OK

Cancel

Once you click the OK button in the Select New Type dialog box, strange and wonderful things occur. A tiny picture of a menu appears in the type picker, a resource picker is created, and an editor opens. Here are the three windows that you'll see:

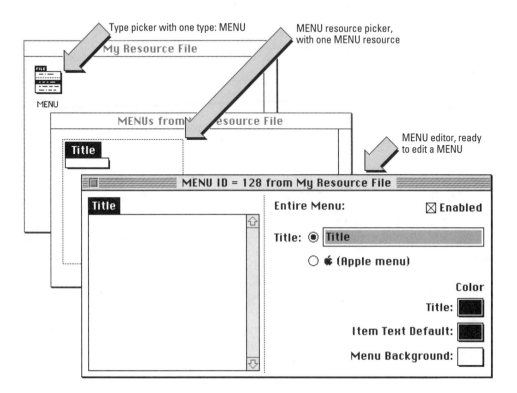

Type picker with one type: MENU

MENU resource picker, with one MENU resource

My Resource File

MENU

MENUs from My Resource File

Title

MENU editor, ready to edit a MENU

MENU ID = 128 from My Resource File

Title

Entire Menu: ⊠ **Enabled**

Title: ⦿ Title

○ ⊛ (Apple menu)

Color

Title:

Item Text Default:

Menu Background:

You've just seen that selecting Create New Resource from the Resource menu does just that — creates a new resource. I've created a *'MENU'* resource that could serve as one menu in a program's menu bar. The menu's title is, generically enough, Title. It has no items in it:

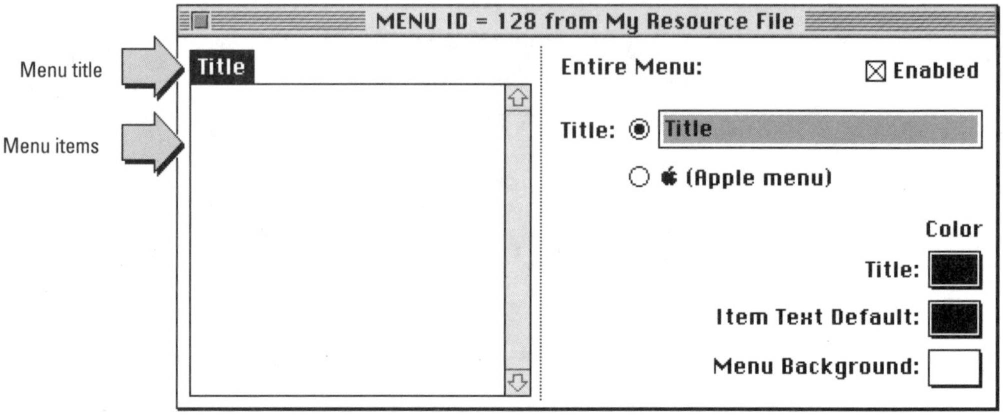

Menu title

Menu items

Programs use resources. A program that tried to make use of my *'MENU'* resource would look like this:

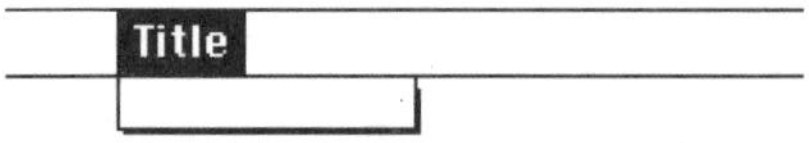

So while I could give myself a pat on the back for making a resource, I won't be quite so self-congratulating. There's still work to be done. Besides, if I were to start patting myself on the back my wife might think I was choking and attempt to administer the Heimlich maneuver!

Adding to a Resource

Each resource type has its own editor. That's because different resources lend themselves to different methods of editing. A menu needs to have words edited — the menu's name and the names of the items that will appear in the menu. A different resource type, such as a window, has different editing needs. For a window you'll want to edit the size of the window and its general look — such as whether or not it gets a title bar along its top. I've discussed the *'MENU'* resource in this chapter, so let's carry on using that resource type in the remaining ResEdit examples.

While there are several tricks a programmer can perform with menus, I'll just focus on the basics. A program's menu consists of a title — the name that will appear in the menu bar that holds the menu — and a list of items, or commands, that appear when the menu is dropped down. I'll create an Edit menu — a menu found in just about every Mac program. Here's how to change the menu's title:

Typing a title here...

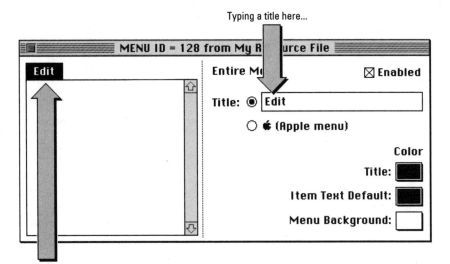

...causes it to also show up here.

Now I'll add an item to the '*MENU*' resource. To do that I select Create New Item from the Resource menu:

If you're observant, this menu choice may look familiar. At the same time, it might look slightly different than a menu selection made earlier in this chapter. Your memory serves you well. To create the '*MENU*' resource I selected the first item in the Resource menu — Create New Resource. To add an item to a '*MENU*', I again selected the first item in the Resource menu. This time, however, the item was Create New Item. ResEdit is no slouch of a program. It knows what you're doing, and it will change some menu commands to commands that are appropriate to the resource being worked on. Here are the two faces of the Resource menu:

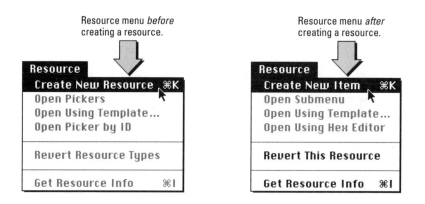

Resource menu *before* creating a resource.

Resource menu *after* creating a resource.

Resource
Create New Resource ⌘K
Open Pickers
Open Using Template...
Open Picker by ID
Revert Resource Types
Get Resource Info ⌘I

Resource
Create New Item ⌘K
Open Submenu
Open Using Template...
Open Using Hex Editor
Revert This Resource
Get Resource Info ⌘I

After selecting Create New Item, ResEdit inverts a section of the '*MENU*' editor. Now, I'll type in the name of the first item I want to appear in my Edit menu. As I type, the characters will appear in two places in the '*MENU*' editor — the text box and under the menu's title:

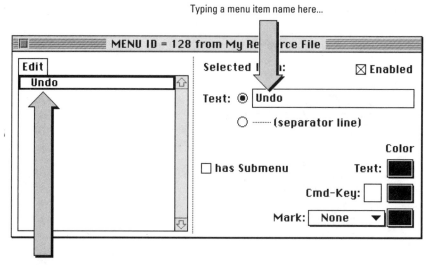

Typing a menu item name here...

...causes it to also show up here.

That's it for adding a menu item. Well, that's *almost* it. You've just seen how to add a menu item that consists of text. There's also a menu item that isn't much of an item at all — the *separator line*. Separator lines allow you to create a menu that has its items grouped into logically related sections — like so:

To add a separator line to a '*MENU*', start out by selecting Create New Item from the Resource menu — just as you did for the first menu item. Now, instead of typing in a name for the item, click on the radio button labeled: (separator line). The new menu item will display a dashed line:

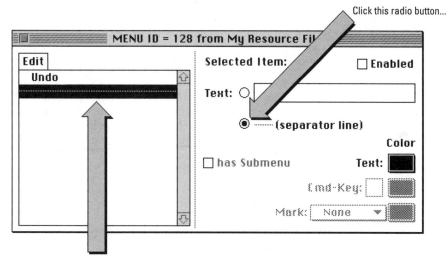

...to make the current item a separator line.

To get a little practice, and to convince yourself that using ResEdit is a breeze, complete the Edit menu by adding three more items. Here's how to add Cut, Copy, and Paste commands to the menu:

1. Select Create New Item from the Resource menu.

2. Type the word: Cut

3. Select Create New Item from the Resource menu.

4. Type the word: Copy

5. Select Create New Item from the Resource menu.

6. Type the word: Paste

Simple, isn't it? After those six steps the '*MENU*' editor will look like the one pictured here:

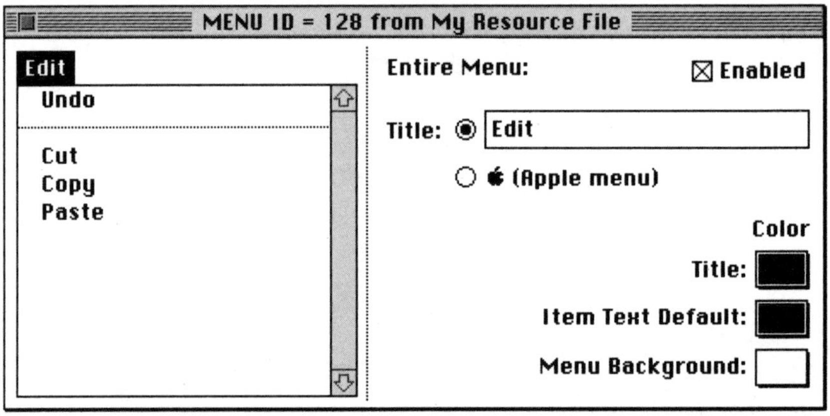

```
▤▤      MENU ID = 128 from My Resource File      ▤▤
┌────────────────────────┐   Entire Menu:          ⊠ Enabled
│ Edit                   │
│ Undo              ⇧    │   Title: ⊙ │Edit                 │
│ ┄┄┄┄┄┄┄┄┄┄┄┄┄┄   │
│ Cut                   │         ○ ❤ (Apple menu)
│ Copy                  │
│ Paste                 │                          Color
│                       │              Title: ▣
│                       │       Item Text Default: ▣
│                  ⇩    │        Menu Background: ▢
└────────────────────────┘
```

Want to see what your new menu would look like in a program? Without writing any source code? I thought that might interest you. ResEdit allows you to preview a menu at any stage in its development. If you look at the last menu in ResEdit's menu bar, you'll see a menu with the same title as the one you're creating. Click on it and it will drop down and show the items you've added to the '*MENU*' resource:

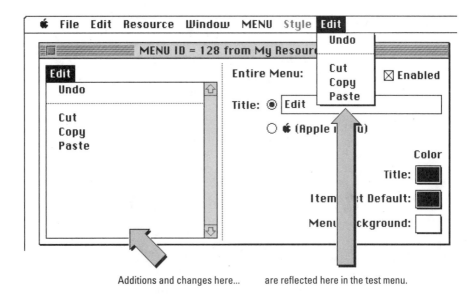

Additions and changes here...   are reflected here in the test menu.

Editing a Resource

ResEdit couldn't really be called a resource *editor* if it wasn't capable of editing a resource you've created. To make a change to one of the items in a '*MENU*' resource, click once on the item to highlight it. Then type in the new item name:

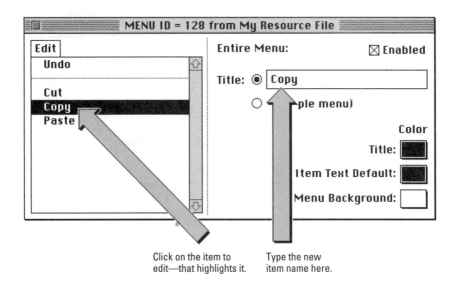

Click on the item to   Type the new
edit—that highlights it.   item name here.

The same procedure works for changing a menu's title. Click on the title, such as Edit in the above example, then type in a new name.

ResEdit allows you to use its own Edit menu to make changes to a resource. Click once on the resource item, then make a selection — such as Cut Item or Copy Item from ResEdit's Edit menu.

When you've completed your additions and changes to a resource file, save it. That's as easy as selecting Save from the File menu. You won't be asked to name the file because you did that when you first started the ResEdit program.

Sorry, Not This Time Around

I'm sure you noticed a few things in the '*MENU*' editor window that I neglected to cover. The number of topics in computer programming is almost endless, so I have to draw the line somewhere. I'm sure you'll forgive me if I tell you that in this book I'll stick to only the most basic concepts. Since you did inquire, though, I'll at least let you know what those other parts of the '*MENU*' editor are for. As is my custom, I'll use a figure. Since I've shown you the '*MENU*' editor window about a dozen times, I'll assume you won't object if I show you just a part of it here:

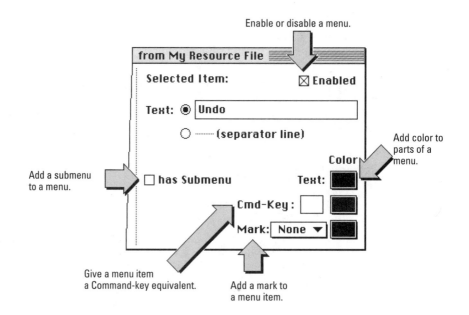

To clarify the above figure, I present yet another figure. Here's an example of each of those '*MENU*' editor features I just pictured:

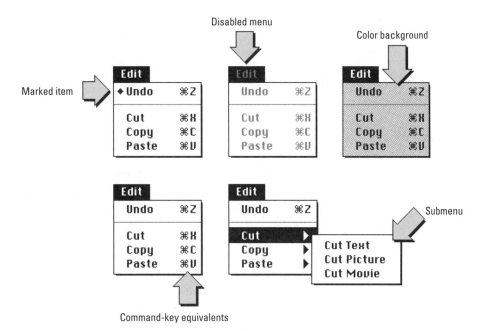

Marked item — ◆ **Undo**

Disabled menu

Color background

Submenu

Command-key equivalents

Sure, you could accuse me of being a tease. I point out all the wonderful things that the '*MENU*' editor is capable of doing, and then I tell you I'll only cover a couple of them. Remember though, creating the resource is only half the battle. To implement a menu in a program you will have to write source code. And the more options you tack onto a menu, the more code you will have to write.

Color is exciting, fun, and visually stimulating. So why don't I cover the topic of color menus in this book? Select the choice that best answers that question:

A. Color menus are "nonstandard" — you rarely if ever see them in a program.

B. I'm saving that topic for the sequel — *Mac Programming for Dummies II.*

C. I couldn't think of a way to add color figures to this black and white book.

The correct answer is letter A. All Macintosh programs have a similar "look and feel" to them. Knowing that all Mac programs behave in a similar way makes users comfortable. A menu with a white background and black text is the norm. Think about the professional software packages you own — do many, or *any*, of them have colored menus?

Now that you know you have the power to add color to your programs, the temptation may be great to add it everywhere — don't. Wait until you have more programming experience, then learn all about color and where to use it effectively. ∎

So why did I bother to show you all of these neat things ResEdit can do? To show you all the neat things ResEdit can do! This book might be just the start of your programming endeavors. Should you survive its hundreds of pages — and I'm betting that you will — you may just want to go on to bigger and better things. Now you know that ResEdit will be the primary tool that will help you do just that.

ResEdit at a Glance

I'll finish off this chapter with three very short reviews. First, a list of the ResEdit menu items used so far:

- ✔ Create New Resource from the Resource menu.
- ✔ Create New Item from the Resource menu.
- ✔ Save from the File menu.

Not much of a review, was it? That's good — it means there's not a whole lot of things you need to memorize. I told you at the outset that ResEdit was easy to use, and I meant it.

The second review is a list of the steps to create a new resource file:

1. Double-click the ResEdit icon to start the program.
2. Click the mouse to get rid of the introductory dialog box.
3. Click the New button.
4. Type in a name for the new resource file and click the New button.

Finally, let's review the steps you'll take to add a new 'MENU' resource to the resource file:

1. Select Create New Resource from the Resource menu.
2. Select the 'MENU' type from the Select New Type dialog box, then click the OK button.
3. Select Create New Item from the Resource menu.
4. Type in a menu item name.
5. Repeat steps 3 and 4 for each menu item.
6. Select Save from the File menu.

All in all, creating a 'MENU' resource wasn't such an overwhelming task, was it? But what about other resource types — are they just as easy to make? Do you have a hunch you might find out in just a page or two?

Chapter 7
The Different Types of Resources

● ●

In This Chapter

▶ Every resource has an ID

▶ Menus live in a menu bar

▶ How to open an existing resource file

▶ Working with the menu bar resource

▶ Creating and editing a window resource

▶ How source code uses a resource

● ●

*R*esources are a good news/bad news kind of thing. The bad news is that there are over 100 different types of resources. The good news is, who cares? — you only need a few types to get a Mac program up and running! I covered the '*MENU*' type in Chapter 6 as an example of creating a resource. '*MENU*' represents a single menu. Here I'll mention the other two types used later in this book — '*MBAR*' and '*WIND*'. These types of resources will allow you to add a menu bar ('*MBAR*') and a window ('*WIND*') to your Mac programs. That'll be it for resources!

Resource IDs

Before jumping right into the new resource types, I'll cover a topic that applies to *all* resource types — resource IDs. Each and every resource has an ID. Why? Because resource editing with ResEdit is getting just too darned simple — it's time to toss around a few numbers just to remind us that we're programming a computer! But of course, you know better than that. There is a very logical reason for giving each resource an identifying number.

At several points in this book I've mentioned that resources and source code work hand-in-hand. In your source code you'll have occasion to work with a particular resource, such as a '*MENU*'. When you do, you'll use the resource's ID. You can't just write source code that in effect says, "Display the '*MENU*' resource in the menu bar," because there might be more than one '*MENU*' resource in your resource file.

Here's how you can find out the ID of each '*MENU*' resource in a resource file:

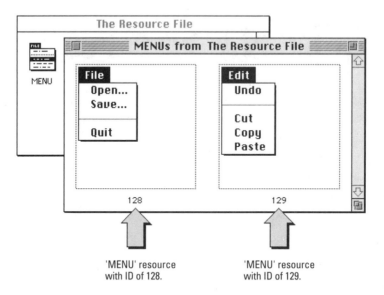

'MENU' resource
with ID of 128.

'MENU' resource
with ID of 129.

Resource type ID numbers generally start at the number 128, and go consecutively from there: 128, 129, 130, and so forth. Don't bother wondering why — you'll never need to know. To see that this is true for '*MENU*' resources, look at the above figure. The two '*MENU*' resources are numbered 128 and 129.

TECHNICAL STUFF

The importance of "128"

If you really *must* know, here's why the resource numbering starts at 128. Every Macintosh has a *system resource file* that contains a whole bunch of resources that are available to all Macintosh programs. It contains resources for things like icons, fonts, and sounds. Having a system resource file means that if you wrote a program such as a word processor, that word processor would have access to all the fonts in the system resource file.

What does the system resource file have to do with the ID numbering limitation? Apple has reserved resource IDs of 0 through 127 for these system resources. That leaves IDs 128 and higher for you.

I won't monkey around with system resources at any point in this book — that's why the information presented in this note is optional reading.

Two traits are used to identify any one resource — its type and its ID number. For that reason you can use the same ID for resources of different types. You're familiar with the '*MENU*' resource, and in this chapter you'll see the resource that defines a window — a '*WIND*' resource. Here's a look at a resource file that contains a '*MENU*' and a '*WIND*' resource — both with an ID of 128:

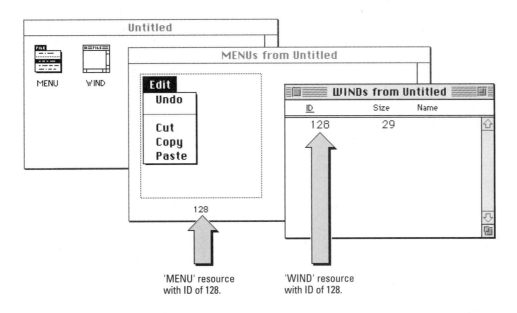

'MENU' resource
with ID of 128.

'WIND' resource
with ID of 128.

That last point can lead to real confusion for many new programmers. It's easy to see why people might mistakenly go to great lengths to ensure that there's no ID duplication in a resource file — they don't want the computer to use the wrong resource. Don't worry — it won't. That's because you'll never write source code that says something like "use resource 128." Instead, your source code will have a meaning more like this: "use window resource 128." The Mac knows the difference between a '*MENU*' resource with an ID of 128 and a '*WIND*' resource with an ID of 128. So it's okay to have both in the same file.

What about accidentally giving two resources of the same type the same ID — such as creating two '*MENU*' resources, both with an ID of 128? Again, there's no reason to worry. ResEdit won't ever assign the same ID to two resources of the same type. ■

What Good Is a Menu Without a Menu Bar?

You'll sometimes hear people casually refer to that white horizontal bar along the top of the Macintosh screen as "the menu." In fact, this is actually the *menu bar*. The menu bar holds one or more menus. Here's a menu bar with six menus in it (the counts as a menu):

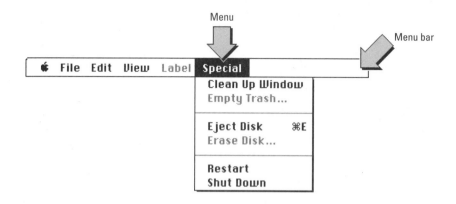

I don't mean to nitpick, but the distinction between the menu bar and the menus is important — and you're about to see why.

Putting Menus in a Menu Bar

In Chapter 6 you saw how to create and edit '*MENU*' resources. To give your Mac program a complete menu bar there's one other menu-related resource type you'll need to create — the '*MBAR*' resource. '*MENU*' resources are individual entities — they are not bound to one another in any way. Not, that is, until you specify which '*MENU*'s are to be a part of your menu bar. The '*MBAR*' takes care of that.

Before going into the details of the relationship between '*MENU*' and '*MBAR*' resources, let's sidetrack a bit. Imagine that you give me a list of the names of some of your relatives. I know they're all related to one another, but until you also tell me where each one lives, I don't know which ones live together:

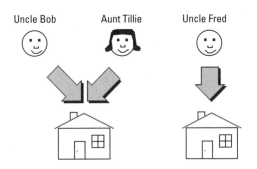

Let's complicate the situation by assuming Uncle Fred owns his own home, and is co-owner of Uncle Bob and Aunt Tillie's house. For a change of scenery, Uncle Fred spends time in each house during different parts of the year:

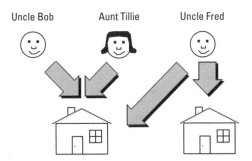

Now, what do these drawings prove? I mean, aside from the obvious fact that my artistic skills are below par? They show that individual objects can belong to more than one group. And the same is true of '*MENU*' resources. You can combine '*MENU*' resources in different ways to form different menu bars. That means you can have more than one '*MBAR*' resource in a resource file. The following figure gives you a general idea of how four '*MENU*' resources might be combined into two '*MBAR*' resources:

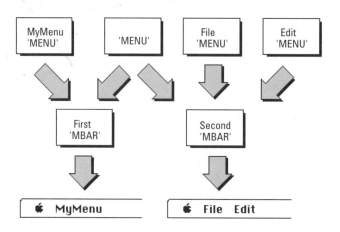

Having more than one menu bar for a single program is a concept that is seldom used — so of course I won't bother to cover it in this book. But even if you only have a single menu bar in your program, you still need an *'MBAR'* resource to define the menu bar.

The multiple menu bar story

Did you ever use a Macintosh program that had a menu change during the running of the program — depending on what action you were performing? It turns out that the resource file for that program has several *'MENU'* resources — which do not all get placed in the menu bar at the same time. That program has more than one menu bar — more than one *'MBAR'* resource — defined for it. During its running, the program will switch menu bars. That's why the ability to group *'MENU'* resources into different *'MBAR'* resources exists.

If you aren't going to have more than one menu bar in a program — as is usually the case — it might seem like the Macintosh should be smart enough to automatically include each *'MENU'* resource in the menu bar of the program it belongs to. The Mac *is* smart enough to do that, but it would be a disservice to programmers who *do* want to use more than one menu bar.

With the introduction of the *'MBAR'* out of the way, it's time to actually make one using ResEdit.

Opening a Resource File

When you run ResEdit, you face a dialog box that lets you create a new resource file or open an existing one. In Chapter 6 you clicked the New button to create a file — I named mine My Resource File. Once you have a resource file, you don't need to create a new one. Click once on its name and then click the Open button:

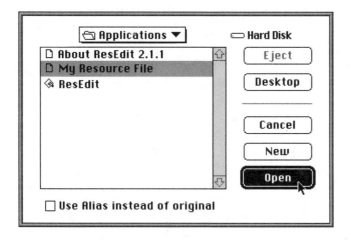

After opening an existing file, the type picker for the file will be displayed. If I open My Resource File its type picker will look like this:

There's only one resource type displayed in this picker — the '*MENU*' type. That's because the only type of resource I've made so far is of the '*MENU*' type.

Opening an existing resource file is a common practice. It's rare for a programmer to create a brand-new resource file, create resources in it, and then never edit that same file. That's because as you work on writing a program you might think of new features you want to add — such as a new menu option for one of the menus. If that happens, you'll open the program's resource file and add that new menu item to an existing *'MENU'* resource. ■

Adding an 'MBAR' to a Resource File

Adding a new resource to a resource file always involves the same steps — you performed them when you created a *'MENU'*:

1. Select Create New Resource from the Resource menu.

2. Select the resource type — such as *'MENU'* — from the Select New Type dialog box, then click the OK button.

3. If the resource has items in it, select the first item from the Resource menu.

To add an *'MBAR'*, select Create New Resource from the Resource menu. You'll see the Select New Type dialog box. Scroll down to MBAR and click once on its name. Then click the OK button.

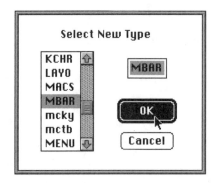

In Chapter 6 you chose MENU from this same dialog box and a *'MENU'* resource picker and a *'MENU'* editor opened. This time, when you select MBAR, you'll again see a resource picker and an editor. This time an *'MBAR'* resource picker and an *'MBAR'* editor open:

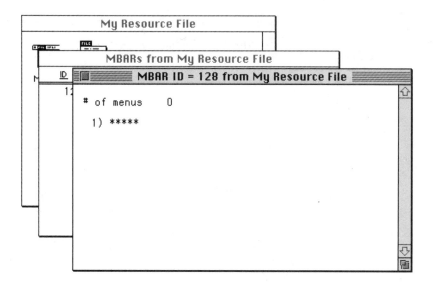

If you've read even just one book on computers, you've read a warning about saving your work — every book includes one. I'm not one to be left out of things, so here's mine. *Save your work, and save it often.* In ResEdit, like most programs, choose Save from the File menu. Or, just press the Command key and the "S" key as a shortcut. Then, if your Mac freezes up, or the power cord gets pulled from the wall (accidentally, or intentionally by an irate spouse), you won't lose your work. It will still be there once you restart your computer. ■

Adding a 'MENU' to an 'MBAR'

The purpose of the '*MBAR*' resource is to list the individual '*MENU*' resources that will be in a menu bar. If you want to include a particular '*MENU*' in the list, what do you use to refer to it? Use its resource ID—that's a topic I covered at the very start of this chapter. Before you start wildly paging back through the book, just look at the figure below. It shows the '*MENU*' resource picker—and the one '*MENU*' it holds — for My Resource File.

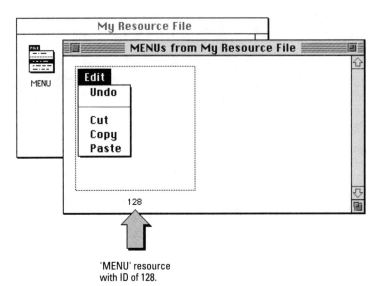

'MENU' resource
with ID of 128.

At any time, you can view the resource picker for any resource type in a file. Simply double-click on its icon in the file's type picker:

Double-click here to see all of
the 'MENU' resources in this file.

Double-click here to
see all of the 'MBAR'
resources in this file.

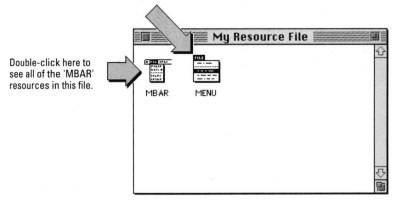

Let's add the one '*MENU*' resource in My Resource File to this '*MBAR*' resource. To add it, click once on the row of five stars in the '*MBAR*' editor. That will place a rectangle around the stars, like this:

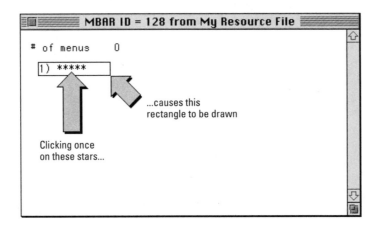

Next, select Insert New Field(s) from the Resource menu. Here's that menu, with Insert New Field(s) selected:

Once again the Resource menu shows its chameleon-like nature by changing the name of the first item in it. You've seen this item as Create New Resource and Create New Item. For an '*MBAR*', you're adding a new field — a new place-holder for the entry of a '*MENU*' resource number. After selecting Insert New Field(s), here's what you'll see:

```
▤▢▥▥▥▥▥▥ MBAR ID = 128 from My Resource File ▥▥▥▥▥  ⇧
  # of menus     1
   ┌──────────────┐
   │1) *****       │
   └──────────────┘
   Menu res ID    ┌────────────────────┐
                  │                    │
                  └────────────────────┘
   2) *****



                                                          ⇩
                                                          ▣
```

The edit box that's been added is the placeholder where you'll type in the
resource ID of a '*MENU*' resource that you want in the '*MBAR*' list. Click the
mouse in the edit box, then type in the number 128. This resource file has just
one '*MENU*' resource in it — and it has an ID of 128. The '*MBAR*' editor now
looks like the one shown below:

```
▤▢▥▥▥▥▥▥ MBAR ID = 128 from My Resource File ▥▥▥▥▥  ⇧
  # of menus     1
   ┌──────────────┐
   │1) *****       │
   └──────────────┘
   Menu res ID    ┌────────────────────┐
                  │ 128                │
                  └────────────────────┘
   2) *****



                                                          ⇩
                                                          ▣
```

If you had more '*MENU*' resources in your resource file, you'd add each of them
in the same manner by following these steps:

1. Click on the row of stars.

2. Select Insert New Field(s) from the Resource menu.

3. Click the mouse in the newly added edit box.

4. Type in the resource ID of the '*MENU*' resource to add.

Menus — Come to Order!

There's one last topic concerning menus and menu bars that I haven't yet covered. What determines the order in which each menu will appear within a menu bar? You'll notice that in just about every Mac program, the File menu comes before the Edit menu (assuming, of course, you read from left to right). How does the programmer guarantee that menus appear in this order? The '*MBAR*' resource takes care of this. The first '*MENU*' listed in the '*MBAR*' will be the first menu on the left in the program's menu bar. The second '*MENU*' will appear next, and so forth. Here's a figure that shows the relationship between an '*MBAR*' with three '*MENU*' resources in it and the menu bar that would result from it:

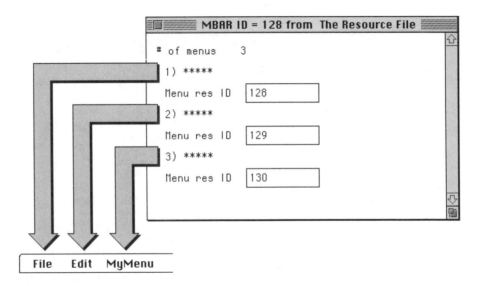

 Hey, where's the Apple? In the preceding figure, and in a few others you've seen here, there's no Ú in the menu bar. Though just about every Mac program has this menu, you can create programs that don't use it. Implementing the Apple menu in a program requires a technique or two that are beyond the scope of this book. ■

Summing Up the Menu/Menu Bar Connection

Now, we'll end this long talk of menus with a killer of a figure that sums up the whole business of combining '*MENU*'s and an '*MBAR*'. Here's the interrelationship between a resource file with two '*MENU*' resources listed in one '*MBAR*', and the menu bar that would result:

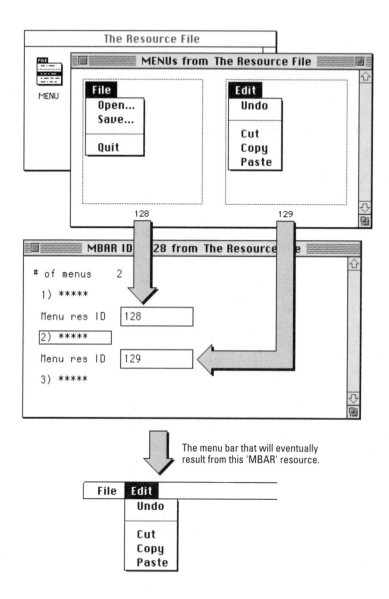

The menu bar that will eventually result from this 'MBAR' resource.

WIND is for Window

Remember that cheap trick I performed back in Chapter 5 — when I showed a window being drawn in a graphics program? I'll take this opportunity to formally apologize for that. I think you'll forgive me if you think back and recall that at the time I pulled that stunt, resource editors hadn't yet been mentioned. Now that you know about ResEdit, it's time to see how a window resource is *really* created.

Opening a Resource File...Again

If you quit ResEdit between the last section and this one, you'll want to reopen your resource file. As you did earlier, run ResEdit and then click once on the name of the resource file to open. Then click the Open button:

The resource file's type picker opens. Mine now has two resource types listed — one for the '*MENU*' resource created in Chapter 6 and one for the '*MBAR*' resource that I just added a few pages back. If you're following along at home your resource picker will look like this:

Breezing Through a 'WIND' Resource

'*WIND*' is the last resource type I'll cover. It defines what a window will look like. Let's add one to My Resource File. Just as you did in Chapter 6 when creating a '*MENU*', and in this chapter when creating an '*MBAR*', select Create New Resource from the Resource menu. The now-familiar Select New Type dialog box will open. Scroll down to WIND, then click once on it. Click the OK button:

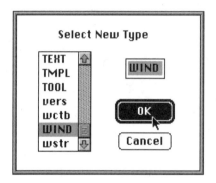

By now you should be getting familiar with what happens next — a resource picker and a resource editor open. Here's a view of the '*WIND*' editor:

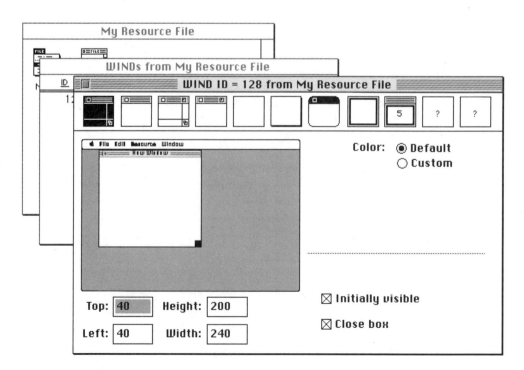

The '*WIND*' editor provides you with an approximation of what your '*WIND*' will look like as a window in a program. It shows a reduced view of a window on a Mac screen. Apple calls this feature of ResEdit the MiniScreen:

The MiniScreen

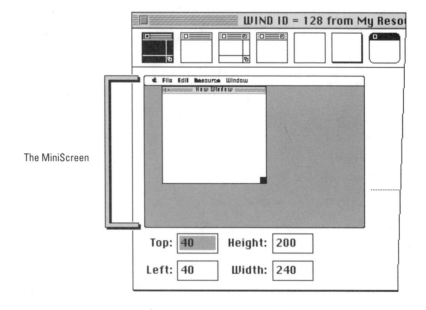

At this point you could save your file and quit ResEdit — you've created a '*WIND*' resource. But, hey, that would be too easy. You've come this far, so why not explore just a little bit? Besides, the longer you play around in ResEdit, the longer you can put off learning how to write source code!

You can change the size of a window by entering different numbers in the four edit boxes. (Click the mouse in a box, or click the Tab key until you're in the right box. The Tab key will highlight, in turn, each of the four edit boxes.)

Changing a Window's Size and Location

In a Mac program, the user can usually move a window to any location on the screen. In many programs, the user can also resize the window. But when it first appears on the screen, how does the window know where it should be, and what size it should start out at? That information is included in the '*WIND*' resource of the window. It's found in the four numbers that appear along the bottom of the '*WIND*' editor:

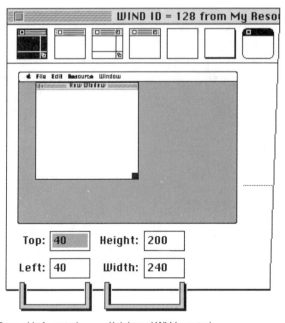

Top and Left control   Height and Width control
a window's placement.   a window's size.

It seems simple enough that by setting the location of the window's top and left sides, and then adjusting the window's height and width, you can place a window anywhere on the screen. What might not be intuitive is just what the numbers are referring to. They're part of the Mac's *coordinate system*. Every point on the screen is numbered so that the Macintosh can keep track of where things are located on its screen. Computers are very ordered creatures, so of course there is a strict order to just how a point on the screen is numbered. I'll go into the details of this numbering system in Chapter 15. For now, you just need to know this much:

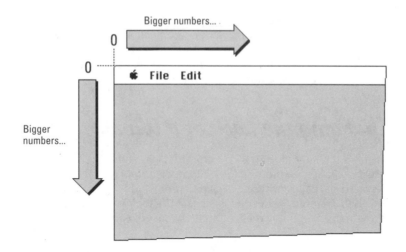

This figure tells you that as numbering goes, the top of the Mac's screen is considered zero and the left side is considered zero. So if I typed in 0 for the Top and 0 for the Left, here's how the change would be reflected in ResEdit's MiniScreen:

Try experimenting with the window's size and placement on the MiniScreen by typing different numbers in all four edit boxes. In Chapter 15 I'll describe in detail all the particulars about these points that make up a Mac screen.

For you anxious types, I'll clue you in right here. Each point on the monitor is called a *pixel*. No, don't worry about getting glitter dust thrown in your eyes — these are *pixels*, not *pixies!* But pixels do have one thing in common with pixies — they're small. Very small. A line just one inch long is made up of over 70 pixels. Now, be patient until Chapter 15. ∎

Changing the Look of a Window

You've just seen that the '*WIND*' editor lets you alter the size of a window. You can also change a window's look. Along the top of the '*WIND*' editor is a row of eleven icons, each representing a different window type. When you create a new '*WIND*' resource, ResEdit assigns it the look of the first icon on the left. You can tell because that is the icon that appears in reverse video:

Highlighted icon when editor of a new 'WIND' opens

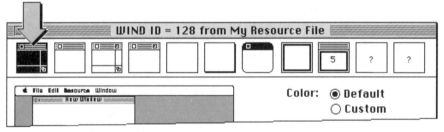

Try clicking on a different icon in the row. In the figure below I've clicked on an icon — the fifth one from the right. Notice that the small window in the MiniScreen has changed its look to reflect the look of the selected window type.

```
┌──────────────────────────────────────────────────────────────┐
│ ▦█   WIND ID = 128 from My Resource File  ▦▦▦▦▦▦▦▦▦▦▦         │
├──────────────────────────────────────────────────────────────┤
│  [▭] [▭] [▭] [▭] [ ] [ ] [█] [ ] [5] [?] [?]                  │
├──────────────────────────────────────────────────────────────┤
│   ⌘ File Edit Resource Window          Color:  ⊙ Default       │
│   □        New Window                          ○ Custom        │
│                                                                │
│                                                                │
│                                                                │
│                                                                │
│                                                                │
│                                                                │
│                                       ⊠ Initially visible      │
│  Top: [40]   Height: [200]                                     │
│                                       ⊠ Close box              │
│  Left: [40]  Width: [240]                                      │
└──────────────────────────────────────────────────────────────┘
```

Here's what a window of this type — once brought to the screen via source code — would look like:

```
┌──────────────────────────────────────────────────────────────┐
│ □                       Window                                 │
├────────────────────────────────────────────────────────────  │
│                                                                │
│                                                                │
│                                                                │
│                                                                │
│                                                                │
│                                                                │
│                                                                │
│                                                                │
└──────────────────────────────────────────────────────────────┘
```

Now click on the second icon from the left. That's the icon I'll be using for any '*WIND*' that I create in this book.

The window type I'll use in this book.

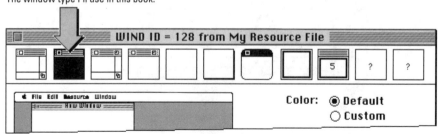

Creating a '*WIND*' with the above icon selected will result in a window with a close box which allows the user to close the window. The window will also have a title bar which gives a window that can be moved around the screen. Here's what a window of this type will eventually look like:

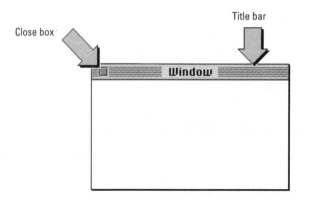

I've covered the major topics concerning the '*WIND*' resource, so it's time to save the file and quit ResEdit. Before I do, take a look at the type picker for My Resource File:

Of the hundred-plus resource types available to you, these are the only three you'll need to get a real live Macintosh program up and running.

Source Code Preview

This chapter started with a discussion of resource IDs. You saw that every resource has an ID number that helps to identify it. Identify it to what, though? In some cases, the ID helps one resource identify other resources, as shown when I listed '*MENU*' resource IDs in a '*MBAR*' resource. That let the menu bar '*MBAR*' resource know which '*MENU*' resources would be in its list of menus. In other instances, a resource ID is used by source code. I showed you this — without explanation — back in Chapter 4. Here's a line from that chapter's ExampleOne program:

```
TheWindow = GetNewWindow( 128, 0L, (WindowPtr)-1L );
```

You know from Chapter 4 that the above line of code displays a window on the screen. But there's almost a dozen different types of windows, and a window can take on just about any size or screen location. How does *GetNewWindow* obtain this information? Yes, yes, I hear you. From a '*WIND*' resource, of course. What if the resource file contains more than one '*WIND*' resource — which one does *GetNewWindow* use? The one whose number appears between the parentheses:

Resource ID of the 'WIND' resource
that holds information for this window.

```
TheWindow = GetNewWindow( 128, 0L, (WindowPtr)-1L );
```

Hopefully the above figure is the proof you need to verify that all your efforts in creating resources with ResEdit are not without purpose. They really are important, and they really will be of use later on when you write your own source code.

Part III
Using a Compiler

"WELL, SYSTEMS INTEGRATION ISN'T PERFECT. SOME DEPARTMENTS STILL SEEM TO GET MORE INFORMATION THAN OTHERS."

In this part . . .

Your Mac isn't nearly as smart as it appears to be. You see, it doesn't understand a single word you type. When you create a source code file by typing in C language commands, the Mac needs the help of a software program to translate your source code into numbers the computer can understand. That very helpful program is called a *compiler*. This book uses the THINK C compiler by Symantec Corporation for its examples.

To save you the trouble of wading through the hundreds and hundreds of pages that make up the THINK C user manual, I've condensed it all down to just three chapters — about fifty pages. Now, the fact that I ripped out and threw away most of my THINK C user manual might seem like a slap in the face to the technical writers over at Symantec. Hold on a minute, though. I'm not saying they're a bunch of rambling, wordy, folks. The entire THINK C manual is very important — to advanced Mac programmers. For the rest of us, the very basics will do just fine. So that's what this part of the book is about.

Chapter 8

Getting to Know You: The THINK C Compiler

● ●

In This Chapter

▶ Why I selected the THINK C compiler

▶ Organizing files in a THINK C project

▶ Creating and naming a project

▶ Adding a library to a project

● ●

Compilers are a topic that often intimidates new programmers. Fortunately for you, you read and completely understood Chapter 3, right? There you learned that a compiler does nothing more than turn your human-readable source code into a computer-readable program. Here in Part III you'll learn all of the specifics of using the THINK C compiler.

Why THINK C?

Different software companies make compilers — so why did I select the THINK C compiler by Symantec Corporation as the one to write about? Because it's got a catchy name. Well, that's one of the reasons. Here are the others:

  ✔ THINK C is easy to use.

  ✔ THINK C is less expensive — by hundreds of dollars — than Apple's compiler.

  ✔ About 80% of the Macintosh C compilers sold today are THINK C.

The THINK C compiler is loaded with features that make Mac programmers drool. Let them drool. You're looking for simplicity, and the THINK C compiler is capable of that, too. It's easy to use, and user friendly. It has "a clean interface," as they say. You'll only be interested in a handful of the many menu options.

It costs *hundreds* of dollars less, huh? That reason alone may be good enough for you to purchase it. But there's still one more…

Sometimes it's good to be different — sometimes it's not. I didn't choose the THINK C compiler just to part of the "in" crowd. I chose it because of support. If you ever have a question about the compiler, you can turn to just about any Macintosh programmer for help. Chances are they will also be using the THINK C compiler.

Yes, I did say earlier that some evil programmers love to see newcomers sweat. But the majority of Mac enthusiasts enjoy extending a hand to someone struggling with a programming problem—they've been down that same road too. As a matter of fact, if you have a modem and you belong to an online information service, such as America Online, you can post Mac programming questions to more experienced programmers. You'll usually get a response that very same day. ■

The THINK C Icons

Chapter 3 discussed compilers, and what they do. In that chapter I presented the following figure:

Chapter 6 covered resources, and mentioned how they work in conjunction with source code. There I updated the previous figure so that it looked like this:

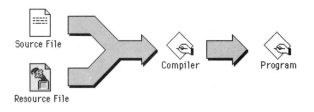

Now it's time to get a little more wear and tear out of this illustration by once again modifying it. Ready?

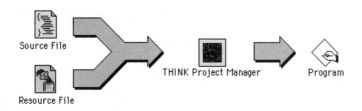

In the above figure I haven't injected any new theory about what a compiler does. The story's the same, but the faces have changed. I've simply replaced the generic text file and compiler icons with the ones THINK C uses.

Earlier I said that source code is held in a text file. That still applies. THINK C has a built-in text editor that allows you to write source code and save it to a text file. The advantage of this approach is that you don't have to run both a text editing program (like TeachText) and a compiler. So that you know a text file was created by THINK C, the compiler gives the file its own special icon:

Now turn your attention to the program icon that replaced the generic compiler icon. It looks like this:

This program, named THINK Project Manager, is the THINK C compiler. Then why is it called a Project Manager? Because projects are an important part of the THINK C way of doing things — as you're about to see.

A Program Starts as a Project

The source code of a program is held in a text file. Sometimes, when there's a lot of source code, a programmer will divide it up into several text files. When it comes time to compile the source code, the THINK C compiler is smart enough to know how to combine the source code from different files into one program. It does need a little help, though. The compiler needs to be told which files to use. A *project* is nothing more than the means to group multiple files together so that the THINK C compiler knows they are related to one another.

Libraries Aren't Just for Books Anymore

All of the examples included in this book will be small enough to fit easily in one text file. But all the projects will contain two files. One of the files will be the source code text file that you create, and the other will be a *library*. A library contains source code that is already compiled and is ready to be combined with your own source code. Who wrote the code in the library? Could be anyone — anyone can make libraries. In this case, the folks at Symantec Corporation are responsible. Who wrote the code and how they turned it into a library aren't important. What is important is that the code will work in conjunction with your own code — with almost no effort on your part.

Introducing a new topic — libraries — means it's time for a new figure. At the risk of being repetitious, I've updated a figure you're all too familiar with:

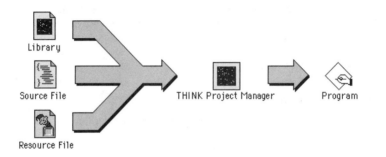

Before panicking at the ever-increasing complexity of this figure, hear me out. *This is the last time this figure will be added to.* That's a promise. And really, the figure isn't *that* bad. Let's take a closer look at the three files lined up on the left of it — the three files that get merged (via the THINK Project Manager) into a new Macintosh program:

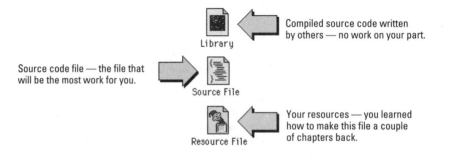

The only one of the three file types you need to know more about is the source code file. You know what a source code file is, but you haven't created one — yet. In the very next chapter you will.

Naming a Project

Every Macintosh program you create using the THINK C compiler starts as a project. You create a new project, give it a name, and then add two files to it. One file — the library — already exists. Several libraries are included on the disks that come with the THINK C compiler. The other file — the text file holding your source code — has to be created by you.

When you start a new project, THINK C will ask you to give it a name. Just about any name will work. THINK C would recognize all of the following examples:

>   My Project

>   MyProject

>   NewProj

>   Dan's C Project

While all of the preceding would work, I'm going to ask that you add a little something to the end of your project's name — no matter what the name. Pick a name, then type a period followed by the *pi* symbol. The *pi* symbol looks like this: π. It is created by pressing and holding down the Option key and then typing the letter "p". If I added this ending to each of the above examples, the project names would now look like this:

>   My Project.π

>   MyProject.π

>   NewProj.π

>   Dan's C Project.π

True, it's a little odd-looking — but it has come to be a THINK *convention*. That is to say, anyone who uses THINK C will immediately recognize a name ending in this way as a THINK C project.

By now you should be getting a pretty good feel for what a THINK C project is. There's no better way to learn about something than by doing it, though. So let's go ahead and make a project.

Creating a Project

Whether you want to write a program that simply opens a window and writes "Hello, World!" or one that does inventory and accounting for a multimillion-dollar business, you'll start each in exactly the same way. You'll create a THINK C project.

Installing THINK C

Of course, before you can create a project you have to install THINK C on your hard drive. If you haven't done so already, install THINK C now. Follow the installation instructions that came with the product.

Creating a Project Folder

The THINK C environment — that is, the folders and files that make up THINK C — are in a single main folder called Development. The installation process created this folder and its contents for you. If you're a neat, tidy person, you'll want to create a new folder to hold your new project. If you're not neat and tidy, create one anyway! Double-click on the Development folder to open it, then select New Folder from the File menu. Give the folder an appropriate name, such as My Folder. That's what I've done here:

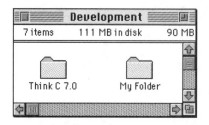

The THINK C compiler comes in different versions. When Symantec, the maker of the compiler, adds new features to the compiler it gives it a new version number. Version 7.0 came out not too long ago. Before that was — you guessed it — version 6.0. Some figures in this book — like the one above — show version 7.0. If you have version 6.0, don't fret. Everything I'll be talking about applies to you too.

Creating a New Project

Open the folder containing the THINK Project Manager — it's the folder titled Think C 7.0. Or, for you version 6.0 users, the folder will be called Think C 6.0. Double-click on the THINK Project Manager icon to start things off. You'll see a dialog box like this one:

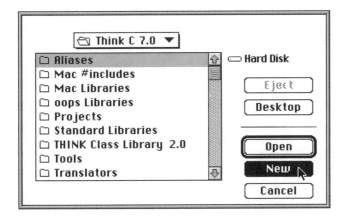

THINK C doesn't do anything without a project open. This dialog box allows you either to open an existing project or to create a new one. You're creating a new project, so click the New button. If you're using THINK C 7.0, you'll see:

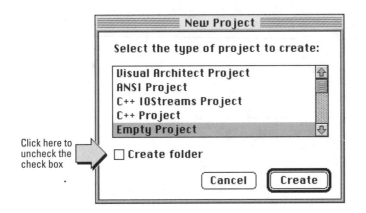

Click here to uncheck the check box

If you're using THINK C 6.0, you won't see a dialog like this. Be patient for just a moment as I attend to the 7.0 users. As shown above, you 7.0 users want to click on the check box to uncheck it — you won't be needing a new folder. Also click once on the words "Empty Project." Next click on the Create button. When you do, a different dialog box will appear:

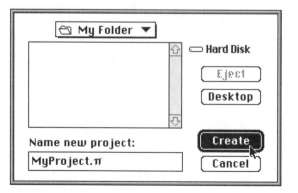

If you're using THINK C 6.0, you'll see the above figure too. Now, whether you use THINK C 6.0 or THINK C 7.0, the remaining steps are the same. In this dialog box you'll want to navigate your way into the project folder you created — the one I named My Folder. Both the Think C folder and My Folder are inside the Development folder. In the figure above I'm backtracking to the Development folder.

From here on in, both versions of the THINK C compiler — version 6.0 and 7.0 — work the same. Because version 7.0 is the most recent version, I use it in the figures in this book. If you're using version 6.0, don't be alarmed. Everything will work just as I describe it throughout the book. ■

Once I see My Folder in the scrollable list of folders I'll double-click on it. Then the dialog box will look just like the one pictured below. Note that My Folder is empty — as it should be. There won't be anything in it until I click the Create button to create a new project. First, though, I type in a name for the project. Of course I remember to use the project-naming convention discussed a couple of pages back.

After clicking the Create button the dialog box disappears and a THINK C project window opens:

```
┌─────────────────────────────────┐
│ ═══════ MyProject.π ═══════      │
├──────────────────┬──────────────┤
│ Name             │ Code         │
├──────────────────┼──────────────┤
│ Totals           │ 578    ⬆     │
│                  │              │
│                  │              │
│                  │              │
│                  │              │
│                  │      ⬇       │
│                  │      ⬚       │
└──────────────────┴──────────────┘
```

There's not much in this window, and there shouldn't be. You have to add to the project. I said that projects will consist of two files—a library and your source code file. I haven't created a source code file yet, so there's nothing I can do about adding that one just now. The library is another story. A library is a file of prewritten, precompiled code. That means it already exists. So you can add that file now.

Adding to a Project

Every project you create will need to have the MacTraps library added to it. The code that is embedded in this library will be used by each of your programs. It helps your program do all those neat Macintosh things like open windows and pull down menus. Do you want the specifics of just how the MacTraps library works in conjunction with your code? Then you better buy another book — 'cause I won't talk about it in this one. The interaction between MacTraps and your source code is invisible to you and to anyone using a program you write. Once you've added the MacTraps library to your project, you can forget all about it. You won't do another thing with it.

At the beginning of this chapter, I said that you'd only need to use some of the dozens of menu items available in THINK C. Here's the first menu item you'll need to use:

Source
Add Window
Add Files...
Remove
Get Info
Debug ⌘I
SourceServer ▶

Check Syntax ⌘Y
Preprocess
Disassemble

Precompile...
Compile ⌘K
Make... ⌘\

Browser ⌘J

The Add Files menu item in the Source menu allows you to — ready for this? — add files to your project. Here I'll add the one and only library I'll use — now and throughout the remainder of the book. When you select Add Files, you'll see this dialog box:

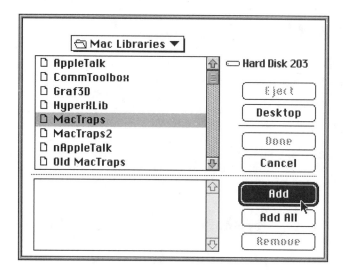

When you see this dialog box, the file names won't match the ones shown in the figure. Not right away. That's because you've got to work your way into the Mac Libraries folder, which resides in the Think C folder, which is in the Development folder. Got it? If not, this might help:

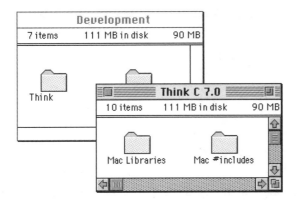

Once you're in the folder containing the Mac libraries, click once on the library named MacTraps, then click on the Add button. The dialog box will now look like this:

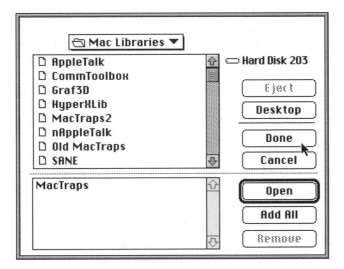

The MacTraps library has been moved to the list at the bottom of the dialog box. The more files you add, the more names will move to this section. But of course, we're only adding this one file — the MacTraps library. Now click the Done button. The dialog box will disappear and you'll see your project window again — with the newly added MacTraps library in it:

```
┌──────────────────────────────────┐
│ ≡≡≡≡≡   MyProject.π   ≡≡≡≡≡       │
├──────────────────────┬───────────┤
│  Name                │  Code     │
├──────────────────────┼───────────┤
│ ▽ Segment 2          │      4  ⇧ │
│   MacTraps           │      0    │
│   Totals             │    582    │
│                      │           │
│                      │           │
│                      │        ⇩  │
│                      │        ▤  │
└──────────────────────┴───────────┘
```

Here's a quick summary of the steps you'll take to add a file to a project. These
steps apply to both source code text files and libraries — a library is just a
different type of file.

1. Select Add Files from the Source menu.

2. Move to the folder that contains the file to add.

3. Click once on the file's name.

4. Click the Add button.

5. Click the Done button.

That takes care of adding a file to a THINK C project. Next, you'll want to add a
source code file to the project. I'll show you how to do that in the next chapter. And
of course I won't let the fact that you don't yet know the C language stop me!

Chapter 9

Writing Source Code— It's Not Hard, Honest!

● ●

In This Chapter

▶ How to open an existing THINK project

▶ Finally, creating a source code file

▶ Adding a source code file to a THINK project

▶ Typing in the source code

● ●

*W*riting source code involves two steps. First, you have to be familiar with the basics: how to create a source code text file, how to make that file part of your project, and how to correctly type in the code. The second step is to know *what* to type in. In this chapter I'll *show* you how to deal with the basics and I'll *tell* you what to type in. At the end of the chapter you'll be comfortable with the process of working with source code, and you'll have the bonus of a source code file that you can compile in the next chapter.

Opening a Project

If you're still in the THINK Project Manager program, exit it by selecting Quit from the File menu. In the last chapter you started THINK C by double-clicking on the THINK Project Manager icon. Now I'm going to show you a second way to run THINK C.

At the start of Chapter 8 you didn't have a THINK C project to work with. When you double-clicked on the THINK Project Manager you saw a dialog box that let you create a new project. Now that you have a project, you can bypass this step and run THINK C directly from the project icon. Double-clicking the icon of a project launches THINK C and opens that project.

Yes, it "launches" the program. To launch a program means to run it. Then why not just say "run" the program? For the same reason the Macintosh interface consists of icons and windows, not just text — Mac users like a little fun and novelty in their computers. And the terminology surrounding the Macintosh sometimes reflects this mood. ■

I made a project in My Folder called MyProject.π in the previous chapter. Here's the icon for it:

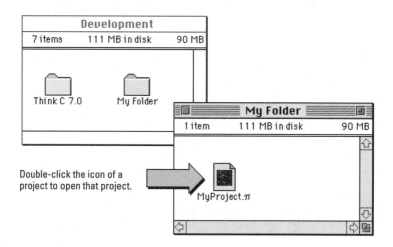

Double-clicking the project icon puts you in THINK C and opens the project window for that project. Here's what I saw after double-clicking MyProject.π:

Name	Code
▽ Segment 2	4
MacTraps	0
Totals	**582**

Now that you know the shortcut for opening a project, it's time to move on to something more productive — like adding a source code file to the project.

Working with a Source Code File

There's not much point in knowing a computer language if you can't figure out how to create and save a file to type code into. So at this point, it's more important that you get the feel for working with source code files. In Part IV I'll fill you in on the details of learning what source code to type in.

Creating a Source Code File

A source code file is a text file. So just as you'd do to create a new text file in a text editor like TeachText, in THINK C you select New from the File menu. When you do, an empty window like this one will open:

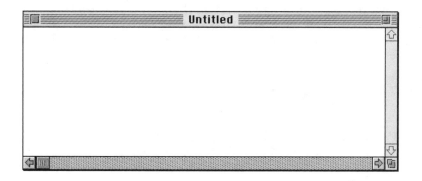

Looks just like a window in a Macintosh text editor or word processor, doesn't it? And if you start typing, it will behave like one, too:

```
This is programming? It isn't quite how I pictured it.
```

Just as I promised you several times, a source code file is nothing more than a text file.

Saving the Source Code File

You've probably already guessed that the words I typed in the window in the preceding figure don't qualify as source code. I'll remedy that in a bit. But first I'll save the file and then add the file to the project. Creating a new text file with the New command does not automatically place the file in your project.

You'll want to add the new file to your project right away so you don't forget. I'll be adding this file to the project in the next section. You don't have to have all your source code typed in before saving a file or adding it to your project. Once the file is added to the project, you can still edit it at any time. ■

You're familiar with the Save and Save As commands in the File menu — they work identically to those found in any Mac text editor or word processor. The Save command saves a file — you should use it periodically to save changes and additions to your source code. The Save As command saves a file, but first allows you to name it. After creating a new file with the New command, select Save As to name it. When you do, you'll see a dialog box like this one:

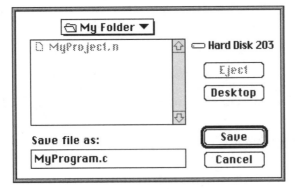

To keep things organized, you'll want to save the source code file to the same folder that your project is in. As you've done in the past, use the menu at the top of the dialog box to move to the folder containing the project. Once it's shown at the top of the dialog box — as it is in the above figure — you can type in a file name.

Give your source code file any name you want — but make sure it ends with a period followed by the letter "c", like this:

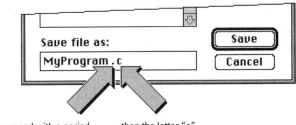

Always end with a period...   then the letter "c".

That ending to the file name is important. When you try to add a source code file to a project, the THINK Project Manager will only allow you to add a file that is C language source code. The letter "c" tells the THINK Project Manager that this file contains C language code. After typing in the name, click the Save button.

This point is worth repeating. A source code file is a text file. But the THINK Project Manager doesn't want to work with just any old text file — it wants source code. Without the ".c" at the end of the file name you won't be able to add the file to the project — the THINK Project Manager will be looking only for libraries and files ending with ".c". In fact, when it comes time to add the file to the project, a source code file with no ".c" at the end of its name won't even appear in the scrollable list of files to add. It will have seemingly disappeared! What happens then? You panic. You think your hours of typing once-in-a-lifetime ideas were wasted. You end it all by jumping out of your window. I can't have that on my conscience — that's why I've devoted all this space to the naming of files. ■

Half of the menu commands you'll use in the THINK Project Manager are in the File menu. Here's a recap of them:

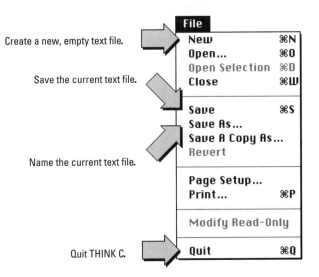

All Macintosh programs have names — yours will too. You'll be giving your program a name at a later time. The program's name can be different than the name of the source code file, so don't spend a whole lot of time thinking of a clever, catchy name right now — you've got work to do! ■

Adding the Source Code File to the Project

With your file named and saved, it's time to add it to the project. Use the same menu command that you used to add the MacTraps library to the project:

```
Source
  Add Window
  Add Files...
  Remove
  Get Info
  Debug           ⌘I
  SourceServer    ▶

  Check Syntax    ⌘Y
  Preprocess
  Disassemble

  Precompile...
  Compile         ⌘K
  Make...         ⌘\

  Browser         ⌘J
```

In the last chapter you saw the dialog box that results from the Add Files command, and here it is again. Work your way into the folder containing the project and source code files.

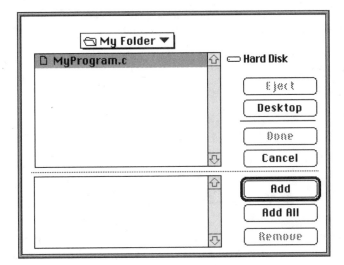

Notice in the above figure that even though there are two files in My Folder — the MyProgram.c source code file and the MyProject.π project file — only one of them shows up in the list. As I repeatedly mentioned, only libraries and files ending with ".c" will be in this list.

Click once on the MyProgram.c name, then click the Add button. Or just double-click on the MyProgram.c name. The result is the same — the file moves to the bottom section of the dialog box:

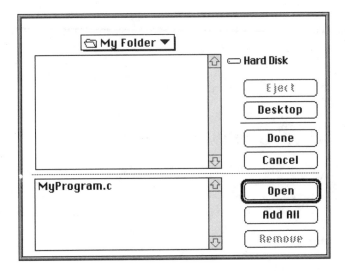

Click the Done button to dismiss the dialog box. You'll then see that the MyProgram.c file has been added to the project:

MyProject.π	
Name	**Code**
▽ **Segment 2**	4
MacTraps	0
MyProgram.c	0
Totals	**582**

These are the only two files you'll need in the project. In general, here are the steps for creating a project that will be used as the basis of a new Macintosh program:

1. Run the THINK Project Manager to create a new project file.
2. Choose Add Files from the Source menu to add the MacTraps library to the project.
3. Choose New from the File menu to create a new, empty text file.
4. Choose Save As from the File menu to name and save the text file.
5. Choose Add Files from the Source menu to add the new text file to the project.

Following the above five steps results in a project that's just about ready to be turned into a Macintosh program. Of course, there's a couple of trivial steps remaining, like writing the source code and compiling it. I'll cover both in the remainder of this chapter. But first, let me digress for a moment to clear up the use of a term you might encounter as you use THINK C.

The THINK C Environment

I said that the THINK C compiler has a built-in text editor. That's what you're using now. If you look across the menu bar, you'll see an Edit menu. It contains all the standard editing commands like Cut, Copy, and Paste. You can use all of these commands on the text in the window that's now open on the screen. But the menu bar also holds some unfamiliar menus, like the Project menu and the Source menu:

É   File   Edit   Search   Project   Source   Windows

These menus are for working with or managing projects and for compiling source code. You don't actually leave the compiler to go to the editor, or leave the editor to manage a project, or leave the project area to compile source code. They coexist, each one always ready for your use. Because of this, programmers often refer to the THINK C *environment*. I'll occasionally use that phrase here in the book. What I won't say is something like, "go to the THINK C text editor" — because there's nowhere to go. You just create a new file or open an existing one and start typing in it.

Sometimes Mac programmers like to throw terminology around rather loosely. Kind of a "Hey, I've been doing this so long that I don't *have* to choose my words carefully" attitude. The program you've been working with is called the THINK Project Manager, not THINK C. So while there is actually no software program called THINK C, you'll hear phrases like "launch THINK C," or "run the compiler." Since I want you to feel like a Mac programmer as soon as possible, I hereby grant you permission to do the same. From here on in you and I will usually simply say "THINK C" rather than the unwieldy "THINK Project Manager environment." ▪

Entering the Source Code

You've come into contact with source code a few times in this book — as early as Chapter 3. In Chapter 4 I introduced a very short Macintosh program that I called ExampleOne. Since I like to stick with familiar territory whenever possible, I'll use that very same source code in this chapter's example.

Opening a Project File

When a source code file is open the source code appears in a standard window that has a close box in the title bar. You can close a source code file anytime. Once the file has become part of a project through the use of the Add Files menu option, it will remain part of that project — even if you close the file. If the file is still open, close it now by clicking in its close box — or go-away box as some people call it.

To reopen a source code file that's part of a project, double-click on the file's name in the project window:

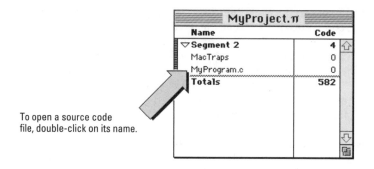

To open a source code
file, double-click on its name.

This trick doesn't work well on a library — such as MacTraps. A library isn't a source code file — it doesn't hold source code you can view and edit. It holds code that has been already compiled by others. If you do accidentally double-click on a library like MacTraps, here's what you'll see:

Name	Code	Data	Jump	Strs
▽Segment 2	7030	206	2224	0
CPstr.Lib	54	0	16	0
DITLFuncs.o	58	0	24	0
EnvironsGlue.a.o	362	0	8	0
GestaltGlue.a.o	646	0	24	0
MacTraps.note	0	0	0	0
OSTraps.a.o	4948	0	1672	0
PackTraps.a.o	252	0	200	0
QDGlobals.a.o	0	206	0	0
SlotTraps.a.o	120	0	64	0
ToolTraps.a.o	582	0	208	0
UnloadA4Seg.Lib	4	0	8	0
Totals	**7608**	**206**	**2336**	**0**

Don't worry, even I don't know what all that means. To get back to the safety and comfort of your project, click and hold the mouse down on the Switch To Project menu item in the Project menu. With the mouse still held down, drag to the right to drop down a second menu. Select your project from this menu. That will close the above window and put you right back where you started.

```
┌─────────────────────────────────┐
│ Project                          │
├─────────────────────────────────┤
│ Close Project                    │
│ Close & Compact                  │
│ Switch To Project    ▶  MyProject.π │
│                         MacTraps  ▸ │
├─────────────────────────────────┤
│ Set Project Type...              │
│ Remove Objects                   │
├─────────────────────────────────┤
│ Bring Up To Date      ⌘U         │
│ Check Link            ⌘L         │
│ Build Library...                 │
│ Build Application...             │
├─────────────────────────────────┤
│ Use Debugger                     │
│ Run                   ⌘R         │
└─────────────────────────────────┘
```

While I was feverishly writing this chapter, I closed the MyProgram.c file so it wouldn't be in my way on the screen. I used the technique of double-clicking on its name in the project window to reopen it. When I opened it, I was back to where I left off:

If your window looks something like mine, or you have some other gibberish typed in it, get rid of it now. Use any of the standard editing techniques you're familiar with. You can click the mouse on the text to highlight it, then select Cut from the File menu or just hit the Delete key. If you have a little time to kill, you can click the mouse at the very end of the text and just backspace over all of it. Whatever works for you is fine with me.

Typing In the Code

The trick to becoming a programmer isn't becoming an accomplished typist — it's knowing *what* to type. In Part IV I'll cover all that — what to type and what it means. But even without knowing quite what the source code means, you can still get a good feel for the process of writing code.

Click the mouse in the MyProgram.c window and start typing the example program I listed back in Chapter 4. I've repeated it below. I've shown it in a window so you can compare it to your own window:

```
main()
{
    WindowPtr  TheWindow;

    InitGraf( &thePort );
    InitFonts();
    InitWindows();

    TheWindow = GetNewWindow( 128, 0L, (WindowPtr)-1L );

    SetPort( TheWindow );
    MoveTo( 30, 50 );
    DrawString( "\pHello, World!" );

    while ( !Button() )
        ;
}
```

As you type in the source code, you may have a few questions about what's important and what isn't. While some rules about writing source code are written in stone, other factors are left to the whim of the programmer. Now then, what should you be concerned with as you enter the code? Keep these points in mind:

✔ Most lines, but not all, end with a semicolon.

✔ Each parenthesis is crucial.

✔ Each brace is crucial.

✔ Proper use of uppercase and lowercase is essential in all words.

The following is a figure that highlights some of the points you *should* be concerned with as you type in the code:

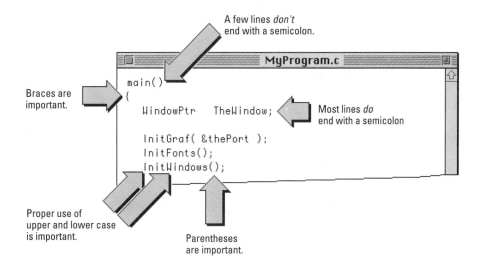

Here's a list that should answer the inquiries about what *isn't* important about entering source code:

- ✔ The number of spaces or tabs between words.
- ✔ The number of spaces or tabs used to indent lines.
- ✔ Whether or not blank lines are used occasionally.
- ✔ Whether or not spaces are between words that lie within parentheses.
- ✔ The font or the size of text used to display the source code.

The following is a figure that points out the *less* important concerns of writing source code:

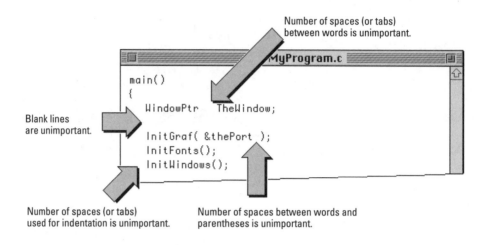

Number of spaces (or tabs)
between words is unimportant.

MyProgram.c

```
main( )
{
    WindowPtr    TheWindow;

    InitGraf( &thePort );
    InitFonts();
    InitWindows();
```

Blank lines
are unimportant.

Number of spaces (or tabs)
used for indentation is unimportant.

Number of spaces between words and
parentheses is unimportant.

If you've got all the code typed, the next step is to compile it. I've talked about compiling several times already, so it's about time you actually got to try it!

Chapter 10

Compiling and Running
Your Source Code

• •

In This Chapter
▶ The importance of the resource file

▶ Compiling a source code file

▶ What to do if compiling doesn't work

▶ Testing a program by running it

▶ Turning code into a final program

• •

*Y*ou've learned what a compiler is, how to create a project, how to make a source code file, and how to enter the source code. You're only a few steps away from being face-to-face with a brand-new Macintosh program you can call your own. So let's not waste any time...

Don't Forget the Resource File

Just about every Macintosh program starts out as a source code file and a resource file. In Chapter 9 you created a source code file — I called mine MyProgram.c. If you want to end up with a program, you'll also need a resource file to accompany the source code file. In Chapters 5 through 7 you learned all about resources and resource files, so creating one here will be a snap.

Begin by running ResEdit. Move into the folder that contains the project, then click the New button — just as I'm about to do here:

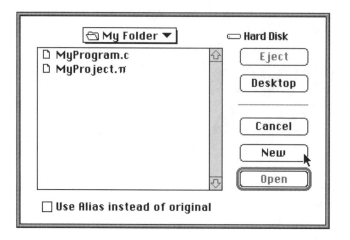

Type in a file name. Now, pay attention to this — it's important. Remember back in Chapter 8 when I explained the THINK project-naming *convention*. There I said that people usually end a project file name with a period and the *pi* symbol, as in: MyProject.π. That *pi* symbol is produced by pressing both the Option and the letter "p" keys. Well, here comes a second naming convention. The resource file that is to accompany a project is the project name followed by a period and the following four letters: rsrc (for resource of course). Since the project name I'm using is MyProject.π, I have no choice but to name my resource file MyProject.π.rsrc. I'm doing that here:

Gotta throw in a caution note here. *The resource file name must be exactly as I described here.* The consequences if you ignore my warning? The THINK Project Manager won't know a resource file exists—even if you've created one. When you try to run your code, you'll get ugly error messages, and there's a very good chance that your Mac will freeze up. It won't be permanently damaged, but you'll have to restart it — and you probably won't remember what caused the problem. ▪

You'll now have an empty resource file. The source code file you created in Chapter 9 makes use of only a single resource. It needs a '*WIND*' resource that serves as the window that will appear on the screen. In case you need a reminder, here's how you create a '*WIND*' resource:

1. Select Create New Resource from the Resource menu.

2. Scroll to WIND in the Select New Type dialog box and click on it.

3. Click the OK button to dismiss the Select New Type dialog box.

A '*WIND*' editor will open. The only change you'll need to make pertains to the row of icons along the top of the editor. Click on the second icon from the left:

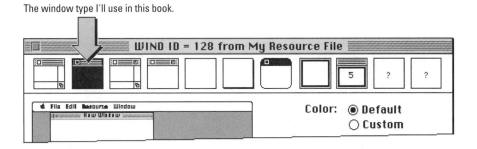

That's it for the resource file. Select Save from the File menu to save the file. Then select Quit from the same menu to exit ResEdit. When you return to the desktop your folder should look something like this:

If the resource file inadvertently ended up in a different folder, move it into the folder that holds the project file and source code file — as shown above.

Take a close look at the above figure. This is the configuration you'll have for any

Mac program you create — a folder that holds a project file, a source code file, and a resource file.

Compiling Your Code

It's time to get on with this much talked-about business of compiling. Here I'll discuss how to compile, and what to do if something should go wrong.

Compiling is incredibly easy — you just select Compile from the Source menu:

```
Source
  Add 'MyProgram.c'
  Add Files...
  Remove
  Get Info
  Debug              ⌘I
  SourceServer       ▶

  Check Syntax       ⌘Y
  Preprocess
  Disassemble

  Precompile...
  Compile            ⌘K
  Make...            ⌘\

  Browser            ⌘J
```

If the Compile option appears dim, you can't select it. THINK C won't *enable* this menu — that is, make it active — unless there's something on the screen for it to compile. Makes sense, right? So if you don't have your source code file open, open it now. Remember, to do that you just double-click on the file name in the project window:

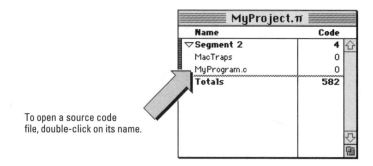

Name	Code
▽ Segment 2	4
MacTraps	0
MyProgram.c	0
Totals	**582**

MyProject.π

To open a source code
file, double-click on its name.

Before you select Compile, take a look at the column of numbers in the project window. They should look something like the ones in this figure:

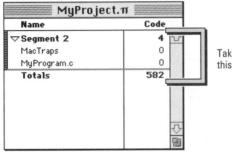

Take note of the numbers in this column.

I'll refer back to this figure in a little while. Now, go ahead and select Compile from the Source menu. I'll wait a minute while you do that.

What Happened?

If you made a mistake when you typed the source code, THINK C will respond by displaying a window titled Compile Errors. If you see that window, sit tight for a moment — I'll cover what went wrong in just a page or two. If you don't see that error message window, then things certainly didn't seem very dramatic, did they? If you typed all the code in correctly, it might seem like not much at all happened. You probably saw the following dialog box, but that's about it:

```
Compiling MyProgram.c...


Lines:          17
```

It might seem like very little happened — but the compiler really did do some work. Look at the project window. Some of the numbers changed:

MyProject.π	
Name	**Code**
▽ **Segment 2**	68
MacTraps	0
MyProgram.c	64
Totals	**646**

These numbers may
change after compiling.

So what *did* happen? THINK C turned the source code in your MyProgram.c file
into *object code* — code that the computer understands. So how come your
source code file is still sitting on the screen, unchanged and very readable? The
compiler does its work behind the scenes. It made a *copy* of your source code
file and worked with that. How can you be sure it really did that? Look at the
column of numbers in the project window. The number in the row with
MyProgram.c changed from 0 to 64 (or thereabouts). That number is the size of
the object code that was created from the source code file.

The numbers in the project window refer to *bytes* of memory. So the number 64
means 64 bytes. About one million bytes is called a *megabyte*, (MB). You're
familiar with that phrase. Your Mac came equipped with megabytes of RAM —
such as 2MB, 4MB, and so forth.

Don't waste your time keeping track of the exact numbers in the project
window. Keeping track of bytes only becomes important far down the
programming road. ■

Compiling code doesn't actually *execute* — or run — the code. The source code
in the ExampleOne program you just typed in and compiled is supposed to put
up a window and write a line of text to it. But it doesn't do that during the compiling stage. To do that you take one of two steps. One way to run the code is to
do so right from within the THINK Project Manager. Another way to see the
code in action is to go ahead and turn the code into a Macintosh program that
will show up on your hard drive after you quit the THINK Project Manager.
You'll see how to perform both these feats later in this chapter.

So, is that it for compiling? Yup, that's it. Unless you made a *typo* — a mistake in
typing the source code.

Can You Type? The Compiler Will Let You Know

After selecting Compile, a window with a message in it *might* pop open on your screen. This is not good. But it also isn't the end of the world. This window only appears when you've made one or more mistakes when typing your source code. When the compiler comes across a mistake it makes a note of it in this window. The window will look like this, though the message in it might be different:

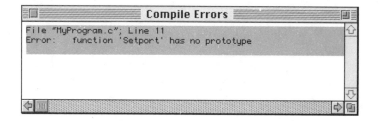

If you made a mistake entering source code, the Compile Errors window gives you a hint as to what went wrong. To get the above message I purposely typed in "Setport" rather than "SetPort". That is, I used a lowercase "p" rather than an uppercase "P". And you thought I was being picky when I said that you had to be careful about upper and lower case!

The Compile Errors window tells you the file name and the line number at which the error occurred. My error is in the file MyProgram.c, at Line 11. If I count down eleven lines from the top of the source code file — including blank lines — I should come across the error. Let's see if that's true:

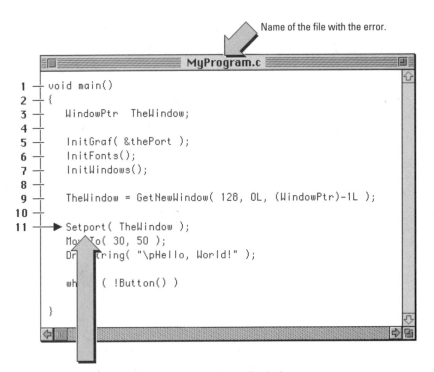

Name of the file with the error.

```
1    void main()
2    {
3        WindowPtr  TheWindow;
4
5        InitGraf( &thePort );
6        InitFonts();
7        InitWindows();
8
9        TheWindow = GetNewWindow( 128, 0L, (WindowPtr)-1L );
10
11       Setport( TheWindow );
         MoveTo( 30, 50 );
         DrawString( "\pHello, World!" );

         while ( !Button() )

     }
```

Here at line 11 is the letter "p" that the compiler finds offensive!

Indeed, the error is on the eleventh line. The compiler was hoping to see "SetPort", but instead found "Setport". A trivial difference to us humans, but not to a computer.

For those without a photographic memory

Trivial indeed! Memorizing the *case* of each letter of each command (or Toolbox miniprogram, if you recall the terminology of Chapter 4) sounds like a real drag. It's not really all that bad, though. First, you don't have to memorize each command — you can find them written down in programming reference books. In fact, you can find many of them in Part IV of this book. You'll also find all the ones mentioned in Part IV, as well as several others, listed by topic in Appendix B.

The second thing that's good to remember — the capitalization of certain letters in a Toolbox command isn't random. It's reserved for the start of what would ordinarily be a new word. For example, the command *SetPort* sets a port. So the "S" of "set" and the "P" of "port" are capitalized.

By the way, don't worry about just what a port is, or why you set one — you'll learn soon enough.

Counting lines of code is tedious — especially if the error occurs well past line eleven. I did it just to demonstrate that I can count past ten — contrary to what people are saying about me. Really, though, I want you to realize that the compiler keeps track of your code by lines. Now that you know that, don't bother counting. Rather, just double-click on the highlighted section of the Compile Errors window. That has the effect of adding highlight to the offensive line of code in the source code window — like this:

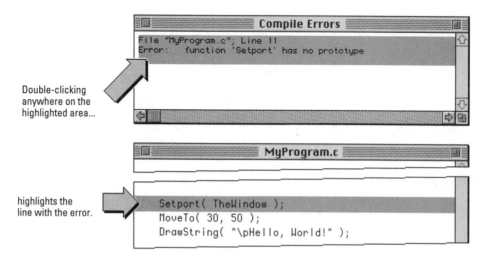

Double-clicking anywhere on the highlighted area...

```
Compile Errors
File "MyProgram.c"; Line 11
Error:    function 'Setport' has no prototype
```

highlights the line with the error.

```
MyProgram.c

      Setport( TheWindow );
      MoveTo( 30, 50 );
      DrawString( "\pHello, World!" );
```

Yes, programmers really say things like "offensive" and "offending" when we refer to a line with an error. Hey, don't shake your head at me — I didn't invent the terminology! ∎

Now that you know exactly how to find your mistake, go to it in your source code file and correct it. You can look back several pages at the ExampleOne program that you used to initially type in this source code to find out what you erroneously typed. If more than one error is listed in the Compile Errors window, correct each one.

After correcting a mistake, you *recompile* the code. Recompile is just the fancy word for saying "compile it again." You can compile the same source code file as many times as you want. THINK C will only save the result — the object code — of your most recent attempt. If you've corrected a mistake, select Compile from the Source menu now.

Running and Building: Sounds Like Quite a Workout!

You've successfully compiled your source code. The computer can now understand it. Now you want the computer to run it so that you can see that you really have created a program. There are two ways you can do that: you can *run* your code or you can *build* a program.

In Chapter 9 I said that THINK C is actually the THINK Project Manager environment. I explained the use of the word "environment" by saying that the THINK Project Manager was capable of doing more than just compiling source code. It also allows you to add files to projects and to edit and save those files. It's actually a project manager, an editor, and a compiler — all rolled into one program.

Besides all of the above-mentioned tasks, the THINK Project Manager can perform one other trick you'll find very useful. It can run your compiled code without actually making a program out of it. On the surface this might not seem like such a big deal, but it is. And that's due to the nature of programming.

It would be nice to sit down at your computer, type in all the source code for a program, compile it once, and be done with the whole business. But that's seldom — if ever — the way it works. When you compile and run your program for the first time, you're bound to see something you don't like. Here are a few possibilities:

- ✔ A window is the wrong size.
- ✔ A menu doesn't do what you thought it would.
- ✔ The words you wrote into a window don't look quite right.

The list goes on and on. So what do you do when something isn't quite right? Start over? Of course not. You make a change to the source code, recompile it, and then run it again and see how things look this time around. This is the reason you don't build — or create — a program right away. Running the program in the THINK Project Manager is quicker than building a program. How so? Here are the steps needed to build a program and test it:

1. Select a THINK Project Manager menu option to build the program.

2. Return to the desktop (leave the THINK Project Manager).

3. Double-click on the new program's icon to run the program.

4. Check out your program.

5. Quit your program.

6. Return to the THINK Project Manager.

Now, here are the steps necessary to run the code *without* making a program out of it:

1. Select a THINK Project Manager menu option to run the program.

2. Check out your program.

3. Quit your program.

You can see that running the code is quicker than building a program, especially if you have to perform the process several times.

When is the time to build a program? When you're finally satisfied with what you see when you run the code. That's when you'll make the menu selection that creates a program that will show up on your Mac's desktop.

Running Code Within THINK C

Now that you know *why* you run your code, you'll want to know *how* to run it. You also might want to see an example why you'd run, then rerun, your code. I'll cover that now.

Running the Code

How to run your code? That's an easy one. Just select Run from the Project menu:

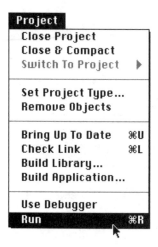

When you make this selection you'll probably encounter this dialog box:

This dialog box doesn't appear every time you select Run from the Project menu. It comes to the screen when one or more of the following is the case:

- ✔ A source code file hasn't been compiled.
- ✔ A source code file has been changed and needs to be recompiled.
- ✔ A library needs to be loaded.

You've already compiled the source code file, so this wouldn't be the cause of its appearance. The second point probably isn't the reason either. I say "probably" because even though I'm trying to keep an eye on you, I might have missed something. Did you make a change to the source code file? Typing even a single space in the source code file is viewed as a change by the THINK Project Manager, and it will want to recompile the file. That leaves the third point as the culprit — a library needs to be loaded.

You added the MacTraps library to the project quite a while ago. But, just as an added source code file needs to be compiled, an added library needs to be *loaded*. That just means that the project needs to figure out what's in the library and set up conditions so that it can access the code that's in the library. Once a library is loaded, you won't have to load it again.

Now, what brought on this conversation? Ah, yes — the dialog box. You don't have to worry about what needs compiling or recompiling or loading. Just click the Update button and let the THINK Project Manager handle everything:

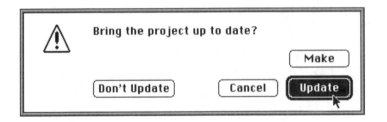

After a few moments, the program will run. The source code file contains the source code for the ExampleOne program that was listed in Chapter 4. If everything works okay, you should see the following window:

```
┌─────────────────────────────────────┐
│ ▣ ▤▤▤   New Window   ▤▤▤▤            │
├─────────────────────────────────────┤
│                                      │
│                                      │
│     Hello, World!                    │
│                                      │
│                                      │
│                                      │
└─────────────────────────────────────┘
```

Don't forget to make and properly name that resource file. Without it, the program can't run. The line of code that has *GetNewWindow* in it looks for the '*WIND*' resource with an ID of 128. If it can't find that resource, the program bombs — it crashes, dies, blows up. Use whichever words you want. ▪

Mac programs really should contain a menu bar. Ours doesn't. If you're still running the program you can verify this by looking at the blank menu bar on the screen. By the time you get to Chapter 19 your programs will have a menu bar. For now, I want to keep things really simple. Since there is no menu that contains a Quit command, I've designed the source code in such a way that the user simply clicks the mouse button to quit the program. Do that now.

When you quit the program that you're running in the THINK Project Manager, you return to the THINK Project Manager. The "Hello, World!" window disappears and the menu bar returns to that of the THINK Project Manager. You've successfully run your first program!

Running It Again. And Again, and Again...

I said that the Run command was of most use while you were developing your program, or making changes to it. Let's make a simple change to the program and rerun it.

If the source code file isn't open, reopen it now. Then go to the *DrawString* line and change the text that appears between the quotes. As tempting as it is to remove the funny-looking "\p" characters, don't. But change any of the other text, as I've done here:

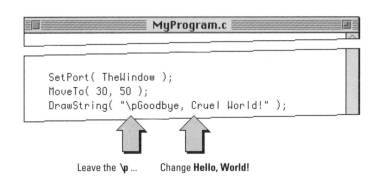

```
SetPort( TheWindow );
MoveTo( 30, 50 );
DrawString( "\pGoodbye, Cruel World!" );
```

Leave the **\p** ...   Change **Hello, World!**

Select Save from the File menu to save the change. Now, select Run from the Project menu. You'll see the "Bring the project up to date?" dialog box. The THINK Project Manager is aware of the change you made to the source code, and it wants to make sure you really want to recompile the source code. Click the Update button. You'll then see a window with the new text in it:

New Window

Goodbye, Cruel World!

Again, click the mouse to end the program and return to the THINK Project Manager. That brief example should give you a feel for the power and usefulness of the Run command. It allows you to change and test source code over and over again — and very quickly.

Building an Application

The Run command is a great way for you to test your source code. But it doesn't make an *application* — a program that is saved on disk. When you're satisfied with the results of your programming efforts, you'll want a *standalone* application. That is, you'll want to have a real Mac program that anyone can run without the THINK Project Manager. You don't want to have to run the THINK Project Manager every time you want to run your program. And if you give a copy of your program to someone else, you certainly don't want to force them to buy the THINK Project Manager in order to run your program.

How a Program Is Built

When the THINK Project Manager creates a program it does so by merging the library and compiled source code of a project with the contents of the resource file that is associated with the same project. I used a figure in Chapter 8 to make this point. It's repeated below:

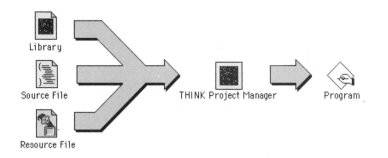

The next figure is based on the above illustration. You may recall that in Chapter 8, I promised you I wouldn't add to the figure. Before you yell, "Aha —gotchya!," give me a chance to explain. I'm not adding to it, I'm just inserting specific names in place of the general ones I used in the above figure. Here's the same figure as it applies to the project I've been using, MyProject.π:

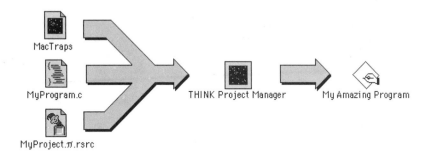

In the above figure the top two files on the left are directly part of the project file — they became part of the project through the use of the Add Files menu item. The other file, the resource file, is indirectly a part of the project. You don't specifically add it to the project. It is associated with the project by its name — it has the project name with ".rsrc" added to it. That can be shown like this:

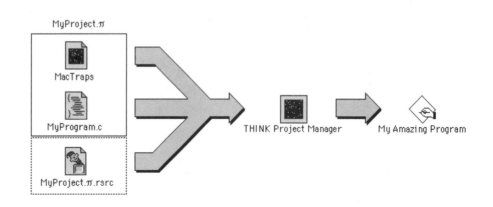

All right, so I lied — I did modify the figure one more time. But my intentions are good — I did it to make everything crystal clear for you. The figure now accurately reflects the interrelationship of all the components involved in building a Macintosh program named My Amazing Program using the THINK Project Manager. I've drawn a solid line around the two files that are directly a part of the project and a dashed line around the one that is indirectly a part of it. Even though you don't actually add the resource file to the project file, it is usually thought of as an integral part of it.

Let's Build It!

A Macintosh program starts as pieces of a whole — separate files in a project. So it makes sense that the word *build* is used when talking about bringing the pieces together to form a complete program — or *application,* as a program is more formally referred to.

When is the right time to build an application? When all of the following are true:

- ✔ Your project holds the MacTraps library.
- ✔ Your project holds a source code file.
- ✔ You've created a resource file to accompany the project.
- ✔ You've compiled the source code.
- ✔ You've tested the code using the Run menu option.

To build an application, select Build Application from the Project menu, like so:

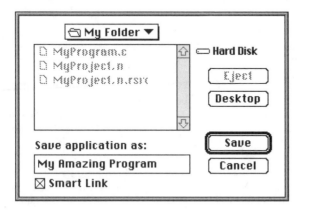

Before building the program, THINK C will give you the opportunity to name it. Choose any name that suits your fancy. I could have named mine ExampleOne — that's what I called it back in Chapter 4 when I first showed off the source code for it. But now that I've had the opportunity to run the code and see firsthand all of the incredibly intricate things it does, I'll give it a more appropriate name:

Note that the pop-up menu at the top of the dialog box shows that I'm now in My Folder. I want to make sure I'm in the same folder that my files are in. That way the resulting program will be saved in the same folder in which all my other files concerning this project are located.

After typing in a name, click the Save button. In response, the THINK Project Manager may or may not display the "Bring the project up to date?" dialog box you saw earlier. If you made changes to the source code, the THINK Project Manager will want to recompile the source code before running it. In that case it will display the dialog box. Click the Update button.

Next, the THINK Project Manager will display two dialog boxes, one after the other. Watch closely as THINK C does its thing, 'cause it's quick. If you have time to read the text in the two dialog boxes, here's what they'll say:

```
Linking My Amazing Program...
```

```
Copying MyProject.π.rsrc...
```

The THINK Project Manager first *links* the program. Compiling source code generates code that is readable by the computer. But compiling a source code file doesn't combine, or merge, the code with the code in the MacTraps library. Linking takes care of that. And, thanks to the THINK Project Manager doing all the work, that's as much as you'll need to know about linking.

The second step in building the application is the merging of the resources in the resource file with the code. To do this the THINK Project Manager makes a copy of all of the resources in the resource file and then performs the merge. Why copy the resources? To preserve your resource file. When the build is complete, you'll of course have a Macintosh application. But you'll also still have your source code file and your resource file — completely intact and seemingly untouched. Then, if you want to make any changes (either now or at a later date), you still have all of your original work.

Checking It Out

When the build is complete, you won't notice any changes in the THINK environment. To see your program you'll have to open the folder in which the program was placed. I placed mine in the folder I named My Folder. Here are its contents:

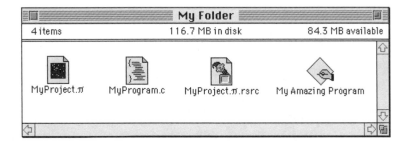

There it is! A program just like any you'd buy. Well, not *just* like any you'd buy. It doesn't do quite as much. But hey, if you can get someone to pay a few bucks for it, more power to you. Really, though — does it behave as any other Mac program? Prove it to yourself by double-clicking its icon to run it. Then, after clicking the mouse to end the program, try copying the program to a disk. Or move the program out of the folder and try running it again. You'll see that your newly created program doesn't need the project, source code, resource file, or the THINK Project Manager to run. It is truly a standalone application.

What Can Possibly Be Left?

That's it. You've written source code, compiled it, corrected errors in the code, and built an application. I guess you don't need *me* anymore. Well, you can't get rid of me quite that easily. You're probably getting comfortable with the idea of using a compiler. But I'll bet you don't feel the same way about writing source code. After all, you really just typed in the code I told you to type. Once you get to know what those strange-looking combinations of characters mean, you'll have this business of programming just about licked. So let's get started!

Part IV
Learning the
C Language

The 5th Wave   By Rich Tennant

In this part . . .

*I*f you thought learning a computer language was a lot like learning a foreign language like, say, French or Japanese, you may have been a little intimidated. I don't blame you. I've never been good at foreign languages myself. Heck, the only thing I can say is "Eat my shorts" in German! Obviously, a programming language can't be as complicated as a spoken language. It isn't, and here's why. A computer language usually consists of less than a hundred words. And to write a simple program, you only need to know a fraction of them.

In programming, it isn't how *many* words you know, it's how you *use* the words you do know. In this part I describe several of the words in a computer programming language called C. And of course, I discuss how to use these elements of the C language. I also talk about the collection of miniprograms called the Toolbox. An easy-to-use Toolbox miniprogram turns a complex task — like displaying a window — into a very easy one.

Chapter 11
What Is C, and Why Use It?

*L*ike spoken languages, computer languages abound. With a spoken language, you don't start out with much of a choice — you learn the language common to the country you're born in. But now that you're about to learn a computer language, you don't have that unnatural restriction — you can choose any one you want. So why pick the C language? And — while I'm on the topic of languages — why is it called C? This chapter will answer these questions.

About Programming Languages

Many programmers know several computer languages. They may have learned one language while in school, and another once they were working. Or they may have learned different languages while working at different jobs. Unless you're a professional programmer, one language is enough.

Why Call It C?

Before discussing other languages I'll clear up a point that might have been nagging at you ever since you heard about the C language — why is it called C? Because "A" and "B" were already taken! Very funny, right? But hold on — this time I'm serious. The C language was designed by Dennis Ritchie of Bell Labs back in 1972. Mr. Ritchie didn't, however, create it entirely on his own. He based it on the B language developed by Ken Thompson, an associate of his.

Those Other Languages

Pascal, C++, FORTRAN, BASIC, and COBOL: they're all programming languages, just as C is. Why so many different ones? There are a number of reasons.

Some languages are created with a specific use in mind. FORTRAN, for instance, is used mainly by scientists and engineers. They need a language that is geared heavily toward math. FORTRAN has a large number of libraries that allow scientists to work easily with topics such as trigonometry and calculus.

A *library*, as you certainly recall from recent chapters, is a collection of code that was written by others. The code is placed in a library so it can easily be incorporated into your own programs. ■

Another reason for the proliferation of computer languages is time. Over time, computers have changed. So it makes sense that languages that are used on computers would change too. If the change to a computer is great, it is more practical to devise an entirely new language than to attempt to modify an out-dated one.

One reason for the existence of different computer languages is the same as the reason different spoken languages exist — they were created independently from one another. The English language and the Japanese language both exist because people in different parts of the world with different ideas developed them independently. Programming languages are no different. People developed different programming languages to suit their particular programming needs. In some cases the results are similar to one another, and in other cases they aren't.

It Sounds Like a Language — But It's Not

The names of computer language are often acronyms. For example, BASIC stands for Beginners All-purpose Symbolic Instruction Code. The names of these languages usually appear in uppercase.

There's a second set of computer names that appear in uppercase, and are often acronyms. But they aren't the names of computer languages — they're the names of *operating systems*. An operating system is your means of communicating with the computer. The operating system allows you to work on your computer even when you aren't running a program. It handles tasks such as copying and deleting files.

The most commonly known operating system is probably DOS, which stands for Disk Operating System. Different software companies make their own versions of DOS, with the Microsoft version far and away the most popular —

MS-DOS. So while the name DOS appears in uppercase and is an acronym, it is not a programming language. And though many people refer to "DOS computers," don't think that there's a brand of computers with that name. The reference is just to the fact that a particular computer uses DOS as its operating system.

A couple of other operating systems that could trick you into believing they're languages are UNIX and OS/2. They're operating systems that are found on many personal computers — but not on the Macintosh.

Strangely enough, the Macintosh operating system doesn't really have a name. It's usually referred to as just "the system." Many Mac owners have System 7 as their operating system, so I guess you could say System 7 is the name of the Mac operating system. But that doesn't provide much comfort to Mac users with an older version, such as System 6.0.7. Perhaps this ambiguous system naming is just another example of the Mac psychology of not fitting into a pre-defined mold. ■

Why Use C on the Mac?

Which is the absolute, one-and-only language to learn for programming the Mac? That depends on who you ask. Different programmers have different thoughts on that — and each will be able to provide valid arguments for their preference. In this book I use the C language, and in this section I'll explain why.

Arguing about a programming language with a programmer is a little like arguing about politics or religion — you'll make little headway, and you certainly won't win. If you *have* to argue about it, my advice would be to do so over the phone. Then you can cradle the phone on your shoulder, keeping both hands free. That allows you to ignore what the other person is saying and keep typing away at your C program on your Mac. ■

Everybody's Using C

Computer languages, like clothing styles, fall in and out of fashion. Well, that's not entirely true. The fashion of dress that most programmers wear has remained pretty much the same for the last twenty years or so — pants that are too short, a wrinkled shirt, and a nicely smudged up pair of glasses. But while their clothing hasn't changed much, the language that most programmers use has.

When the Mac came out about a decade ago, almost everyone programmed it using the Pascal language. Then, about a half dozen years ago or so, many programmers switched to C. Most felt it was a little more powerful than Pascal. When talking about a programming language the word "powerful" is hard to define precisely. But it's safe to say that in this instance it means that programmers felt they could get their programs to do more by using C.

If you decide to program in C, and if you need a little help at some point, you'll find a wealth of Mac programmers who can give you a hand. That's because just about all of them know C. That alone may be enough reason to use it.

That's a good one! I just realized I said, "...*if* you need a little help at some point...". Using the word "if" means you might, then again, might not, need help. You *will* need help. I'm not criticizing you personally, it's just a fact. Programming can be a little tricky at times, and we all need to ask others for advice. I need to, and do — just about every day. One of the most important lessons you can learn about programming is to cast aside your fear of being ridiculed and *ask for help* whenever you don't understand something. ■

So, is it a sound practice to select a computer language just because everyone else is using it? Do we really want to be thought of as nothing more than lemmings heading for the sea? Of course not. Selecting C because the majority of programmers use it is only *one* of the reasons for choosing it — there are several...

...Other Reasons for Using C

How's that for a lead-in to a new section? To satisfy your curiosity, here are a few more reasons why you're being asked to learn C.

- ✔ It can be used to produce both mammoth, amazingly complex programs, *and* short, extremely simple ones.

- ✔ The best-selling Macintosh compiler on the market is the THINK C compiler — that means you'll be using a powerful, easy-to-use compiler with plenty of support.

- ✔ It's a highly *structured* language, meaning that it follows certain set rules — learn the rules, and the rest falls into place.

- ✔ It is not as complicated a language as its newest rival, the C++ language.

- ✔ The single-letter name, C, sounds rather cryptic and mysterious — so it impresses friends and coworkers when you inform them that you've mastered it.

Who could ask for more persuasion than all of the above? Now that you've accepted the notion that C is good, it's time to learn it!

Chapter 12

Keeping Track of Things: Data Types and Variables

A computer program wouldn't be very useful if it didn't keep careful track of things. After, all that's primarily what a computer is used for — remembering things, calculating things, and ordering things. That's a lot of things. Many people think of the computer as a machine that works with numbers. I specifically used the word "things" instead of "numbers" because a computer works with much more than numbers — it also works with words and pictures. And in the case of a computer with a graphical user interface, it also works with objects such as windows and menus. In this chapter I'll take a look at the two primary programming tools you'll use to keep track of all these things — data types and variables.

Data Types and Variables: Different, But Related

Back in Chapter 3 you got a first peek at data types and variables. There, in my introduction to source code, I mentioned the *int*. The *int* is a C language word that stands for an integer — a whole number. In Chapter 3 I said that the *int* was a symbol for an integer. I also told you that C allows you to make up your own symbols — I gave the example of "trucks" as a symbol. What I didn't say in Chapter 3 was that these two kinds of symbols are very different from one another, and that each has its own special name.

Data Types

Data is information, and information is what you're keeping track of when you program. As I mentioned at the beginning of this chapter, there are different types of data — numbers, words, pictures, and so forth. So a computer language has different *types* to keep track of data. Thus the phrase *data types*.

Just about everything can be divided into types. We're all people, but we can be divided into types by sex: the male sex, the female sex, and insects. Oops, let's start over: the male sex and the female sex. The same is true with numbers — there are different types. Numbers without decimal points — whole numbers — are often called integers. Because "integer" is such an incredibly long word, the C language refers to a number that is an integer as an *int*. Numbers with decimal points are called floating-point numbers. In C, a floating-point number is called — you guessed it — a *float*.

Back in Chapter 4 I established some conventions. One of them was that I would use *italics* for source code words that appeared in the text of this book. That lets you immediately see that a word is indeed source code, and not just part of the text. ▪

C language data types are predefined for you. By predefined I mean that there are a set number of them you can use. The *int* and the *float* are just two of the dozens of types that exist. Don't worry though — you'll only need to know about ten of the types in order to write some pretty interesting programs.

Variables

In Chapter 3 I said that in C you can make up symbols of your own. I used *trucks* as an example. You create a symbol for the purpose of keeping track of something. I made up the symbol *trucks* with the intent of keeping track of the number of trucks an auto dealer had on his lot. A made-up symbol like *trucks* is called a *variable*.

A variable always has a name — mine is called *trucks*. A variable also always holds a value. In Chapter 3 I demonstrated how you give a variable a value:

```
trucks = 5;
```

I'll describe this method of *assigning* a variable a value in more detail in a bit.

For now, let's look at a figure that shows the two parts of a variable — its name and its value:

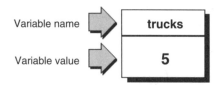

My *trucks* variable has as its value the number 5. From our talks about numbers you know that the number 5 is a whole number — an integer. Many of the variables you create will hold integers — but a variable doesn't have to hold only an integer value. In the figure below I've created two more variables. One I've called *TheWords*, and it holds, not surprisingly, some words. The second variable I've named *DogPicture*. It holds a picture of a dog (at least, it's *supposed* to be a dog). Here they are:

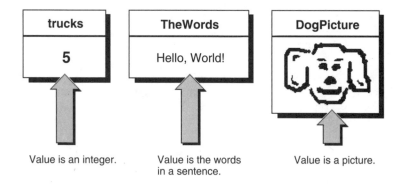

In my examples *trucks*, *TheWords*, and *DogPicture* are all variables — variable names, actually. I said every variable has a value associated with it. In general terms, here are the values of each variable:

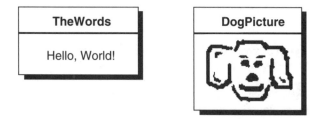

In the above figure I've drawn different sized boxes to hold each of the three variables. I had to — the things they hold are different sizes. That brings up an interesting point — how does the THINK C compiler know how big this thing is that you are creating and holding in a variable? And how does it know what you're storing there? The answer is that you must *tell* the compiler what you're storing in a variable. And that's where data types come in.

Every Variable Has a Type

Every variable has a value, but not just any kind of value. You must let the compiler know what type of information — what kind of data — a variable will hold. If you want a variable to hold an integer value, tell the compiler:

```
int  trucks;
```

The above line of code does two things. It creates a variable named *trucks*, and it tells the compiler that it will hold an integer — a value that is of the *int* data type. A line of code like the one above is called a *declaration*. You are declaring that a variable named *trucks* will be created, and declaring that it will hold data of the *int* type.

Amazingly, sometimes computer terminology actually makes sense. When you come across a new term, like *declare*, think of the meaning you know the word by. Not a computer-related meaning, but one you might use in normal conversation. The dictionary says that to declare is "to make clearly known; state or announce openly." Now that definition fits squarely with the computer use of the word, which is to make a variable — and its data type — clearly and openly known to the compiler. ■

Here's the format you'll follow every time you declare a variable:

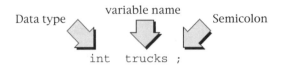

Data type   variable name   Semicolon

```
int    trucks ;
```

The above figure states that to declare a variable you first state the data type that the variable will hold, then give the name the variable will have, and then end it all with a semicolon.

What's with all the semicolons? One seems to pop up in just about every line of code. In the C language, a semicolon marks the end of a line of code. Kind of like a period ends a sentence in English. In fact, a semicolon in C has pretty much the same meaning a period does in the English language. The semicolon lets the compiler know where a line, or instruction, ends — just as a period lets the reader know when a sentence, or thought, ends. ∎

Every Variable Has a Value

You already know that every variable has both a name and a value. In the previous section you saw that the value of a variable must be of a particular type. The declaration creates the variable and lets the compiler know what type of value it will hold — but it doesn't give the variable a value. That's done with an *assignment* statement.

```
trucks = 5;
```

An assignment statement gives a variable a value — it assigns a value to the variable. But then, you already knew that — I stole the above line of code, and the following figure, straight out of Chapter 3:

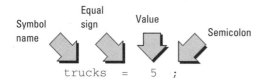

The above figure tells you that to give a variable a value you first list the variable's name, followed by the equal sign, and then end the line with a semicolon.

Order Is Everything

Now, for today's quiz. Does the following source code look all right to you?

```
trucks = 5;
int trucks;
```

You probably answered "No" to the question I posed. And you probably answered that way because you know by now that if I ask a question I'm probably up to something. The answer is indeed "No," and here's why. Before you can assign a variable a value, you must first declare it. When you compile your source code the compiler looks at each line of source code *in order*, from top to bottom. So in the above example the first thing it would see is:

```
trucks = 5;
```

Since the compiler hasn't reached the declaration yet — the second line — it doesn't know what the heck *trucks* is. Even if it is clever enough to assume that *trucks* is a variable, it doesn't know what type of data *trucks* can hold. The compiler will become so frustrated in fact, it will stop compiling and pop open its error message window. It'll put a message in it like this:

```
========================= Compile Errors =========================
File "MyProgram.c"; Line 5
Error:   'trucks' has not been declared
```

Why can't the compiler peek ahead somehow and see that on the very next line *trucks* is in fact declared? Because you're dealing with a computer, my friend. And with computers, *order is everything*. So the moral of this story is to declare your variables before using them. That is, before assigning them values. I'll remedy the offending code by simply switching the two lines around, like so:

```
int trucks;
trucks = 5;
```

Common Types

I said that C has dozens of data types. I also said that you'd only need a handful to create a Macintosh program. I'll mention a few of them here. The rest of them will make more sense to you if they are presented in the context in which they're used. So I'll cover the remaining half dozen or so types throughout the remainder of the book.

Data Types for Whole Numbers

You've already seen one of the three most common number data types — the *int*. The other two are the *short* and the *float*.

A variable declared to be of the *int* type holds an integer — but not any integer. The biggest number you can store in a variable of type *int* is 32,767. I know, I know — it would simplify things if an *int* held a number up to, say, 10,000 or

100,000. But it doesn't. Just remember that for most of your whole numerical needs, an *int* will work. After all, it's unlikely that your auto dealership will ever have more than 32,767 trucks, right?

Why are there any restrictions at all on how big a number you can store in a variable of a certain data type? Because a variable is held in computer memory. One variable occupies a certain number of bytes of memory. An *int* variable will be stored in two bytes. In the system of math that the computer uses, 32,767 is the biggest number it can fit in two bytes of memory. ■

A variable declared to be a *short* is very similar to one declared to be an *int*. Variables of either type hold whole numbers, and both hold numbers up to 32,767. So why have two data types that are essentially the same? Because there is a subtle difference between the two:

A *short* can *never* hold a whole number greater than 32,767.

An *int* can *sometimes* hold a whole number greater than 32,767.

The clever programmer can get variables of type *int* to hold numbers greater than 32,767 — but it isn't recommended that this be done. So, for all practical purposes, the *short* and the *int* are one and the same. Which one should you use? I've looked at a lot of source code that programmers who work for Apple have written, and they seem to go bonkers about the *short* type. So that's the type I'll use in the remainder of this book. Since it's not so intuitive that something called a *short* holds an integer, I'll remind you of this fact in a couple of places later in this book.

If you want to create a variable that holds numbers larger than 32,767, use the *long* data type. A variable that is declared to be of type *long* can hold a number larger than two billion. That should definitely handle all your whole number needs.

I'll bet you just thought you figured something out: if the *long* type can hold such a huge number, as well as much smaller numbers, why not just play it safe and always use it? Why ever bother with the *short* type? That's a good observation, but there is a reason why both types exist — memory. In order to hold such a large number, more memory has to be reserved for a variable that is a *long* than one that is a *short*. If your program is keeping track of, say, the number of children a day care center takes care of, use a *short* — it's pretty unlikely the day care center will ever have more than 32,767 kids, right? On the other hand, if you're writing a program that keeps track of the number of people living in your state, you'll want to use a *long*. ■

A Data Type for Fractional Numbers

You'll find that the *short* data type and the *long* data type — both of which hold only whole numbers — are useful for most of your programming needs. After all, that auto dealership you're writing a program for won't be selling *fractions* of a truck. Regardless of how shady the salesman appears, he probably can't get away with that. But if you were writing a program that kept inventory of automobiles, you would want to include the price of each — and that involves fractions. More specifically, it involves decimals — numbers like $9,295.95. If a number includes a decimal point, a *short* won't cut it.

A floating-point number contains a decimal point. A number with a decimal point isn't required to have a certain number of digits before, or a certain number of digits after, the decimal point. The decimal point moves about — thus the term "floating-point." Here's a couple of examples:

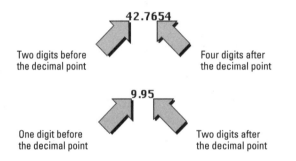

Two digits before   Four digits after
the decimal point   the decimal point

One digit before   Two digits after
the decimal point   the decimal point

Just as integers are represented by a C data type, floating-points are also represented by a C data type — the *float*. You'll want to use the *float* data type for:

 Keeping track of things that don't come neatly packaged in whole numbers.

 Keeping track of less than one thing — a fraction of something.

 Keeping track of things that exceed the limit of a *long* type — more than 2 billion.

Here are a few specific examples of when a Mac program would require the use of the *float* data type:

 Keeping track of how far you jog, such as 3.5 miles.

 Keeping track of money, such as $19.95.

 Keeping track of the size of an amoeba — about 0.02 inches long.

 Keeping track of numbers greater than a *long* can hold, like 5,500,000,000.0.

The next section deals with a very different kind of data type — one that has nothing to do with numbers. Before moving on to it, let's see if you have a handle on the different data types that involve numbers. It's time for a very short quiz. Which of the following is true:

A. The *short* data type holds whole numbers up to 32,767.

B. The *int* data type holds whole numbers up to 32,767.

C. The *long* data type holds whole numbers up to about two billion.

D. The *float* data type holds a number with a decimal point.

E. The author must be a total nerd since he knew the size of an amoeba.

F. All of the above.

The answer, of course, is letter F.

Common Variables

In the previous section I showed you some of the commonly used C data types. So it makes sense that I now show you a few of the commonly used variables, right? Wrong! Data types are a part of the C language. There are a limited number of them, they each have a specific way in which they must be spelled, and each has a specific way in which it can be used. Variables, on the other hand, aren't predefined for you. You make them up. Because of this I can't give you particular instances of variables that every programmer uses as I can with data types.

But I can give you a couple of examples of how some programmers might do things. Some programmers like to use underscores in their variable names — like this:

```
short bowling_score;
```

Other programmers would rather use an uppercase letter as shown in the example below:

```
short bowlingScore;
```

This makes a two-word variable name stand out. ■

A Few Examples

In the next chapter you learn the C language. In this chapter I've given you a head start by introducing two concepts very important to a programming language — declarations and assignments. Since you've made it to this point without throwing down the book in disgust, I'll assume that those two programming ideas made at least a little sense to you. If they did, you're ready for a few brief examples.

Declaring Variables

The declaration of a variable informs the compiler that you've just created a new variable. It also lets the compiler know what type of information the variable will hold. Here are a few examples:

```
short bookstores;
long  books;
float price;
```

Most programs use more than one variable. For example, the three variables that I just declared might all appear in a single program that keeps track of books sales for this *For Dummies* book. The *short* variable *bookstores* would hold the number of bookstores that carry the book. The *long* variable *books* holds the number of copies of this book sold. The *float* variable *price* holds the cost of a single copy of the book.

I made a couple of assumptions when I chose the data types for my variables. Variable *bookstores* is a *short*. Since the largest value a *short* can have is 32,767, I'm assuming fewer bookstores than that will carry it. For the *books* variable I selected the *long* data type. If this book sells more than 32,767 copies, my program will still be able to keep track of sales. What about the *price* variable — did I have a choice in what data type I would use? Not really. Book prices aren't usually whole numbers, like $20. Instead, they are often a dollar amount plus 95 cents — like $19.95. This means two things:

✔ Since the number has a decimal point, you must use the *float* data type.

✔ You were tricked into thinking you paid less than you really did for the book.

Technically, the line of source code that declares a variable is called a *declaration statement*. You'll see this term in many computer programming books. In this book I'll just say that I'm "declaring a variable." ▪

Assigning Values to Variables

Declaring a variable is the necessary first step you must perform before you can use it — that is, before you can give it a value. Once declared, you give a variable a value by assigning it one. Let's assume we have three variables declared. Better yet, let's just go ahead and declare them:

```
short bookstores;
long books;
float price;
```

Once declared, you can give any or all of them values. I'll do that now:

```
price = 19.95;
bookstores = 295;
books = 40521;
```

Variable *price* is a *float*, so I've included a decimal point in its value. Variable *bookstores* is a *short*, so its value must be less than 32,767 — and it is. The *long* variable *books* can — but doesn't have to be — greater than 32,767. Notice that the value I gave *books* doesn't include a comma — like 40,521. THINK C doesn't like commas in a number.

Also notice in the above example I didn't write:

```
price = $19.95;
```

The variable *price* was declared as a *float* — a number with a decimal. Something like a dollar sign isn't a part of a number — it's a label that precedes a number. Adding extra information, such as labels, will cause the THINK compiler to complain — in the form of an error message when you try to compile your program. ■

The line of source code that assigns a variable a value is called an *assignment statement*. Like the term "declaration statement," you'll see this phrase in some computer programming books. Here, I'll just say that I'm "assigning a value to a variable," or I'm "giving a variable a value." ■

At this point you know about data types, variables, declarations, and assignments — and you haven't even read the chapter on learning C. You're in way too deep to back out...so it's on to the rest of the C language!

Chapter 13

Learning the Language — Just the Basics, Please

The entire C language can't be covered in a single chapter of a single book. But then, who needs the entire language? You just want to know enough to get a Mac program going, right? That much I can cover here and now — so let's begin.

Care To Comment on That?

Sometimes source code can look confusing — I'll grant you that. You and I aren't the only ones who feel that way. Because so many people are befuddled by code, compilers offer you a way to add *comments* to your source code. These comments, or explanations, appear within your source code — but aren't source code themselves. A comment is text that is readable by you, but is ignored by the compiler when it comes time to compile the source code. Take this line of code for example:

```
short tickets;
```

What do you think the variable *tickets* will be used for? You might have a few ideas — and one of them may even be right. But if I wrote the source code, and you're looking at it, you won't know for sure. Now look at the same line of code — this time with a comment added to it:

```
short tickets;  /* the number of concert tickets sold */
```

Much clearer, right? And when you compile the above line, the THINK Project Manager won't return an error message to you — even though the words that follow the semicolon obviously aren't valid C code. How does the compiler know the difference between code and comments? Here's the answer:

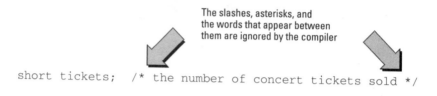

The slashes, asterisks, and the words that appear between them are ignored by the compiler

```
short tickets;   /* the number of concert tickets sold */
```

A slash, immediately followed by an asterisk, signals the start of a comment. An asterisk, immediately followed by a slash, marks the comment's end. As an example, I'll add comments to a few lines of code I used in the previous chapter:

```
short bookstores; /* number of bookstores carrying my book */
long  books;    /* number of books sold        */
float price;    /* price of a single copy of my book   */
```

Sure, it does take a little extra time to add comments to your source code. But the clarity they add will be well worth the effort.

Variable Names

Now that you've been exposed to several different variables, it's time for the lowdown on variable names. Here are the rules you must follow for each variable name:

✔ Use any combination of upper- and lowercase letters, digits, and underscores.

✔ Use a letter for the first character in the name.

The following are examples of valid variable names:

books

testScore

TotalScore

final_result

total2

Here's a look at a few invalid names, and why they're illegal:

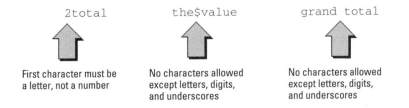

2total — First character must be a letter, not a number

the$value — No characters allowed except letters, digits, and underscores

grand total — No characters allowed except letters, digits, and underscores

Additionally, keep in mind that C is case-sensitive. The THINK compiler knows the difference between uppercase and lowercase letters, and will thus view *dog* and *Dog* as two different variable names.

When picking a name for a variable, make it descriptive of what the variable is to stand for. If a variable is to hold the total number of days you worked, name it *TotalDays* rather than something obscure like *number*. It makes it easier for someone else to figure out what your code is supposed to be doing. And, should you set unfinished code aside for a while and then return to it, these descriptive names will make things easier for you too!

Operating Without a License

Computers work with numbers, and the programs you write will certainly do the same. You've already seen a simple case of this:

```
trucks = 5;
```

To give a variable a value, you must *operate* on it. The word "operate" might sound a little pretentious for the simple act of assigning a variable a value, but it's not meant to. Here, "operate" just means "to work with." A machine operator works with a machine, and a telephone operator works with numbers — telephone numbers. In C, certain symbols — like the equal sign — are also called *operators*.

In the following line of code the equal sign works with the variable *trucks* and the number 5. The equal sign is responsible for placing the number 5 in the variable *trucks* — without it, the variable would not receive a value:

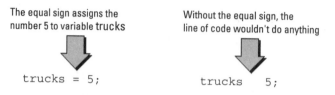

The equal sign assigns the number 5 to variable trucks

```
trucks = 5;
```

Without the equal sign, the line of code wouldn't do anything

```
trucks    5;
```

In C, the equal sign is called the *assignment operator* — it's used to assign a value to a variable. While the equal sign is by far the most commonly used C operator, there are plenty of others — as you're about to see.

Minimal Math

In your Macintosh programming endeavors, which of the following do you hope to accomplish:

> A. Write a program that uses a menu and a window.

> B. Write a program that disproves Einstein's Theory of Relativity.

If your choice was "A," then the C language and this book are for you. If you chose "B," then C might be for you, but this book ain't. C has several operators that allow you to include a wealth of mathematical tricks and techniques in your programs — but I'll only cover four of them. Those four, however, should meet just about all your arithmetic needs.

The Addition Operator

In programming, the act of addition is just as you'd expect it to be — you place the plus sign between two numbers to add them together. The result of the addition, the sum of the two numbers, is stored in a variable:

```
trucks = 5 + 10;
```

The above line of code is performing two tasks — it's adding together the numbers 5 and 10, and saving the result in the variable named *trucks*. Because two tasks — or operations — are being performed, two operators are used:

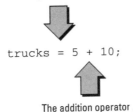

The assignment operator

```
trucks = 5 + 10;
```

The addition operator

The *addition operator* is used to add two numbers together. That being the case, try to determine why this following snippet is actual, real-live, functioning C code:

```
short  pickups;
short flatbeds;
short trucks;
pickups = 5;
flatbeds = 10;
trucks = pickups + flatbeds;
```

The above code appears to be adding two variables together, rather than two numbers. Keep in mind that a variable has a name and a value. The computer is more interested in the value of the variable. So when you add two variables together, it's the values of the variables that get added. Take a look at the source code up to, but not including, the line that adds the variables:

```
short pickups;
short flatbeds;
short trucks;
pickups = 5;
flatbeds = 10;
```

Here's a figure that represents the variables:

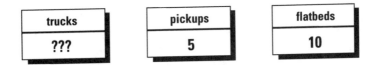

trucks	pickups	flatbeds
???	5	10

I put question marks as the value of *trucks* because I don't know what the value of *trucks* is — I haven't assigned it a value at this point. Now, the addition line:

```
trucks = pickups + flatbeds;
```

Let's see what happens to the variables now:

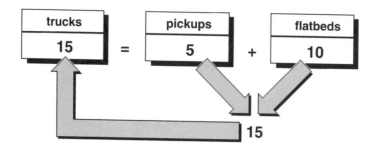

What exactly is the purpose of using variables rather than just using numbers? The computer is great at keeping track of values, but people are better at keeping track of names:

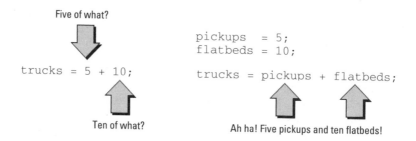

Now that you know that the compiler views a variable by the value it holds, you shouldn't be surprised to hear that all four of the following assignments will result in variable *trucks* being assigned a value of 15:

```
pickups = 5;
flatbeds = 10;
trucks = 5 + 10;
trucks = pickups + flatbeds;
trucks = pickups + 10;
trucks = 5 + flatbeds;
```

The Subtraction Operator

If you fully understood the previous section, then the remaining three basic math operators will be a snap. To subtract one value from another and assign the result to a variable, use the minus sign — the *subtraction operator.*

```
trucks = 10 - 5;
```

The subtraction operator works with variables — just as the addition operator does:

```
pickups = 5;
flatbeds = 10;
trucks = flatbeds - pickups;   /* The result of each of these  */
trucks = flatbeds - 5;      /* four lines of code? Variable */
trucks = 10 - pickups;       /* trucks will have a value of 5 */
trucks = 10 - 5;
```

The Multiplication Operator

In C, multiplication is performed by placing the *multiplication operator* — an asterisk—between the two numbers to multiply:

```
TotalDays = 7 * 10;   /* TotalDays will have a value of 70 */
```

Here's a few examples using variables:

```
short DaysPerWeek;
short Weeks;
short TotalDays;
DaysPerWeek = 7;
Weeks = 10;
TotalDays = 7 * 10;
TotalDays = DaysPerWeek * Weeks;
TotalDays = DaysPerWeek * 10;
TotalDays = 7 * Weeks;
```

The Division Operator

The only other mathematical operator I'll cover is the *division operator* — a slash. This operator divides the first number by the second:

```
dozens = 48 / 12;   /* dozens will have a value of 4 */
```

Like all the other operators, the division operator works on numbers, variables, or combinations of both:

```
short totalDozen;
short eggs;
short oneDozen;
eggs = 48;
oneDozen = 12;
totalDozen = 48 / 12;
totalDozen = eggs / oneDozen;
totalDozen = eggs / 12;
totalDozen = 48 / oneDozen;
```

They All Work Together

You don't have to restrict your use of math operators to one per line. You can use them just as you would if you were figuring something out on paper:

```
short grandTotal;
short score1;
short score2;
short penalty;
score1 = 75;
score2 = 90;
penalty = 10;
grandTotal = score1 + score2 - penalty;
```

They All Work with Floats, Too

Though I haven't shown it, each of the four math operators works with floating-point numbers as well as with whole numbers. Here are a few examples:

```
float height1;   /* first height, in meters */
float height2;   /* second height, in meters */
float totalHeight; /* sum of the two heights  */
height1 = 8.5;
height2 = 7.4;
totalHeight = height1 + height2;  /* totalHeight becomes 15.9 */
```

Repeating Yourself — By Looping

One of the greatest powers of a computer is its ability to do repetitious work — and do it at incredible speed. Computer programs perform this feat by running the same lines of code repeatedly — that is, by *looping* through the lines.

The Need to Loop

You know that *DrawString* is the command you use to draw some text into a window. Let's say I want to write the word "Again" three times in a row in a window. Don't ask me *why* I want to do this — just humor me. To write the word "Again" three times in a row I could do this:

```
DrawString("\pAgain Again Again ");
```

A second way to achieve the same result would be to use the *DrawString* command three times, like this:

```
DrawString("\pAgain ");
DrawString("\pAgain ");
DrawString("\pAgain ");
```

Either of the above methods would result in text that looked something like this:

```
┌──────────────────────────────────────────────┐
│ ▣         ▬▬▬▬▬▬  Window  ▬▬▬▬▬▬              │
├──────────────────────────────────────────────┤
│  Again Again Again                            │
│                                               │
│                                               │
│                                               │
└──────────────────────────────────────────────┘
```

That's all well and good — but what if you wanted to write the word "Again" ten times, or a hundred times? You might fill pages of source code with the *DrawString* command. A better method would be to have a line of code that tells the program to repeat the line or lines that follow — something like this:

```
Repeat the code between the following braces 10 times
{
  DrawString("\pAgain ");
}
```

You probably have figured out that the above example isn't real C source code. But if I replaced the first line — the one written out in English —with some C that did what those words say, I'd have the technique of looping all figured out.

The while Loop

Looping is an important part of a programming language — most have some means of letting you easily add looping capability to your source code. The powerful C language is no exception. To create a loop in C you use a *while* statement.

Words that are part of C, like *short*, *float*, and *while*, are called *keywords*. The keywords make up the language itself. Because each keyword has a specific use and purpose, you can't use these words for other purposes. For instance, you can't create a variable named *while*. ■

In general terms, here's what a *while* loop does:

```
while something is true...
{
    ...run the code that is between the braces
}
```

The word "something" is a little vague for a computer, so you won't be surprised to hear that instead of "something," the *while* loop performs a *test*. This kind of test isn't graded like the ones in school — there's no letter grade here. Instead, the test is scored by either a pass or fail — there's no "average."

In C, if a test passes we say the test is *true*. If the test fails, we say it is *false*. I'll rewrite — again, in general terms — what the *while* loop is shaping up as:

```
while test is true...
{
    ...run the code that is between the braces
}
```

Let's take a look at an actual *while* loop. Before I write the loop, I know I'm going to need a single variable that will be used as part of the test. I'll declare the variable, then assign it a value of 0:

```
short count;
count = 0;
```

Now for the loop. I'll write it out, and then explain what's going on:

```
while ( count < 10 )
{
    DrawString("\pAgain ");
    count++;
}
```

The test in the above loop lies between the parentheses — that's where you'll always find it. If the test is true, the code following it will run:

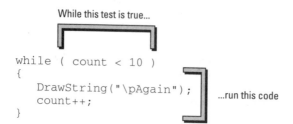

While this test is true...

```
while ( count < 10 )
{
    DrawString("\pAgain");
    count++;
}
```

...run this code

That figure helps, but it might not be descriptive enough. Let's take a closer look at what's going on in the test. You should recognize the "<" symbol. It, along with the ">" symbol, are called *comparative operators*. Like the basic math operators, comparative operators may look familiar to you. You discovered them early in school — though they probably weren't referred to as comparative operators at that time. Here's a chart that tells how comparative operators are used in the *while* loop test:

Operator	Name	Test is true if...
<	less than operator	left side is less than right side
>	greater than operator	left side is greater than right side

So the *while* statement in my example is read, "while *count* is less than 10." While *count* is less than 10, do what? Run the code that follows the test. Is the value of variable *count* less than 10? Yes — I assigned it a value of 0, remember?

```
short count;
count = 0;
```

Because *count* has a value of 0, the test passes. That is, it *evaluates* to true. That means the code within the braces will run. The word "Again" will be written, and the variable *count* will *increment* by one.

```
while ( count < 10 )
{
    DrawString("\pAgain");
    count++;
}
```

Write the word "Again"

Add one to the value of variable *count*

"Slow down" you say! What's this about "incrementing" a variable — and what's with the "++" symbol? You know that you can assign a variable a value:

```
count = 0;
```

But did I mention that later in your source code you can assign that very same variable a *different* value? You may already have known that — or figured it out. If not, think of the meaning of the word "variable." As is my habit, I'll quote Mr.

Webster: "apt or likely to change or vary; changeable, fluctuating." Didn't I tell you that programming terminology actually makes sense at times?

If you didn't know before, you do now — a variable can take on different values during the running of a program. That's what's happening in my *while* loop— variable *count* is being assigned a new value. To do that, I've used the *increment operator* — that's two plus signs in a row. That's the last operator you'll need to know about. Of course, there's still about a dozen chapters left, so there might be one or two I haven't thought of yet. Regardless, you can take comfort in the idea that there aren't a whole lot of operators you need to remember.

Let's evaluate where we stand at this point. Before the *while* loop, variable *count* has a value of 0. So when *count* is compared to the number 10, it is indeed less than 10. That means the test passes and the code between the braces runs. When that code does run, the word "Again" is written to a window. Additionally, the variable *count* takes on a new value — its old value of 0 incremented by one. So *count* now has a value of 1.

So, where's the loop? Here's what happens. Once the code between the braces runs, the program makes a U-turn and heads back up to the *while* statement. Code normally doesn't do that. When a loop isn't present, code runs one line after another:

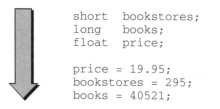

```
short   bookstores;
long    books;
float   price;

price = 19.95;
bookstores = 295;
books = 40521;
```

With a loop, the program keeps ending up back at the *while* statement, kind of like this:

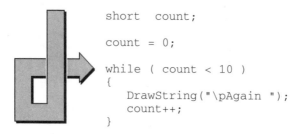

```
short   count;

count = 0;

while ( count < 10 )
{
    DrawString("\pAgain ");
    count++;
}
```

Back at the *while* statement for the second time, the same test is performed again. This time, however, variable *count* has a value of 1, not 0. Remember that *count* got incremented in the loop *body*. The body is the code between the braces. Is *count* still less than 10? Yes. So the program runs through the body of the loop again. The very same two lines of code are run. The word "Again" gets written, and variable *count* is again incremented — this time from 1 to 2. Then it's back up to the *while* statement for still another test.

When does a loop end? When the test fails. After the tenth running of the loop body, variable *count* will have a value of 10. When the program loops back up to the *while* statement, the test will fail. Variable *count*, with a value of 10, will be compared to the number 10. Is 10 less than 10? No — the test is false, and the body of the loop will be skipped:

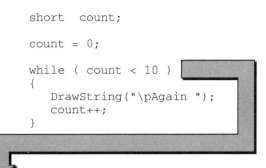

```
short   count;

count = 0;

while ( count < 10 )
{
    DrawString("\pAgain ");
    count++;
}
```

When count is no longer less than 10,
the loop body is skipped, and whatever
code follows the body will now run

What happens if you forget to increment the variable that serves as the loop counter? For example, what would the following code do?

```
short count;
count = 0;
while ( count < 10 )
{
  DrawString("\pAgain ");
}
```

The above loop is called an *infinite* loop. It would run forever — or at least until you shut the computer off. That's because the variable *count* is first given a value of 0, and then never assigned a new value. The test, *count < 10*, will always be true — and the loop body will always run. If you compile and then run one of your programs, and it just seems to sit there waiting, check your source code for this error. ▪

Loops are one way of changing the *flow* of a program as it runs. You saw that without a loop, the program runs one line after another. With a loop, that even flow is broken up. Some lines of code — the ones in the loop body — are run more than one time.

Changing Directions — By Branching

Computers are thought of as decision-making machines. Your Mac can't actually think for itself, of course. But you can write source code that makes it seem like a program running on the Mac is actually making a decision. For that, you'll need to know how *branching* works.

The Need to Branch

Imagine you've written a program that has a single menu in the menu bar. The menu has just two items in it:

> **Animation**
> **Animate a Square**
> **Animate a Circle**

If the user selects the first menu item, a square will be drawn, and it will race across the window from left to right. If the user selects the second menu item, a circle will be drawn and it will move across the window. What draws the square and moves it? Your source code. What draws the circle and moves it? Your source code — but *different* source code:

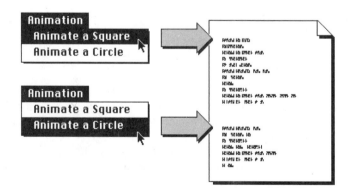

How does the program know which source code to run? It determines that from the menu item that was selected. It's obvious then that some technique is needed to allow a program to *branch* down different source code paths.

By the way — by the time you finish this book you'll be able to write a program that has a menu similar to the one shown above. Not only that, your program will be able to move an object across the screen.

The switch Branch

Handling a menu selection is a very practical application of a branching statement — I'll continue to use it for the branching example. Rather than talk about animation, though, let's start very simply. Assume I have a menu in my program that has these two menu items in it:

When the user selects the first item, the words "Item 1!" are written to a window. When the second item is selected, the words "Item 2!" are written to the same window:

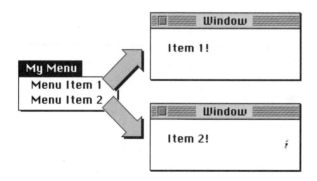

That's all that happens — from the user's perspective. From the programmer's viewpoint, a lot more action took place. If the user selects the second menu item, the program will assign a variable the value of 2. I called the variable *TheMenuItem*:

TheMenuItem = 2;

If the user had selected Menu Item 1, then *TheMenuItem* would have been assigned a value of 1. That's an example of *why* a variable is allowed to be assigned different values. In Chapter 17 I discuss menus in detail, and there I'll demonstrate how this actually takes place.

Next, the code has to take care of whatever needs to be done in response to the selection of the second menu item. Not by accident, I've picked an example where not much has to be done. The program simply has to write "Item 2!" to a window — a window we can safely assume was created earlier in the program.

Here's where the decision-making comes in. You know that the program is going to write to the window, regardless of which menu item the user picks. But which words should it write? A decision has to be made as to whether to write "Item 1!" or "Item 2!". What should the program base the decision on? The value of variable *TheMenuItem* — it holds the number of the menu item. So I need to write source code that does something like this:

```
what is the value of TheMenuItem?
{
  in case its value is 1:
    DrawString("\pItem 1!");
  in case its value is 2:
    DrawString("\pItem 2!");
}
```

Once again you probably realize that the above words aren't actual code. Here's the real source code for making a decision:

```
switch ( TheMenuItem )
{
  case 1:
    DrawString("\pItem 1!");
    break;
  case 2:
    DrawString("\pItem 2!");
    break;
}
```

The *switch* statement is the C language way of selecting one group of source code to run — from a collection of two or more groupings. The program doesn't always run the same group of code — it switches, depending on the circumstances at the time the program meets the *switch* statement. To write a *switch* branch, first write the word "switch" followed by a variable name between parentheses:

```
switch ( TheMenuItem )
```

The variable should be an *int* or a *short*. Following the *switch* line comes a pair of braces. In between the braces will be two or more *case labels*. My example uses two labels, "case 1:" and "case 2:". Each label is followed by one or more lines of code, and ends with a *break* statement.

A *switch* statement works by comparing the value of the variable between the parentheses on the *switch* line to each of the values associated with the *case* labels:

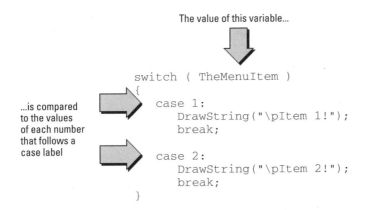

Let's say the user of my program selects the second menu item. My code will then have an assignment statement like this:

```
TheMenuItem = 2;
```

Then comes the *switch* statement. The value of *TheMenuItem*, 2, will be compared to the values listed in each *case* label. When a label with the same value as *TheMenuItem* is found, the code under that label will run:

```
TheMenuItem = 2;

switch ( TheMenuItem )
{
   case 1:
      DrawString("\pItem 1!");
      break;

   case 2:
      DrawString("\pItem 2!");
      break;
}
```

Only the code that follows the matching case label will run

It's important to realize that not all of the code between the braces will run during a pass through the *switch*. Only the code that follows one label will run. Once the program starts running some of the code, what signals the program that it's time to leave the *switch*? That's where the *break* statement comes in. No matter what *case* label code is running, when the program reaches a *break* statement, the *switch* ends. That is, the program jumps out from the braces and moves on to the line of code that follows the *switch* — whatever that may be. So it's important that every group of code that follows a *case* label ends with a *break*:

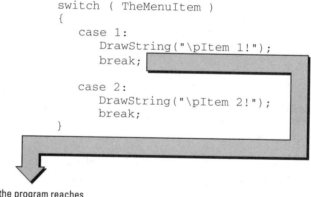

```
switch ( TheMenuItem )
{
   case 1:
      DrawString("\pItem 1!");
      break;

   case 2:
      DrawString("\pItem 2!");
      break;
}
```

When the program reaches a break statement, the rest of the switch code is skipped

With the explanation complete, another look at the *switch* statement is in order — it should make sense to you now. Here's the code, with one line in brackets. That bracketed line isn't code — it's just my way of showing that you'd need some additional code added to make things happen. As mentioned, you'll see that code in Chapter 17.

```
short TheMenuItem;
[ When a menu selection is made, set TheMenuItem equal to it ]
switch ( TheMenuItem )
{
  case 1:
    DrawString("\pItem 1!");
    break;
  case 2:
    DrawString("\pItem 2!");
    break;
}
```

The if Branch

The *switch* branch is very useful when you want your program to be able to choose from several possibilities. But many situations arise where you'll only want your program either to run a section of code or not run it. While the *switch* branch can be used for such occasions, a different type of branch is more practical — the *if* branch. Now that you're a master of the *switch*, the *if* branch will look very simple. Here's an example:

```
short VacationDays;
if ( VacationDays > 0 )
{
  MoveTo( 20, 30 );
  DrawString( "\pYou've got vacation coming!" );
}
```

An *if* branch uses a test condition to determine if the code under the *if* should run or not run. In the above example the *if* examines the value of the variable *VacationDays* to see if it is greater than 0. If it is, then the two lines of code between the braces will run. If *VacationDays* isn't greater than 0, the lines will be skipped and no message will be written.

That's All There Is to C?

No, there's plenty more. If that was it, there wouldn't be much need for software engineers like myself. I know with that line I'm setting myself up for some rude comments from you, but show a little mercy.

While this chapter didn't cover all the C there is, it did cover the basics. The remaining bits and pieces that you need in order to write a Macintosh program will be doled out throughout the remainder of the book. And once you're done, you can refer to Appendix A. There I've listed several other elements of the C language, along with examples of each. You won't need any of them to complete the programs in this book, but the examples will be helpful if you decide to try to modify my programs.

Chapter 14

To Build a Program You Need a Toolbox

*I*f every Mac programmer had to write every program completely from scratch, they'd all be in a world of hurt. There's just too much to do. Apple realized that long ago — and they kindly did something about it. Many of the strange and wonderful things that are done in Mac programs were achieved by Macintosh programmers who used just a few lines of code. They, you, and I all have the Macintosh Toolbox to thank for that.

Why Have a Toolbox?

Back in Chapter 4 you were introduced to the Macintosh Toolbox. There I said it was a collection of miniprograms that you can incorporate into your own programs. You've surely heard the expression "don't reinvent the wheel." Now, I'm not usually real big on clichés, but this one does work perfectly when describing the Macintosh Toolbox.

Many of the things you'll want to accomplish as a Macintosh programmer are the very same things every other programmer wants to accomplish. We all want to create and move windows, draw to them, and display menus — to name just a few common tasks. If you, I, and every other programmer want to do these things, we have to write the code to do it. Sounds like a lot of repetition, doesn't it? Apple thought so too.

Apple programmers anticipated the problem of everyone trying to figure the same things out, and writing the same code once they did. So they went and wrote much of the code for you. Why be so generous? You may not have been aware of this thing called the Toolbox when you bought your Mac, but for some people it's a big selling point. Programmers like to program, of course, but they don't like to do a whole lot of the work involved in programming the mundane tasks — things such as making a menu drop down when the user clicks on the menu bar, or closing a window when the user clicks the mouse in the window's close box. Programmers just want to type in a single command to have something like this take place. A programmer can then devote his programming time to matters of more importance — like giving his programs the ability to sound the Mac's speaker to scare his dog.

Miniprograms are Functions

Now that you have more than half the book under your belt, it's time for me to use correct terminology. Each of these things I've been calling a miniprogram is actually a *function*. A function, you may recall, is a collection of instructions that generally serve a single purpose. I say "generally" because it is possible to write a function that does all sorts of not necessarily related things — though that's not the preferred way of doing it.

GetNewWindow, MoveTo, DrawString — and any other part of the Toolbox — are each functions. Sometimes programmers refer to functions as *routines* — the terms mean one and the same, and are interchangeable. I'll use the word "function" in the remainder of this book.

How Your Program Works with the Toolbox

Are you the type of person who just can't stand it when something works, but you don't know *how* it works? If you are, read this section — it describes how code that you didn't write and didn't add to your project gets used by your program. In short, it tells how a call to the Toolbox works. If you're the type of person who doesn't care *how* something works, as long as it *does* work, skip the next few pages. You'll be able to write programs that work just as well as those written by the overly curious people who do read this!

Since this part of the chapter deals with microchips, some people might immediately think it's going to be way over their head. Personally, I don't think this section is super-complicated. I don't think you will either. But just to give fair warning to everyone, I'll give it the feared and dreaded *double* Technical Stuff icon:

Plenty of Chips, But No Dip

To really know how your program makes use of the Toolbox you have to know a little bit about computer chips. A very little — so don't go slamming the book shut just yet.

Your Macintosh has several different computer chips inside it. They hold different information, and serve different purposes. Of the many kinds of chips, three are of most importance: RAM chips, ROM chips, and the CPU chip. Calling these three chips the most important is a little like saying that in a human, the heart, lungs, and brain are the most important organs. It might be true, but you wouldn't want to try to get along without the rest of your insides, right?

RAM chips are memory chips. They hold computer programs. When you run a program by double-clicking on it, the Mac actually makes a copy of the program and places the copy into RAM memory. So when the salesperson at the local computer store says "get more RAM, upgrade, upgrade, you can never have too much RAM!" he isn't just giving you a line. Not this time, anyway. The more RAM your Mac has, the more programs you can have running at once. I'm going to show a RAM chip in a few upcoming figures. When I do, I'll represent the chip like this:

```
┌──────────────────┐
│  RAM Chip        │
│                  │
│                  │
│                  │
│                  │
│                  │
└──────────────────┘
```

A ROM chip is also a memory chip. But while the contents of a RAM chip change (as programs are stored and removed in it), the contents of a ROM chip don't change. That's the big difference between the two types of memory. The ROM chip doesn't hold copies of your programs, as a RAM chip does. Instead, the information in a ROM chip is placed in the chip at the Apple factory — before the computer reaches the dealer or you. RAM and ROM chips look pretty much alike, so my drawings will too. Here's how I'll draw a ROM chip:

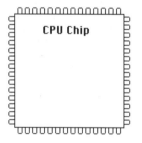

The last chip I'll cover is the CPU, or central processing unit. You may have heard this chip referred to as the "brains of the computer." As a matter of fact, I was going to add a little drawing of a brain to my rendering of the CPU, but I couldn't accurately draw one. I couldn't find a nice clip art picture of a brain to use either. So my CPU chip looks a lot like my RAM and ROM chips — I've just changed the shape a little:

Harmonious Chips

Computer chips work in almost perfect harmony with one another. That's a little surprising, since computer chips are made by people — and people don't get along harmoniously. I'll leave that one to the philosophers and sociologists. Here, I'll just cover what it is these chips are working so hard at.

When you run a program, a copy of it gets stored, or loaded, into part of a RAM chip. If it's a big program, it might occupy more than one chip. Let's say I've double-clicked on a program icon, and the copy of the program code is in RAM. While you can't actually see the contents of the chip from the outside, I've figuratively shown a RAM chip here with the program occupying a part of it:

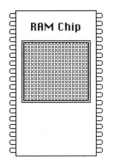

As a program runs on the Mac, the RAM chip interacts with the CPU. The CPU is able to move stuff around in RAM — pulling numbers out, adding them, rearranging them, and putting them back into memory. Thankfully, you and I don't have to ever know any of the details of just what the CPU is up to. That being the case, I can just show this action in a simplistic way:

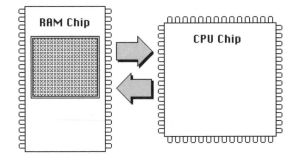

Toolbox functions are stored in ROM chips — right where Apple engineers tucked them. Let's show the code for the *GetNewWindow* Toolbox function like this:

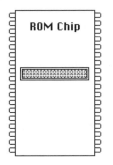

Now for the part that is really of interest to you. If a program includes Toolbox calls — and all Macintosh programs do — RAM and the CPU also end up interacting with ROM. Why? Because when the program calls a Toolbox function — like *GetNewWindow* — the CPU moves information back and forth between the RAM chip and the ROM chip. The code for the program is in RAM and the code for the Toolbox function is in ROM. The CPU acts as a sort of middleman, helping to run all the code in conjunction:

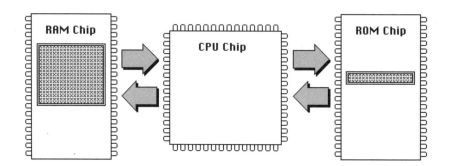

What's the result? To a user of the running program, everything appears to be going along smoothly and effortlessly:

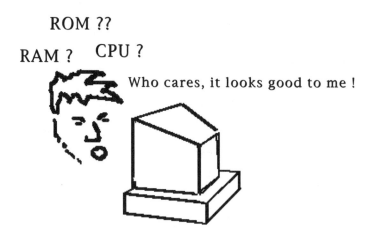

 The Toolbox is such an integral part of Mac programming that you won't be able to talk to a Macintosh programmer for more than a couple of minutes without it being brought up. Programming books, magazine articles, and fellow programmers will all mention it. So the more you know about the Toolbox — including how it interacts with chips — the more you'll gain from reading computer literature and from listening to Mac conversations. If all this talk about chips isn't thrilling you, just try to remember these key points:

  ✔ A program that is running is in RAM memory chips.

  ✔ The Toolbox functions are built into ROM memory chips.

  ✔ A program using the Toolbox communicates with ROM via the CPU. ■

Helping Out the Toolbox

Using the Toolbox functions that were written by Apple and stored in ROM chips is an essential part of programming the Mac. They are very useful and very powerful. Those Apple engineers are a pretty clever bunch, so you know there's no way you could contribute to their efforts — right? Wrong! A Toolbox function carries out a task almost as if it were a small program — hence my reasoning for calling them miniprograms earlier in the book. But just calling a Toolbox function usually isn't enough to get the function to do its work. You also must supply the function with some additional information to help it out.

Function Parameters

To use a Toolbox function in your program's code you write its name and follow the name with a pair of parentheses. Between the parentheses lie the function *parameters*. The parameters provide the Toolbox with information it needs in order to properly run the Toolbox function. For example, the Toolbox function *DrawString* needs to know what words to write to a window. You give it that information in the form of a single parameter. Without it, the Toolbox wouldn't know what to write. Here's a call to *DrawString*:

```
DrawString("\pTesting 1 2 3");
```

Even though there are several separate words between the parentheses, they are all considered a single parameter. The *DrawString* function always requires just a single parameter:

One parameter

```
DrawString("\pTesting 1 2 3");
```

The word is pronounced pah-ram-ah-ter. I thought I'd mention that for you British readers, who might be tempted to say para-meter — as in centimeter!

The dictionary says that in math, a parameter is a quantity whose value varies with the circumstances of its application. That's about the same definition we use in computer programming. Function parameters vary, depending on the circumstances. At the start of a program a parameter to *DrawString* might be:

```
DrawString("\pWelcome!");
```

However, the parameter to *DrawString* might be:

```
DrawString("\pGoodbye!");
```

at the end of a program. ■

Some Toolbox functions need more than one parameter. To let the Toolbox know where one parameter ends and the next begins, separate parameters with a comma. Back in Chapter 4 I briefly mentioned the *MoveTo* function. It tells the Toolbox where to print the next line of text. I describe *MoveTo* in the next chapter. For now, here's another bit of code from ExampleOne:

```
MoveTo( 30, 50 );
DrawString( "\pHello, World!" );
```

The next figure shows the two parameters of *MoveTo*. It also gives you a hint at what they tell the Toolbox to do.

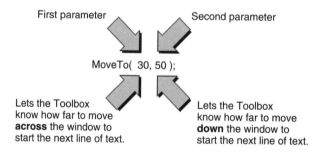

First parameter   Second parameter

MoveTo(30, 50);

Lets the Toolbox know how far to move **across** the window to start the next line of text.

Lets the Toolbox know how far to move **down** the window to start the next line of text.

Some Toolbox functions don't require any parameters. Functions that don't need additional information obviously can perform only one unvarying task. Here are a couple of lines of code I lifted from the ExampleOne program of Chapter 4:

```
InitFonts();
InitWindows();
```

The above two calls to Toolbox functions don't have parameters — though they still include the parentheses. Calls to functions always end with a pair of parentheses — regardless of the number of parameters. Since these two functions don't need parameters, you know they will always do the same thing. *InitFonts* will always initialize the fonts so that your program can make proper use of fonts. *InitWindows* will always initialize things in the Toolbox so that it can work properly with windows.

Function Return Values

Because you're kind enough to help the Toolbox out by passing it parameters, the Toolbox occasionally reciprocates by giving something back to you. Well, back to your program, actually. Some functions provide your program with a *return value*. If a function *doesn't* have an equal sign (the assignment operator) in a call to it, it *doesn't* have a return value. For instance, a call to *MoveTo* doesn't return a value:

```
MoveTo( 30, 50 );
```

If a call to a function does include the assignment operator, then it does return a value:

Return
value

Assignment
operator

```
TheWindow = GetNewWindow( 128, 0L, (WindowPtr)-1L );
```

To see how the above line of code works, let's take a look at some code that you're a little more familiar with. To give a value to a variable you first declare it, then assign it a value:

```
short  books;
books = 300;
```

Those are the same steps you take when writing the code for a function that has a return value:

```
WindowPtr  TheWindow;
TheWindow = GetNewWindow( 128, 0L, (WindowPtr)-1L );
```

The first line is the declaration of a variable named *TheWindow*. Its data type is *WindowPtr*. The second line is the assignment statement. The variable *TheWindow* is getting assigned a value. Here's a figure to spell that out:

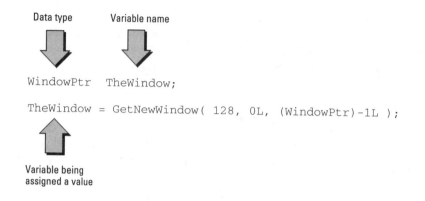

```
WindowPtr    TheWindow;

TheWindow = GetNewWindow( 128, OL, (WindowPtr)-1L );
```

Variable being
assigned a value

From the previous chapter you know about data types such as the *int, short*, and the *float*. Variables of any of these types are always numbers. There are plenty of other data types, and many of them *don't* represent numbers. The *WindowPtr* is one such type. A variable that is a *WindowPtr* represents a window. The variable is said to point to a window. In fact the "*Ptr*" part of "*WindowPtr*" stands for "Pointer." You create a different variable of the *WindowPtr* type for each window you create. This way, when you want to do something to a window — such as write text in it — you have a means of specifying which window to use:

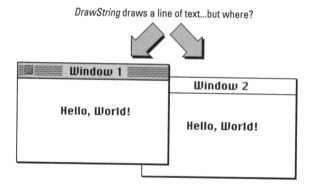

DrawString draws a line of text...but where?

In the next chapter I'll go into all the sordid details of how your program will choose which window to draw to by using a *WindowPtr*. For now, you should be aware that a *WindowPtr* variable gets its value when a window is created.

When you decide to give a *short* variable a value, you simply assign it one:

```
books = 300;
```

It's not quite that easy to do when the value of the variable isn't a number. That's when the Toolbox takes over and does the assignment for you — in the form of a return value. Now the call to the Toolbox function *GetNewWindow* should start to be making a little more sense to you:

```
WindowPtr  TheWindow;
TheWindow = GetNewWindow( 128, 0L, (WindowPtr)-1L );
```

TheWindow is a variable. It gets its value when the Toolbox function *GetNewWindow* returns it — right after the function creates the window. Now, what about the parameters of *GetNewWindow*? Sorry, this section deals with return values, not parameters. But if you keep reading, you'll learn about the parameters for several of the most commonly used Toolbox functions.

A Sampling of the Toolbox

Now you know why the Toolbox is important, and you know how the Toolbox works. The only remaining information you need about the Toolbox is the contents of it. There are over 2,000 functions in the Toolbox, so I'm sure you'll forgive me if I don't cover them all. I will, however, cover one call in detail here — *GetNewWindow*, an important Toolbox function used in just about every Mac program.

Some Toolbox functions have no parameters, others have one, and still others have more than one. To make matters worse, functions require all different *types* of parameters. *DrawString* requires one or more words as its one parameter. *MoveTo* requires two numbers for its two parameters. How on earth can one person memorize which functions require which parameters? It's another one of those good news/bad news situations. The bad news is, there is no possible way you can memorize all this information. The good news is, you aren't expected to!

Macintosh programming books *tell* you what parameters to use. For example, in the next chapter I list several commonly used Toolbox functions along with a brief description of what each function is used for. I also list the parameters for each. I provide that same information for several other Toolbox functions in Appendix B. So, how did *I* memorize all of this information so that I could pass it on to you? Feel free to tell people that I'm incredibly brilliant and was blessed with a photographic memory. But the truth of the matter is I just looked them up in reference material supplied by Apple.

So every time you use a Toolbox function you have to look it up in a book? Yes — if you are writing one and only one Macintosh program. If you plan on writing more than one you'll start to become familiar with the more common functions. For example, you've seen the function *DrawString* several times throughout this book. You're probably already aware of the fact that this function requires one parameter — the text that is to be written to a window. So from here on in, you'll never have to look up that function to check on what parameters it needs. ▪

Speaking of reference material, you may want to look into a series of books from Apple Computer called *Inside Macintosh* — I've made use of them in preparing this book. There are over a dozen books in this series, and they vary in complexity. You'll find that the two titled *Overview* and *Macintosh Toolbox Essentials* are the most useful and easy to read.

I'll finish this chapter by further elaborating on the *GetNewWindow* function. *GetNewWindow* creates a new window for your program to use. The window will have the characteristics — such as size and location on the screen — that are specified in a '*WIND*' resource. A call to *GetNewWindow* returns a *WindowPtr* to your program. That is, the function assigns a *WindowPtr* value to the variable on the left side of the assignment operator. Here's a declaration of a *WindowPtr* variable and a typical call to *GetNewWindow*:

```
WindowPtr  TheWindow;
TheWindow = GetNewWindow( 128, 0L, (WindowPtr)-1L );
```

You've had some pretty heavy exposure to *GetNewWindow* in this book. But I never did describe the mumbo-jumbo that's tucked in between the parentheses. You now know that they're parameters. *GetNewWindow* requires three of them:

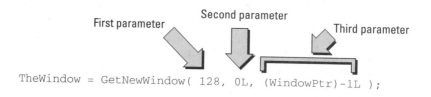

```
TheWindow = GetNewWindow( 128, 0L, (WindowPtr)-1L );
```

The first parameter to *GetNewWindow* is the ID of the '*WIND*' resource for the window you want to create. In Chapter 7 you saw how to create a '*WIND*' resource using ResEdit. When you make a resource in ResEdit, the program gives it an ID. ResEdit usually gives the first resource of each type an ID of 128 — that's why you'll see the number "128" scattered about Macintosh source code. If you want to double check on a resource ID, run ResEdit and open the resource file. I did that to verify that my '*WIND*' resource did indeed have an ID of 128:

The ID of a resource can be found using ResEdit.

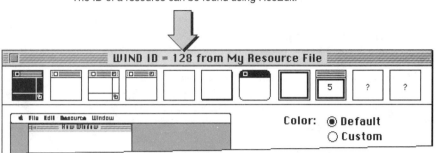

The second parameter to *GetNewWindow* is used to reserve memory for the window. Reserving memory is a tricky business, so it's good that you have the option of letting the Mac do it for you. If this second parameter has a value of *0L*, the Toolbox will figure out where the new window should be stored. By the way, that's the number zero followed by an uppercase letter "L".

The third and final parameter to *GetNewWindow* specifies whether the new window should open in front of any other open windows or behind them. I'm not exactly sure why you would ever want a new window to be hidden by other windows on the screen, but I guess it's nice to know you have the option to do so. If you want your window to open up in front, as I always do, always use *(WindowPtr) -1L* for this parameter.

No, I'm *not* going to explain what the heck *(WindowPtr) -1L* means. Just make sure to type it correctly. Include the parentheses, a minus sign, the number one, and an uppercase letter "L". ■

Reserving memory for a window is a very advanced programming technique — it's very unlikely that you'll ever do it.

In any program I've ever worked with, a new window always opens up on top of any existing windows. Yours should too.

What do the above two points mean to you? You can essentially forget about what the second and third parameters to *GetNewWindow* are all about. If you always use *0L* for the second parameter, and *(WindowPtr) -1L* for the third, you're safe. That means you only have to remember what the first parameter stands for — the ID of the '*WIND*' resource of the window you want to open. ■

Here's a summary of the *GetNewWindow* function:

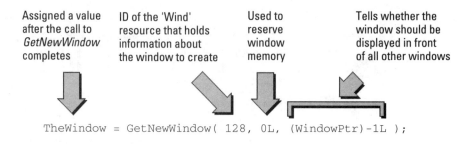

Assigned a value after the call to *GetNewWindow* completes

ID of the 'Wind' resource that holds information about the window to create

Used to reserve window memory

Tells whether the window should be displayed in front of all other windows

```
TheWindow = GetNewWindow( 128, 0L, (WindowPtr)-1L );
```

In this chapter I've concentrated on the *GetNewWindow* function. That makes sense, since every Mac program displays at least one window. But the Toolbox is capable of much more than making windows — as you'll soon see.

Chapter 15

Drawing: Why Have a Mac If You Can't Draw?

● ●

In This Chapter

▶ QuickDraw is a part of the Toolbox

▶ Specifying the window location to draw to

▶ Drawing lines

▶ Drawing rectangles

▶ Specifying which window to draw to

● ●

The Macintosh is best known for its graphical user interface. Note the word "graphical" in that phrase. Graphics may not be the most serious side of programming, but then, who wants to always be so serious? If you can't play around on the Mac by drawing a few lines and shapes now and then, why have one?

Quick on the Draw

The Macintosh Toolbox is divided into separate areas. One area holds functions that work with windows. Another area holds functions that work with menus. And still another area contains functions used for drawing. Stop right there! That's the one we're interested in — at least in this chapter. These different parts of the Toolbox have names, and the part that deals with drawing is called *QuickDraw*.

You'll most likely hear QuickDraw used in a phrase such as, "use a QuickDraw function to handle that." Remember, the Toolbox is nothing more than a huge collection of functions. So each part of the Toolbox is simply a set of functions. When you refer to QuickDraw, you're referring to one or more of the functions that are used to draw in a window.

The Coordinate System

Before I get down to the business of drawing, there's one issue I have to clear up — an issue I discussed briefly back in Chapter 7. I've mentioned it in passing several times: when you tell the Mac to draw something, how does it know *where* to draw that something? You know that you use the Toolbox function *MoveTo* before you use *DrawString*, right?

```
MoveTo( 30, 50 );
DrawString( "\pHello, World!" );
```

But that only hints at what's happening. What do the numbers that lie in the parentheses of the call to *MoveTo* mean? For the answer to that question, you must return to your grade school days...

Remember the number line? In school, you used it to count and to prove to yourself that numbers lined up in order. I don't know about your grade school, but in mine it looked something like this:

With the number line mastered, you felt pretty good. That is, until a few years later when you were introduced to the coordinate grid. Math teachers loved the ol' number line so much they stuck two of them together to form something like this:

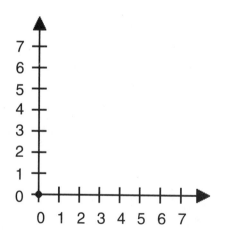

To keep you bored, and to keep their jobs, math teachers had to next think up something to *do* with all their coordinate grids. So they had you plot points — remember? In the figure below I've plotted the point (5, 2). That notation means I moved five places along the horizontal line and two places up the vertical line.

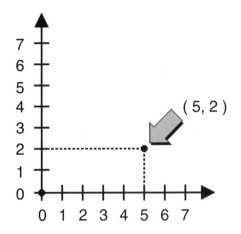

By now you're surely wondering whether I introduced this subject just for the sheer fun of it, or for the sake of nostalgia. Neither. It applies directly to the topic at hand — how the Mac draws things in a window. So let's make the connection and wrap things up. Imagine flipping our coordinate grid and placing it in a window. It would look like this figure:

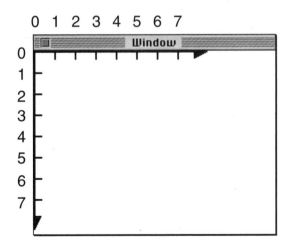

Now, if you want to move to a particular point in a window, you just do so using *MoveTo* — just as you did on the coordinate grid in school. Here I've moved to the point (5, 2):

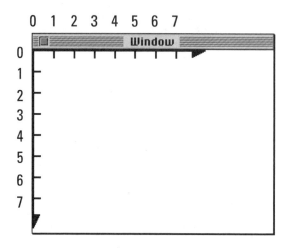

After a call to *MoveTo*, I'll call *DrawString*. Where does the text start? Right where I moved to:

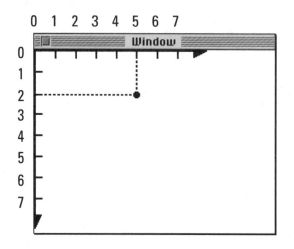

The above figure is very close to the truth — but not quite. You see, I used a number line and coordinate grid with nice big numbers and a nice wide spacing between numbers. That was for your benefit, so that everything would look nice and clear. On a Mac, the coordinate grid is much, much smaller. The distance between points on the grid of the Mac is so small that I can't draw it accurately in a figure. Instead, I've only labeled every 30 points:

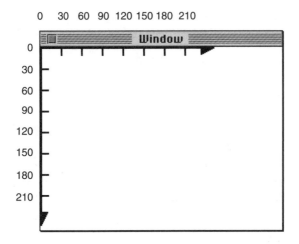

That small grid size is good — it gives you more freedom to pick and choose just where you'll draw things. If I want to write text in the upper left corner of a window, I'd write this code:

```
MoveTo( 15, 30 );
DrawString("\pCorner Text");
```

If I wanted text to start near the center of the window, I'd use this code:

```
MoveTo( 150, 120 );
DrawString("\pCenter Text");
```

Here's a look at the result of both of these *DrawString* calls:

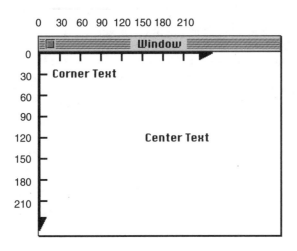

The above figure is now accurate — except for one obvious point. The coordinate grid I've superimposed on the window doesn't appear on a real window. You'll have to use a little guesswork to determine just where to place text. It should help, however, if you realize there are about 70 grid marks per inch of window.

Let's Draw!

I didn't make you do your number line schoolwork as a punishment. The idea of a coordinate grid, or *coordinate system* as some call it, is a very important piece of information when it comes to drawing on the Mac. That's because the QuickDraw functions — the Toolbox drawing functions — rely on it.

Drawing a Line

I always like to start simple, so I'll begin the discussion of shape drawing by using the simplest shape I can think of — a line. Is a line really a shape? I'm not sure, but a few of them together make up a shape — and that's good enough for me.

To draw a line you move to the window location that will serve as the start of the line, and then call the Toolbox function *Line*. You have the freedom to draw a line of any length and in any direction. To let the Toolbox know what your line is to look like, you pass the *Line* function two parameters. The first tells the horizontal length of the line and the second tells the vertical length of the line. Here's an example:

```
MoveTo( 60, 100 );
Line( 200, 0 );
```

The above call to *Line* would result in a line that is 200 pixels in length in the horizontal direction, and 0 pixels in length in the vertical direction. The next figure shows where the line gets drawn to. I've cluttered up the window with a few extra arrows and numbers — they're only in the figure to help point out what's going on. The only thing that would actually appear in the window is the one solid, horizontal line.

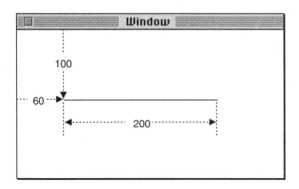

To draw a horizontal line, as I've done above, set the second parameter of *Line* to 0. That tells QuickDraw to go zero pixels in the vertical direction. I introduced the word *pixel* earlier, but didn't provide much detail. The screen is composed of thousands of individual dots that can be turned on and off — and each one is called a pixel. A few pages back I told you that there are about 70 grid marks per inch of window. I was referring to pixels. So pixels are very small. If you touch your nose to your monitor, you might be able to see the individual pixels. Make sure your eyes are open and your monitor is on, of course!

How about a vertical line? To draw one, set the first parameter of *Line* to 0. That tells QuickDraw to draw zero pixels in the horizontal direction:

```
MoveTo( 30, 30 );
Line( 0, 100 );
```

The above code first uses *MoveTo* to move 30 pixels in from the left and 30 pixels down from the top. Then *Line* draws a line 0 pixels in the horizontal direction and 100 pixels in the vertical direction:

A line doesn't have to be vertical or horizontal — it can be drawn at just about any angle. Here's one example, followed by a window that displays the line.

```
MoveTo( 30, 30 );
Line( 250, 60 );
```

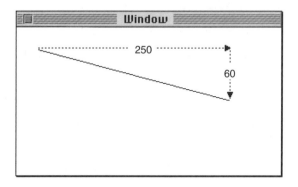

Drawing a Rectangle

Drawing a rectangle, like drawing a line, requires a knowledge of the Mac's coordinate system. It also requires that you be familiar with a data type you haven't seen yet — the *Rect*. The *Rect* holds information about a single rectangle. It's an interesting data type in that it holds four different numbers at the same time.

A variable that is of the *Rect* type holds the four *coordinates* of a rectangle. Any rectangle can be defined by using the coordinate system to specify the left, top, right, and bottom of the rectangle. Let's say you want to draw a rectangle that looks like this:

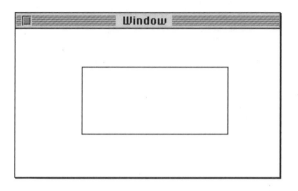

If you want to define the above rectangle using the numbers of the coordinate system you could say something like this:

- ✔ The left side of the rectangle is 100 pixels in from the left of the window.

- ✔ The top side of the rectangle is 50 pixels down from the top of the window.

- ✔ The right side of the rectangle is 300 pixels in from the left of the window.

- ✔ The bottom of the rectangle is 150 pixels down from the top of the window.

I've added a few dashed lines to the window to further illustrate where these numbers are coming from:

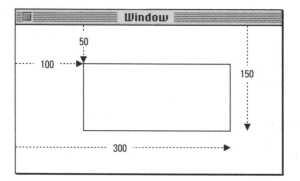

The Toolbox exists to make your life easier, and *SetRect* is one example of how that's true. The *SetRect* function performs four separate assignments, all in one call to it. Here's how I would assign the four coordinates of the above rectangle to a *Rect* variable named *TheRect*:

```
Rect  TheRect;
SetRect( &TheRect, 100, 50, 300, 150 );
```

Order is important! If you switch numbers around, the result will not be what you wanted. Think of *SetRect* like this:

SetRect(&TheRect, left, top, right, bottom);

Here's still another way to remember the order: litterbug. The word "litterbug" has the first letter of left, top, right, and bottom in the correct order — LITTERBUG. ∎

Notice the "&" symbol that precedes *TheRect* in the *SetRect* function call. That's important. How important? This important:

Without that innocent-looking "&" symbol, you'll get an error message when you try to compile the program. *SetRect* and several other QuickDraw functions require it — so keep an eye open for it as you type in source code. ■

After calling *SetRect*, here's what my window looked like:

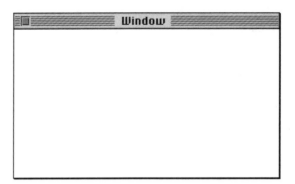

Misprint? Nope. *SetRect* doesn't draw a thing. But then, it's not supposed to. All *SetRect* does is assign a *Rect* variable the coordinates of a rectangle. An assignment statement just gives a variable a value, it doesn't draw anything. You know that from your previous work with other data types, like the *short*:

```
short  books;
books = 50;
```

To do the drawing, you use another Toolbox function — *FrameRect*. It's possible to have more than one *Rect* variable in your program, so you have to help *FrameRect* out by telling it which rectangle you want drawn — or framed. Here's how you draw a rectangle, from start to finish:

```
Rect  TheRect;
SetRect( &TheRect, 100, 50, 300, 150 );
FrameRect( &TheRect );
```

And here's the result of my efforts:

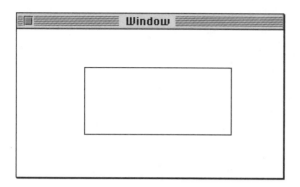

Lines and rectangles are just a small sampling of the drawing capabilities of QuickDraw — but it's enough to give you an idea of how drawing works. When you've completed the book, make sure to check out Appendix B for a description of several other QuickDraw drawing functions that you can easily incorporate into your own programs.

Drawing to a Port

In Chapter 14 I promised that I would go into the details of the *WindowPtr* data type, and how it's used to select different windows. Hoping I forgot, huh? No such luck.

Why Have Ports?

Here's the dilemma: your program opens two windows, and you want your program to write to one of them. You could write code like this:

```
MoveTo( 50, 50 );
DrawString("\pHello, World!");
```

But the question that arises is, which window will the text be drawn to? I introduced this problem in the previous chapter. I even drew up a figure to describe it — here it is again:

DrawString draws a line of text...but where?

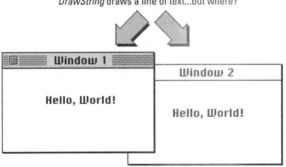

The solution to the problem comes in the form of *ports*. Every window has one port. It's a kind of identifier that keeps each window unique, and allows you to pick and choose among open windows.

A port, or portal, is a gateway or a place of entry. That definition fits in pretty well with the programmer's use of the word. You'll use a window's port as your means to draw in it and move it about the screen. Without a window's port, you're locked out. By the way, the word "port" also is the name of a sweet, dark-red wine — but I don't *think* Apple was referring to that when they selected the word. ■

Before you write or draw to a window you'll tell the Mac which port you want to work with. Only one port can be *set* at any given time — that prevents writing or drawing from taking place in two windows at once. Before writing a line of text to a window you'd want to write something a little like this:

```
Set the port to the port belonging to Window 1
MoveTo( 50, 50 );
DrawString("\pHello, World!");
```

That's *about* how you do it. To find out *exactly* how you do it, read on...

WindowPtrs and Ports

In the previous chapter you saw that some Toolbox functions return a value. You also saw that *GetNewWindow* is one such function. It assigns a value to the *WindowPtr* variable that appears in the same line of code as *GetNewWindow*. Before the call, variable *TheWindow* had no value. After the call, it does. What value isn't important — be content to know that the value is a collection of information about the window that just opened.

Let's examine a program that opens two windows. This program would have two *WindowPtr* variables declared — cleverly named *TheWindow1* and *TheWindow2*:

```
WindowPtr   TheWindow1;
WindowPtr   TheWindow2;
```

First, one window is created and displayed:

```
TheWindow1 = GetNewWindow( 128, 0L, (WindowPtr)-1L );
```

Notice that I used the name of one of the *WindowPtr* variables, *TheWindow1,* in the above line. After the call is complete, *TheWindow1* points to the newly opened window. It serves as a reference to it:

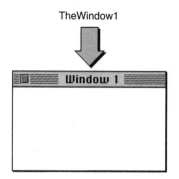

Next, I'll open and display the second window. Here I use the other *WindowPtr* variable, *TheWindow2:*

```
TheWindow2 = GetNewWindow( 129, 0L, (WindowPtr)-1L );
```

The new window opens up in front of the old window, and the variable *TheWindow2* points to it:

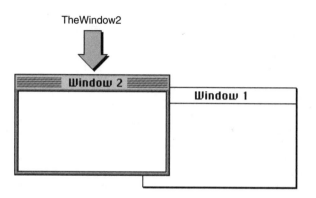

Now my program has two windows and two separate pointers — each pointer referencing one window:

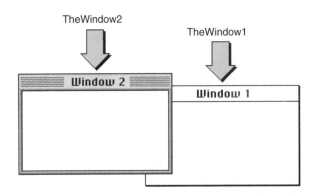

Now the setup is over. It's time to write to one of the windows. Which one? That's up to me — because now that I have a *WindowPtr* for each, I have the means to pick the window I want to use. The way to tell the Mac which window you want to work with is to call the Toolbox function *SetPort*. This function is simple to use — just pass it the *WindowPtr* variable for the window you want to draw to. Here's an example that sets the port to the port of the second window I opened and then draws to it:

```
SetPort( TheWindow2 );

MoveTo( 50, 50 );
DrawString("\pHello, World!");
```

Just to reinforce things a little, here's a more comprehensive example. In the following code I open two windows, just as I did above. Then I write one line of text to one window and a different line of text to the other window. I'll follow the code with a figure of what the windows should look like.

```
WindowPtr   TheWindow1;
WindowPtr   TheWindow2;
```

First, one window is created and displayed:

```
TheWindow1 = GetNewWindow( 128, 0L, (WindowPtr)-1L );
TheWindow2 = GetNewWindow( 129, 0L, (WindowPtr)-1L );

SetPort( TheWindow1 );
MoveTo( 50, 50 );
DrawString("\pWindow One");
SetPort( TheWindow2 );
MoveTo( 10, 20 );
DrawString("\pWindow Two");
```

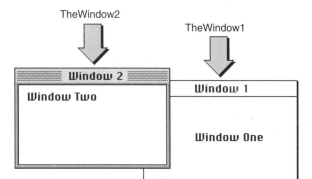

Using different resource IDs

If you're very observant you might have noticed something that I tried to slip by without explanation. Here are the lines of code that might have caught your eye:

```
TheWindow1 = GetNewWindow( 128, 0L,
(WindowPtr)-1L );

TheWindow2 = GetNewWindow( 129, 0L,
(WindowPtr)-1L );
```

Notice that the two calls to *GetNewWindow* use different *'WIND'* resource IDs — that is, the first of the three parameters in the two function calls differ. One uses *'WIND'* ID 128, the other uses *'WIND'* ID 129. That means that the resource file for my program has to include two *'WIND'* resources — one for each ID used in my program. You can tell the two windows are based on different resources because they look different from one another — they were defined that way in the *'WIND'* resources.

What if your program only uses one window? Sorry, you still have to call *SetPort* before drawing or writing to it. Sure, it might seem ridiculous to tell the Mac to set the port to your window when that's the only window on the screen. But the Macintosh is a computer, and computers never do things without some kind of reason. In this case, there's a pretty darned good one. It turns out that the entire screen of your Macintosh also has a port — just as each window on the screen has one. So if you don't call *SetPort* when your one window is on the screen, subsequent drawing might miss your window and take place right on the screen! If you think back to my ExampleOne program, I used *SetPort* even though the program opens a single window. Here's that entire short program so you can see for yourself:

```
main()
{
    WindowPtr  TheWindow;                 /* the window                 */
    InitGraf( &thePort );                 /* standard initializations */
    InitFonts();
    InitWindows();                        /* next line opens a window */
    TheWindow = GetNewWindow( 128, 0L, (WindowPtr)-1L );
    SetPort( TheWindow );                 /* set the drawing port     */
    MoveTo( 30, 50 );                     /* set the drawing position */
    DrawString( "\pHello, World!" ); /* draw some words           */

    while ( !Button() )                   /* do nothing until         */
        ;                                 /* button is clicked        */
}
```

I think I just explained things pretty clearly, but one point is worth repeating. Even if your program uses only one window, you should still call *SetPort* before writing text or drawing shapes in it. If you don't, what was supposed to be drawn might not get drawn — and you might spend a lot of time trying to figure out why. ■

That concludes Part IV, which means it's on to bigger and better things — including the creation of your first program that includes both a window and a menu.

Part V
The Moment of Truth: Writing a Program!

The 5th Wave   By Rich Tennant

"MISS LAMONT, WILL YOU GET ME TECHNICAL SUPPORT AT STRIPOC INTERACTIVE PLEASE?"

In this part . . .

*W*hat do I mean by "the moment of truth"? Heck, you saw a Mac program way back in Chapter 4. True enough. But you haven't seen the source code for a real Mac program. One that has a menu that allows the user to make choices. That's what Mac programs are all about — giving the user the power to decide what to do.

The program that's covered in the chapters of this part has a functional menu and a movable window — two important program features not covered up to this point. It also demonstrates how to effectively use the part of the Toolbox that draws shapes in windows — QuickDraw. And, as if that weren't enough, this shows you exactly how to turn your source code into an honest-to-gosh application — a program that you can save on your hard drive or copy to a floppy disk.

Chapter 16
Examining a Simple Mac Program

● ●

In This Chapter

▶ A thorough look at the source code of ExampleOne

▶ Functions — with and without the Toolbox

▶ Initializing the Toolbox

▶ Events — how a program responds to the mouse

▶ Getting closer to writing a "real" Macintosh program

● ●

*I*n this chapter I'll give you one last look at the ExampleOne program that you first laid eyes on in Chapter 4. Whether you know it or not, you've learned many of the elements that are key to writing a Macintosh program. So now it's time for a thorough dissection of each of the dozen or so lines that make up ExampleOne.

While the ExampleOne program demonstrates several of the important concepts of Macintosh programming, it isn't something to really brag about. In this chapter I'll start to rectify that by adding to the source code to get a little bit closer to what a Macintosh program is really all about.

ExampleOne — One More Time

Since I'll be discussing all of the ExampleOne program in this chapter, it might be helpful to see it once again in its entirety — it's listed just below. For better or worse, this is the last time you'll see the ExampleOne program. Or is it? You see, almost every line of code that makes up ExampleOne will be used in every Macintosh program you write. So bits and pieces of the infamous ExampleOne will always live on.

```
main()
{
    WindowPtr  TheWindow;               /* the window              */
    InitGraf( &thePort );               /* standard initializations */
    InitFonts();
    InitWindows();                      /* next line opens a window */
    TheWindow = GetNewWindow( 128, 0L, (WindowPtr)-1L );
    SetPort( TheWindow );               /* set the drawing port    */
    MoveTo( 30, 50 );                   /* set the drawing position */
    DrawString( "\pHello, World!" );    /* draw some words         */

    while ( !Button() )                 /* do nothing until        */
        ;                               /* button is clicked       */
}
```

Functions Aren't Just for the Toolbox

Every miniprogram in the Toolbox is a function. But the Toolbox isn't the only place you'll find functions. They also exist in the source code of every C program — and that includes programs you write. It might not have sunk in when I mentioned it way back in Chapter 4, but the ExampleOne program has a single function, and its name is *main*.

If the Toolbox has functions, why does your program also have to have them? Keep in mind that the primary purpose of a function is to group source code together in an attempt to better organize it. Apple has done that with its own source code, and then placed it in the Toolbox. Now you'll have to do that with your own source code within your source code file.

There are a couple of approaches you can use here. If your program consists of more than a page full of code, you might want to divvy it up into separate functions. You'll then have to learn about calling your own functions — just as you call Toolbox functions. You'll also have to learn a lot more about parameters — those variables and numbers that appear between the parentheses of a function name. The second approach — used if your program doesn't consist of a whole lot of code — is to just pack it all into one function and forget about function calling and parameters. Which way sounds easier to you?

All right, one function per program it is! Here's how you do that. All programs written in C must have a function named *main*. That's not just a whim or a preference of mine — it's The Law. So, if your program is going to have just one function, and all C programs must have a function named *main*, guess what the name of your function will be?

Let's look at the form that all functions take. A function begins with its name, followed by a pair of parentheses. All the source code that follows the function name, and that is to be part of the function itself, gets nested between a pair of braces. Here's a figure straight out of Chapter 4:

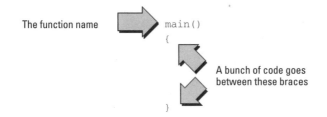

The function name → `main()`
`{`
A bunch of code goes between these braces
`}`

Look back at the source code for the ExampleOne program. Does it follow this format? Yes. It has a single function named *main*. Between the braces that signify the start and end of the function are ten lines of code that initialize the Toolbox, open a window, and write some text to the window.

Initializing the Toolbox

You know what the ExampleOne program does, but you probably aren't exactly sure how it does it. Throughout the preceding chapters you've been given most of the information you need to understand the program — but it has been given to you piecemeal. The next several sections of this chapter will sum it all up — starting with the initialization of the Toolbox.

A Mac program starts to run when the user double-clicks on its icon. During the running of a program, the program will be communicating with the Toolbox. And the Toolbox, in turn, will be communicating with the program. As is the case with humans, before any serious communication can take place these two have to get introduced to one another. That's what the *initialization* process is all about. Those calls to the Toolbox that begin with "Init" are getting this communication under way. Here's how my ExampleOne program carries out its initialization:

```
InitGraf( &thePort );
InitFonts();
InitWindows();
```

I've used three initialization calls — but there are others. To prepare your program to work with menus, there's a Toolbox function called *InitMenus*. For using dialog boxes there's *InitDialogs*. If your program does fancy things with the cursor, you'll want to call *InitCursor*. And if your program is to have text editing capabilities, you'll call *TEInit*. Most programs will also call a Toolbox function named *FlushEvents*. Now, *FlushEvents* doesn't have "Init" in its name, but it is still a part of the program initialization process. Events are something I cover later in this chapter. For now, realize that events are things that can linger in memory from one running of a program to the next. When a program starts, you want it free of old events — so you flush them. Please don't make me further the explanation with an analogy, okay?

A program that has all the above features, such as windows, menus, dialog boxes, and so on, will have initialization source code that looks like this:

```
InitGraf( &thePort );        /* standard initializations */
InitFonts();
InitWindows();
InitMenus();
TEInit();
InitDialogs( 0L );
FlushEvents( everyEvent, 0 );
InitCursor();
```

The question naturally arises as to which of these calls to Toolbox initialization functions should be included and which should be excluded. That's an easy one — just include the above eight lines in *every* Mac program you write. You can't overdo it. If an initialization is unnecessary, it won't hurt your program, and it won't hurt your Mac. What about unnecessary code? You may have heard somewhere that source code should be efficient so that a program runs quickly. That's true. But a call to a Toolbox function like *InitWindows* takes only *microseconds* to run — that's *fast*. No one will ever notice.

On the one hand, extra initializations take almost no time to run, aren't harmful, and are unnoticeable to the user of a program. On the other hand, a necessary initialization that *isn't* included in your source code will cause the program to bomb when someone attempts to run it. Now, you tell me — which hand do you choose?

No matter what your program does, always start it off with these eight lines — just as they're presented here:

```
InitGraf( &thePort );        /* standard initializations */
InitFonts();
InitWindows();
InitMenus();
TEInit();
InitDialogs( 0L );
FlushEvents( everyEvent, 0 );
InitCursor();
```

If you include the above eight lines, in the order shown, your program will always be properly initialized. ■

When programmers talk about efficient code they are often talking about time-consuming programming tasks — like redrawing all of the graphics that appear in a window. An issue like that becomes important in programs that work with large, complex graphics. If you're working with a program that displays photos, for example, you don't want to wait minutes for the Mac to redraw a picture that you just rotated. ■

Working with a Window

I've covered opening a window, and the *GetNewWindow* Toolbox function, several times in this book — so I'll just summarize things for you. But even if you think you've got this window business licked, read on. Over the course of the next few pages I'm going to add a little new code to ExampleOne.

Opening a Window

To open a window you first create a '*WIND*' resource in your program's resource file. Then, in your source code, you declare a *WindowPtr* variable. Finally, call the Toolbox function *GetNewWindow* to open and display the window. Here's the code:

```
WindowPtr  TheWindow;
TheWindow = GetNewWindow( 128, 0L, (WindowPtr)-1L );
```

Writing to a Window

Once a window is on the screen, feel free to work with it. But first, don't forget to let the Mac know that the port you'll be writing to is that of the new window:

```
SetPort( TheWindow );
```

If you want to write text, move to the desired location in the window by calling *MoveTo*, then write:

```
SetPort( TheWindow );
MoveTo( 30, 50 );
DrawString( "\pHello, World!" );
```

What about that "\p" that always precedes the words you want to write? That has to do with *strings*. A string is the computer's way of keeping track of several characters — letters, digits, and symbols — in one grouping. In the old days (about 10 years ago), programmers almost exclusively used the Pascal language to program the Mac. To this day the Mac still looks for strings that are in a Pascal format. So the "\p" before the start of a string is a way of saying to the Mac, "Here comes a string from the C language, but feel free to put it into the Pascal format you are more familiar with." ▪

Planning an Addition

Mac programs contain graphics — except for mine. I'll remedy that by drawing a rectangle to the window that ExampleOne opens. Programming requires planning.

Sometimes a little, sometimes a lot. Adding a rectangle is easy, but still, I'll take a moment to plan it out.

To add a rectangle I need a *Rect* variable and the use of two QuickDraw functions. Here's the code I wrote in Chapter 15:

```
Rect  TheRect;
SetRect( &TheRect, 100, 50, 300, 150 );
FrameRect( &TheRect );
```

In my ExampleOne program, I want to have a box around "Hello, World!" to draw the user's attention to it. I'll draw my rectangle in such a way that it frames the text that's written with *DrawString*.

Here's the source code that I use to move to a location and then draw a line of text:

```
MoveTo( 30, 50 );
DrawString( "\pHello, World!" );
```

The result is shown in the following figure. I've marked the starting point of the text:

My job is to determine the coordinates for a rectangle that is to surround this text. For that I'll use my knowledge of the Mac's coordinate system, and do a little calculating to come up with where the rectangle should be placed. Whenever Jethro of the Beverly Hillbillies needed to do a little math he "commenced to ciphering." I'll do the same. I used the following reasoning to come up with the rectangle's coordinates:

- ✔ The top must be less than 50 — I chose 30.

- ✔ The bottom must be greater than 50 — I chose 60.

- ✔ The left side must be less than 30 — I chose 20.

✔ The right side must extend beyond the end of the text — I chose 120.

Here's what a rectangle of the above dimensions would look like:

```
┌──────────────────────────────────────────┐
│ ▣ ▨▨▨▨▨▨▨▨  Untitled  ▨▨▨▨▨▨▨▨▨▨         │
├──────────────────────────────────────────┤
│      ┊ 30                                  │
│      ▼───────────────── ┊                 │
│   ┌─────────────────┐  ┊ 60              │
│ 20│  Hello, World!  │  ┊                  │
│   └─────────────────┘  ▼                  │
│   ┊────────────────▶                      │
│           120                             │
│                                           │
└──────────────────────────────────────────┘
```

Here's what my *SetRect* call looks like, using the above coordinates:

```
SetRect( &TheRect, 20, 30, 120, 60 );
```

Don't forget the order that *SetRect* expects those four coordinates to appear in — left, top, right, bottom.

This note isn't really Mac Psychology — but I didn't have any other icons at my disposal that made more sense. Anyway, for years I thought that Jethro was just incorrectly using a word when he said he had do some "ciphering." I just found out that "cipher" means "to solve arithmetical problems." I have to admit it's more than a little humbling to realize a hillbilly who barely "gradjeated the third grade" knows things I don't! ▪

More Planning for the Addition

Now I'll incorporate the rectangle-drawing code into my program. Programmers list a program's variables right near the top of their programs so that the compiler is sure to find them first. Back in Chapter 4, that's what I did with the *WindowPtr* variable named *TheWindow*:

```
main()
{
    WindowPtr  TheWindow;

    InitGraf( &thePort );
    InitFonts();
    [ rest of the code here ]
```

I'll add the *Rect* variable up front, right by the *WindowPtr* variable. By the way, the order in which the two variables appear doesn't matter. So it isn't important which of the two variables I list first:

```
main()
{
   WindowPtr   TheWindow;
   Rect        TheRect;

   InitGraf( &thePort );
   InitFonts();
   [ rest of the code here ]
```

Next, I'll look for the appropriate place to add the *SetRect* and *FrameRect* calls. Because I'm drawing to a window, I'll want to keep a couple of things in mind as I determine where to add the new code:

  ✔ Has a window been opened?

  ✔ Has the port been set to the opened window?

The above two points mean that my new code should go *after* the call to *GetNewWindow* and *after* the call to *SetPort*. I've done this in the code below. I've also added the remaining Toolbox initializations — as I recommended earlier in this chapter. To avoid any confusion with the ExampleOne program, I've given this source code a brand-new name — BoxedText.

```
main()
{
   WindowPtr   TheWindow;
   Rect        TheRect;

   InitGraf( &thePort );
   InitFonts();
   InitWindows();
   InitMenus();
   TEInit();
   InitDialogs( 0L );
   FlushEvents( everyEvent, 0 );
   InitCursor();

   TheWindow = GetNewWindow( 128, 0L, (WindowPtr)-1L );
   SetPort( TheWindow );

   MoveTo( 30, 50 );
   DrawString( "\pHello, World!" );

   SetRect( &TheRect, 20, 30, 120, 60 );
   FrameRect( &TheRect );
   while ( !Button() )
      ;
}
```

After compiling and running the above program, I get a window that looks just like this:

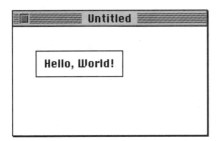

Notice in the BoxedText listing I only called *SetPort* once — even though I draw to the window twice. That's because I'm not doing anything between the drawing of the text and the drawing of the rectangle. What if I opened a new, second window between these two drawing operations?

```
TheWindow = GetNewWindow( 128, 0L, (WindowPtr)-1L );
SetPort( TheWindow );
MoveTo( 30, 50 );
DrawString( "\pHello, World!" );

TheWindow2 = GetNewWindow( 129, 0L, (WindowPtr)-1L );

SetRect( &TheRect, 20, 30, 120, 60 );
FrameRect( &TheRect );
```

Here's this chapter's quiz. Which window, *TheWindow* or *TheWindow2*, would the rectangle get drawn to?

The answer is *TheWindow*. Why? Because its port is the current, or active, port. Why? Because the most recent call to *SetPort* specified that *TheWindow* be the current port. Now, part two of the quiz. How would you modify the above code to have the rectangle drawn to *TheWindow2*? The answer is shown below:

```
TheWindow = GetNewWindow( 128, 0L, (WindowPtr)-1L );
SetPort( TheWindow );
MoveTo( 30, 50 );
DrawString( "\pHello, World!" );

TheWindow2 = GetNewWindow( 129, 0L, (WindowPtr)-1L );

SetPort( TheWindow2 );
SetRect( &TheRect, 20, 30, 120, 60 );
FrameRect( &TheRect );
```

Add another call to *SetPort* — this time specifying that *TheWindow2* becomes the current port. The new line is shown in bold above.

What If...

What would it have meant if I ran the program and the window looked like the one in the following figure, rather than the one I just showed?

```
┌─────────────────────────────────┐
│ ▣  ▤▤▤▤ Untitled ▤▤▤▤▤          │
├─────────────────────────────────┤
│                                 │
│    ┌──────────────┐             │
│    │ Hello, World!│             │
│    └──────────────┘             │
│                                 │
│                                 │
│                                 │
└─────────────────────────────────┘
```

That would have meant I guessed wrong about the size of the rectangle. I based the size of the rectangle on the fact that there are about 70 pixels to an inch. How did I know there are 70 pixels in an inch? I've been programming the Mac for 10 years; I just know stuff like that. How would *you* know there are about 70 pixels to an inch? You just finished Chapter 15 — where I mentioned this fact! Looking at the words "Hello, World!" I see that they're about an inch long. That's 70 pixels. I then added a little clearance to each side, making the total length of my rectangle 100 pixels. Let's double-check.

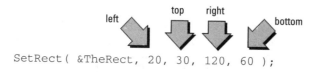

```
SetRect( &TheRect, 20, 30, 120, 60 );
```

The left side of the rectangle is 20 pixels in from the left side of the window. The right side of the rectangle is 120 pixels in from the left side of the window. Jethro could quickly tell us that 120 minus 20 is 100. Now, back to my original question. What would it have meant if I ran the program and the window looked like this?

```
┌─────────────────────────────────┐
│ ▣  ▤▤▤▤ Untitled ▤▤▤▤▤          │
├─────────────────────────────────┤
│                                 │
│   ┌──────────────┐              │
│   │ Hello, World!│              │
│   └──────────────┘              │
│                                 │
│                                 │
│                                 │
└─────────────────────────────────┘
```

It would mean that my rectangle wasn't big enough. How would I fix this? Make the rectangle bigger by setting it bigger during the call to *SetRect*. Here's what the code currently looks like:

```
SetRect( &TheRect, 20, 30, 120, 60 );
FrameRect( &TheRect );
```

To make the rectangle a larger I could make it 130 pixels in length by changing the right side to 150 pixels in from the left side of the window rather than 120:

```
SetRect( &TheRect, 20, 30, 150, 60 );
FrameRect( &TheRect );
```

An Eventful Experience

Through some mystical process, your Macintosh is aware of everything you do. Well, everything that involves the Macintosh. Whether you move the mouse, click the mouse button, press a key, or insert a disk, the Mac knows. This power to spy on you, in the hands of an evil computer, could be disastrous. Fortunately, the Mac is a user friendly computer. Because it's friendly, it's willing to share. So when the Mac notices that a user has taken some action — like pressing the mouse button — it passes this information on to whatever program is currently running. And if that program happens to be yours? Well then, you can have your program make note of this fact and respond accordingly.

Actions Are Events

In Macintosh lingo, an action such as a mouse click is called an *event*. Events are the heart and soul of a Macintosh program. They are what make a Macintosh program run. For example, if the Mac wasn't aware of events it would never know when the user clicked the mouse on a menu item. It would never know when a key was pressed. It would never…you get the picture. The Mac would not be the Mac. Events drive a program to do certain things. So, not surprisingly, Macintosh programs are called *event-driven* programs.

The Outdated Event Loop

All Macintosh programs have an *event loop*. From Chapter 14 you know what a loop is, and in this chapter you just learned what an event is. There are two lines of code in the ExampleOne program that I haven't yet described in this chapter. They just happen to represent the event loop of the ExampleOne program:

```
while ( !Button() )
   ;
```

The code beneath a *while* loop is usually enclosed in braces, like this:

```
while ( BooksSold < 100 )
{
   MoveTo( 10, 30 );
   DrawString("\pPoor sales! You'll never write in this town
            again!");
}
```

There is an exception to this, however. If one and only one line of code will appear beneath the *while* statement, then the braces are optional. I've omitted them in ExampleOne. I could have written the ExampleOne *while* loop this way:

```
while ( !Button() )
{
   ;
}
```

and it would have had the same effect. ∎

The purpose of a program's event loop is to repeatedly look for and process events until the user quits the program. At each pass through the loop, the program checks to see if an event has occurred. If an event did occur, the program usually responds in some way. If an event didn't occur, nothing happens. In either case, a moment later, the program is back looking to see if another event has occurred.

I won't spend a great deal of time explaining how the event loop of ExampleOne works. That's because it's not very practical. Why did I try to pawn off a second rate event loop on you? I used it because the ExampleOne program is meant to be the simplest of programs, and the two-line event loop I used is the simplest of event loops.

While the event loop of ExampleOne isn't of very high quality, you have seen it several times. So I feel I would be derelict in my duties if I didn't offer at least a modest explanation of how it works.

The event loop of a program is generally the last piece of source code in the program's *main* function. Once the event loop is reached, that's where the program remains until the user quits. In ExampleOne you might think of the flow of the program this way:

```
main()
{
    WindowPtr   TheWindow;

    InitGraf( &thePort );
    InitFonts();
    InitWindows();

    TheWindow = GetNewWindow( 128, 0L, (WindowPtr)-1L );

    SetPort( TheWindow );
    MoveTo( 30, 50 );
    DrawString( "\pHello, World!" );

    while ( !Button() )
        ;
}
```

Because you'll probably never see another event loop like this one, I said I wasn't going to go to great depths to explain it. So I'll just say that like any loop, the event loop checks the condition between the parentheses to determine if it's true. In this case the odd-looking text between the parentheses is a call to a Toolbox function called *Button*. Anytime it's called, *Button* will tell your program whether or not the mouse button was just pressed by the user.

If the mouse *wasn't* pressed, the loop runs. Here the exclamation point assists in the decision. Yes, I know that's an evasive explanation, but trust me — you don't want all the details. What happens when the loop runs? This line of code runs:

```
;
```

What does a semicolon, all alone, do? Absolutely nothing. And for this simple program, that's all I want to happen: nothing. Once ExampleOne places a window on the screen and writes to it, the program doesn't do anything at all. It just loops continuously, waiting for the user to click the mouse button. What happens when the user finally does click the mouse button? If not clicking the mouse causes the loop test to pass and the loop to run, then a press of the mouse must cause the loop test to fail and end the loop. That's exactly right. And where does the program go after a loop ends? To the next line of code that follows the loop, the closing brace:

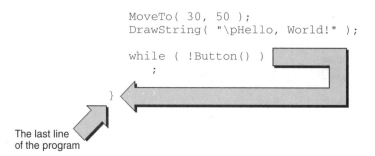

```
MoveTo( 30, 50 );
DrawString( "\pHello, World!" );

while ( !Button() )
    ;

}
```

The last line
of the program

As long as the mouse button isn't pressed, the *while* loop continues to cycle. Once the button is pressed, the *while* test condition fails and the line following the loop code is run. That line is the closing brace of the program. There's nothing left to run, so the program quits.

The ExampleOne event loop isn't nearly as powerful as the full-fledged event loop you're going to see later in this chapter. But you can learn a couple of important points about event loops from it:

- ✔ An event loop is usually based on a C *while* loop.
- ✔ Once the event loop is reached, it repeats itself until the program ends.

Holding Onto an Event

The event loop of ExampleOne only looked for a click of the mouse button. But a mouse click isn't the only kind of event the Mac recognizes. The computer also notices when the user presses a key, inserts a disk, and several other actions. As a programmer, you aren't only interested in *if* an event occurred, you want to know *what* event has occurred. Why? You want your program to react in different ways to events, depending on the type of event. For example, if the user clicks the mouse button in the menu bar you want your program to drop down a menu. If the user inserts a disk in the Mac, that's also an event — but you won't want a menu to drop down for this event.

Obviously, some means of storing information about an event is needed. If I were the Mac, I'd log information about events like this:

What type of event?	Where was the mouse?
mouse click	in the menu bar
key press	event doesn't involve the mouse

I got tired of entering event types in the above table and quit after just two. Fortunately, the Mac doesn't get tired—it keeps all the information I show above, and a lot more. It doesn't use a table, of course. Instead, it uses a C data type called the *EventRecord*. When you declare a variable to be of the *EventRecord* type you then have the means to hold all sorts of information about one event. Here I've declared an *EventRecord* variable named *TheEvent*:

```
EventRecord   TheEvent;
```

An *EventRecord* variable holds lots of information about an event, but the most important bits of info are the two I've listed in my chart: the event type and where the event took place. With some data types, the clever C language allows you to dig two or more separate bits of information out of one single variable. The *EventRecord* is one such data type. How do you get information about what the event is? You follow the variable name with a period and the word "what" as I'm doing here:

```
TheEvent.what
```

Here's a summary:

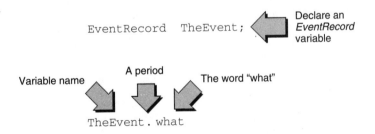

How do you suppose you go about finding out where an event took place? Use the same method as above, but use the word "where" instead of "what":

```
TheEvent.where
```

I've told you how to get information out of an *EventRecord* variable, but how does the information get in the variable in the first place? As with most tasks on the Mac, a call to a Toolbox function does the trick. It's called *WaitNextEvent*, and here's a typical call to it:

```
WaitNextEvent( everyEvent, &TheEvent, 0L, 0L );
```

When your program calls *WaitNextEvent* the Mac performs its spy work to see if the user is up to anything. If an event has just occurred, *WaitNextEvent* gathers all the important information about the event and stores it in the variable named *TheEvent*. Here's what's going on:

Before `WaitNextEvent`,
`TheEvent` holds no information

`WaitNextEvent( everyEvent, &TheEvent, 0L, 0L );`

After `WaitNextEvent`,
`TheEvent` is full of information

As long as you declare an *EventRecord* variable named *TheEvent*, you can use the same four parameters that I did whenever you call *WaitNextEvent*. You don't have to know anything about the other three parameters, but if you're feeling adventurous you can examine this next figure:

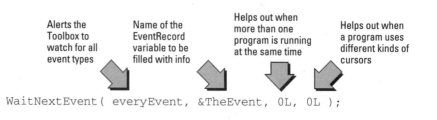

Alerts the Toolbox to watch for all event types

Name of the EventRecord variable to be filled with info

Helps out when more than one program is running at the same time

Helps out when a program uses different kinds of cursors

`WaitNextEvent( everyEvent, &TheEvent, 0L, 0L );`

Don't forget to type in the "&" character before the *EventRecord* variable name in the call to *WaitNextEvent*. THINK C won't like it if you forget! ■

A call to *WaitNextEvent* informs the Toolbox that it should grab hold of the next event it sees and tuck all event-related information into the *EventRecord* variable. But that only takes care of one single event. In a Mac program, events could be happening all the time. If the user clicks the mouse twice, that's two separate events. So that your program doesn't miss events as they happen, it seems like it might make good sense to call *WaitNextEvent* over and over. In fact, that is exactly what your program should do. I'll lay out what needs to be accomplished, and in the next section I'll go about doing it:

✔ Get information about *events*.

✔ *Loop* through code that calls *WaitNextEvent* over and over.

New Improved Event Loop — With More Stain-fighting Power!

No, it can't fight stains. But that's about the only thing the new improved event loop can't do. I'll make good use of the *EventRecord* data type and the *WaitNextEvent* function by using both in this section's event loop.

Imagine that I've written a program that initializes the Toolbox and then opens a window — just as ExampleOne or BoxedText do. So that I can concentrate on just the new event loop, I'll omit that code from my program and just show the loop:

```
AllDone = 0;
while ( AllDone < 1 )
{
   WaitNextEvent( everyEvent, &TheEvent, 0L, 0L );
   switch ( TheEvent.what )
   {
      case keyDown:
         MoveTo( 10, 20 );
         DrawString( "\pKey pressed" );
         break;

      case mouseDown:
         AllDone = 1;
         break;
   }
}
```

The new event loop is much larger than the old one, but you've seen most of its elements in the past. Let's take a close look at what it's doing. First the loop test. I'm using a *short* variable called *AllDone* and comparing it to the value 1. Is *AllDone* less than 1? Of course — I assigned it a value of 0 just before the *while* statement. When will the loop stop looping? When *AllDone* has a value of 1 or greater. Near the end of the loop is a line that assigns *AllDone* a value of 1 — that takes care of ending the loop. But more on that later.

The first thing that happens inside the loop is a call to *WaitNextEvent*. Notice that the four parameters of this function are just as I described in the preceding section. After the call to *WaitNextEvent* is complete, the variable *TheEvent* holds information about whatever event just occurred.

The primary purpose of a program's event loop is to recognize an event and *handle* it. That means it should take some action appropriate to the type of event that has occurred. That's the purpose of the *switch* statement. You'll recall from Chapter 13 that a *switch* statement is a branching statement that allows the program to run only one section of two or more groups of code. The *switch* statement begins with the word "switch" followed by a variable name in parentheses.

For my *switch* statement I use the *EventRecord* variable *TheEvent* — but not the whole variable. Here I'm only interested in what type of event occurred. So naturally I'm going to examine the *what* part of the variable. That's handled by this line:

```
switch ( TheEvent.what )
```

Next come the *case* labels. Where did the words *keyDown* and *mouseDown* come from, and what are they? They're both part of C. So that programmers can have a way of referring to different event types, each event has its own name. You can use these names in the *case* sections of the *switch* statement. Here's that code:

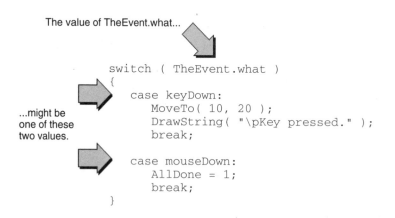

```
                    switch ( TheEvent.what )
                    {
                        case keyDown:
                            MoveTo( 10, 20 );
                            DrawString( "\pKey pressed." );
                            break;

                        case mouseDown:
                            AllDone = 1;
                            break;
                    }
```

The value of TheEvent.what...

...might be one of these two values.

Notice that in the above figure I say that the variable *TheEvent.what* might have a value that matches one of the two *case* values. What if it doesn't? The two *case* labels only account for two types of events — a key being pressed (*keyDown*) and the mouse button being clicked (*mouseDown*). What if the user inserts a disk? (That's called a *diskEvt.*) My *switch* statement doesn't look for an event of this type. So if one does occur, nothing will happen:

```
switch ( TheEvent.what )
{
    case keyDown:
        MoveTo( 10, 20 );
        DrawString( "\pKey pressed." );
        break;

    case mouseDown:
        AllDone = 1;
        break;
}
```

If the event doesn't match any of the event types I have listed by the *case* labels, the program returns to the top of the loop to see if it should run the loop again. Will it? Let me answer that question with another question. Did the value of *AllDone* change? No. It is still 0. Since 0 is less than 1, the loop will run again, and once again *WaitNextEvent* will be called to capture another event.

Let's assume that the user presses a key on the keyboard. That constitutes a *keyDown* event. The call to *WaitNextEvent* picks up on that and sets *TheEvent.what* equal to *keyDown*. When the *switch* statement is reached, the *keyDown case* will run. Assuming a window is open, the words "Key pressed" will be written to it:

If *TheEvent.what* is a *keyDown* event...

```
switch ( TheEvent.what )
{
    case keyDown:
        MoveTo( 10, 20 );
        DrawString( "\pKey pressed" );
        break;

    case mouseDown:
        AllDone = 1;
        break;
}
```

...then only this code runs.

What happens if instead of pressing a key, the user clicks the mouse button? The event type is then *mouseDown*. In my example I do only one thing when a *mouseDown* event occurs — I set variable *AllDone* to a value of 1. Now, what happens when the program returns to the top of the loop statement and makes its test? *AllDone* has a value of 1 — which is not less than 1 — and the test fails. The entire *while* loop is skipped and the program ends.

An Eventful Program

There's no better way to really understand some code than to see it placed in a complete program. In this section I'll describe a Mac program that uses an event loop like the one I've discussed in this chapter.

The Source Code Listing

Since I'm creating a new program, I need to think of a new program name. The purpose of the program is to demonstrate that the Mac knows about events — so EventTest is what I've dubbed it. I'll show you the complete source code listing for the program now. In the sections that follow I'll break it down and describe it.

```
main()
{
    WindowPtr     TheWindow;      /* A window to write to        */
    EventRecord   TheEvent;       /* Hold info about one event   */
    short         AllDone;        /* Tell the program when to end */
    Rect          WhiteRect;      /* A rectangle to cover text   */
    long          count;          /* A loop counter              */

    InitGraf( &thePort );
    InitFonts();
    InitWindows();
    InitMenus();
    TEInit();
    InitDialogs( 0L );
    FlushEvents( everyEvent, 0 );
    InitCursor();

    TheWindow = GetNewWindow( 128, 0L, (WindowPtr)-1L );
    SetPort( TheWindow );
    AllDone = 0;
    while ( AllDone < 1 )
    {
        WaitNextEvent( everyEvent, &TheEvent, 0L, 0L );
        switch ( TheEvent.what )
        {
            case keyDown:
                MoveTo( 10, 20 );
                DrawString( "\pKey pressed" );
                count = 0;
                while ( count < 100000 )
```

```
        count++;
        SetRect( &WhiteRect, 10, 10, 100, 25 );
        FillRect( &WhiteRect, &white );
        break;

    case mouseDown:
        AllDone = 1;
        break;
        }
      }
   }
```

A Friendly Reminder

My EventTest program is here as an example of how an event loop fits into a Mac program. You don't have to type in the code and run it to understand what's happening. But if you have the THINK C compiler I realize you might want to do that so you can test it out. If you don't remember all the steps of writing a program you have a couple of options.

The first option is to wait until you've read Chapter 18. There I fully describe a complete Macintosh program from start to finish. That includes creating the resource file, project file, and source code file. The second option is to go back and review a few chapters. This program uses one window, so it needs a resource file with a single 'WIND' resource. If you don't remember the exact steps to creating a resource file you can refer back to Chapter 6. Chapter 7 discusses the 'WIND' resource in detail. A THINK C program starts as a project. Creating a project is covered in Chapter 8.

The Basic Stuff

About the first half or so of my EventTest program consists of the basic stuff that you've become quite accustomed to seeing. Like all programs, this one starts with the declaration of variables. Here I've commented all of the variables. I'll describe each variable as I get to the code that uses it.

```
WindowPtr     TheWindow;    /* A window to write to        */
EventRecord   TheEvent;     /* Hold info about one event   */
short         AllDone;      /* Tell the program when to end */
Rect          WhiteRect;    /* A rectangle to cover text    */
long          count;        /* A loop counter               */
```

After the variable declarations come the Toolbox initializations. These eight lines were lifted directly from another program I wrote. Remember, they never change:

```
InitGraf( &thePort );
InitFonts();
InitWindows();
InitMenus();
TEInit();
InitDialogs( 0L );
FlushEvents( everyEvent, 0 );
InitCursor();
```

The last bit of code that I call "basic stuff" is the opening of a window. Calling *GetNewWindow* provides my program with a *WindowPtr* that can be used in other Toolbox calls, like *SetPort*. You've seen these two lines throughout the book:

```
TheWindow = GetNewWindow( 128, 0L, (WindowPtr)-1L );
SetPort( TheWindow );
```

The Event Loop

The event loop of EventTest should be a welcome sight to you. It is the very same event loop I showed you earlier in this chapter — with just five extra lines added to it. Here it is:

```
AllDone = 0;
while ( AllDone < 1 )
{
   WaitNextEvent( everyEvent, &TheEvent, 0L, 0L );
   switch ( TheEvent.what )
   {
      case keyDown:
         MoveTo( 10, 20 );
         DrawString( "\pKey pressed" );
         count = 0;
         while ( count < 100000 )
            count++;
         SetRect( &WhiteRect, 10, 10, 100, 25 );
         FillRect( &WhiteRect, &white );
         break;

      case mouseDown:
         AllDone = 1;
         break;
   }
}
```

The new lines all appear under the *keyDown case* of the *switch* statement. Here's how the old *keyDown* section looked:

```
case keyDown:
   MoveTo( 10, 20 );
   DrawString( "\pKey pressed" );
   break;
```

In the old *keyDown* code, a press of a key caused the program to write to the window — like this:

```
╔═══════════════════════════════════════╗
║ ▣ ▦▦▦▦▦▦ New Window ▦▦▦▦▦▦▦ ║
╠═══════════════════════════════════════╣
║                                       ║
║  Key pressed                          ║
║                                       ║
║                                       ║
║                                       ║
║                                       ║
║                                       ║
╚═══════════════════════════════════════╝
```

That's fine. But what happens if the user again presses a key? The same code will run, and the same words will be written to the window — in the exact same spot. After the first press of a key the window goes from one that is blank to one that has words written in it. But after that, the user has no way of knowing that words are being written. The solution? Erase the words soon after displaying them. A key press will then result in the words "Key pressed" flashing on and off. Let's see how EventTest does that.

After writing the words "Key pressed" to the window, the variable *count* is assigned a value of 0. Then the program goes into a very simple loop:

```
case keyDown:
    MoveTo( 10, 20 );
    DrawString( "\pKey pressed" );
    count = 0;
    while ( count < 100000 )
        count++;
```

The loop doesn't appear to be doing much except counting. Variable *count* starts with a value of 0, and increases by a value of 1 each time through the loop. That "++" symbol is the increment operator. You should recall from Chapter 13 that when it appears next to a variable name the variable is incremented by one. So, what good is a loop that does nothing but count from 1 to 100,000? Not much, unless you want to kill some time. That's exactly what the loop is doing. While the Mac is busy counting up to 100,000, it doesn't do anything else. That means the loop is delaying the rest of the program from running. So what's really important is what *follows* the loop — what code is getting delayed?

The loop has the extra benefit of showing just how fast a Mac runs. The loop runs 100,000 times and takes a little less than one second to run on an old Mac Plus. It takes only about a quarter of a second to run on a much newer Mac II model. In either case, that's a pretty fast way to count to 100,000! ■

The two lines of code that follow the loop are calls to the Toolbox functions *SetRect* and *FillRect*. Chapter 15 showed you that *SetRect* establishes the coordinates of a rectangle — but doesn't draw it. The coordinates I selected are ones that will create a rectangle that surrounds the words "Key pressed." But I don't want to place a frame around these words — as the Toolbox function *FrameRect* would. Rather, I want to fill this rectangle with the same color of the window. The window is white with black text. If I draw a white rectangle over the black text I will effectively obscure the text — it will be erased. I use *FillRect* to do this.

The *FillRect* function draws a solid rectangle — with no frame. You give *FillRect* two parameters — the *Rect* variable that should be filled and the shade to fill it with. Here's the code that sets up a rectangle, then fills it with *white*:

```
SetRect( &WhiteRect, 10, 10, 100, 25 );
FillRect( &WhiteRect, &white );
```

The use of one Toolbox routine differs depending on whether you have version 6.0 or 7.0 of THINK C. That routine is *FillRect*. In the above example you see it used like so:

```
FillRect( &WhiteRect, &white );
```

Notice the "&" character before *white*. That's the way you use it if you have THINK C 7.0. If you have version 6.0, use *FillRect* like this:

```
FillRect( &WhiteRect, white );
```

With version 6.0, you *don't* include the "&" character before *white*. All my *FillRect* examples are written for THINK C 7.0 users. If you have THINK C 6.0, omit the "&" symbol before *white*. Yes, it is a very subtle and annoying difference. So much so that I'll make reference to it several more times in this book.

How do you know if you have version 6.0 or 7.0 of the THINK C compiler? You can find out by selecting About THINK Project Manager from the Apple menu of THINK C. Or, look at the user manual that came with the program. ■

Let's sum up what happens when a key is pressed, using, of course, a figure:

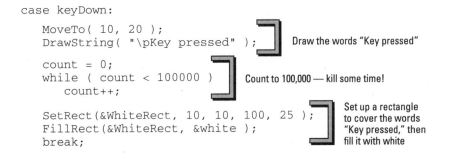

```
case keyDown:
    MoveTo( 10, 20 );
    DrawString( "\pKey pressed" );        Draw the words "Key pressed"

    count = 0;
    while ( count < 100000 )              Count to 100,000 — kill some time!
        count++;

    SetRect(&WhiteRect, 10, 10, 100, 25 );    Set up a rectangle
    FillRect(&WhiteRect, &white );             to cover the words
    break;                                     "Key pressed," then
                                               fill it with white
```

Events and the event loop are two of the most important and powerful concepts in Macintosh programming — that's why this chapter is one of the longest in the book. The event loop gives a Mac program the ability to react differently in different circumstances. One of those circumstances is a mouse click in the menu bar. None of the examples to this point have included a menu. Now that you've gained knowledge about the event loop, it's time to change that.

Chapter 17

Menus That Drop
and Windows That Move

- -

- -

Sometimes a chapter in a book ends with a review. Just to be different, I'll start a chapter with one. Here's a review of what your Mac programs can do — so far:

✔ Initialize the Toolbox.

✔ Open a window.

✔ Draw text and graphics in a window.

✔ Respond to user actions, such as mouse clicks.

These are some very important topics in Macintosh programming. But there are a couple of things that are missing — things that prevent your programs from having that true "look and feel" of a Mac program.

The first missing feature deals with windows. Yes, you can open a window. But it sits lifeless on the screen as if it were frozen. The user can't move it or close it. In fact, if the user tries to do anything with the window by clicking the mouse on it, the program ends. The second missing feature is a biggie — menus. To avoid the scorn and ridicule of other Mac programmers, your programs need menus. I'll take care of both of these issues in this chapter.

Bringing a Window to Life

A true Mac program doesn't just display a window, it lets the user work with the window. A user expects to be able to drag, or move, a window. And when done with it, the user will want to be able to close that same window. Those are the two topics I'll cover here.

The Parts of a Window

In Chapter 16 you saw that there is a name for each of the different event types, such as *mouseDown* and *keyDown*. Knowing that, it might not come as a surprise to you to learn that the different parts of the screen, and windows on the screen, also have names.

When the user clicks the mouse button, a *mouseDown* event gets reported to your program. What should your program do next? In past programs I've simply used a mouse click as a signal to quit the program. A better response would be to determine where the mouse click took place, and then act accordingly. If the mouse click took place in the menu bar, my program should drop a menu. If it took place in the close box of a window, my program should close that window. And if the mouse click took place in the title bar of a window, my program should start dragging the window.

The Mac screen and any window on it has several different parts. I've listed the three most common part names below.

- *inMenuBar* is anywhere in the menu bar.
- *inGoAway* is the go–away, or close box, of a window.
- *inDrag* is the drag bar, or title bar, of a window.

Notice that the part names begin with "in." That gives you a hint as to how these part names will be used by your program. If the mouse is clicked "in" the menu bar, drop a menu. If the mouse is clicked "in" a window's close box, close the window. Here's a figure that emphasizes where the three main parts are located:

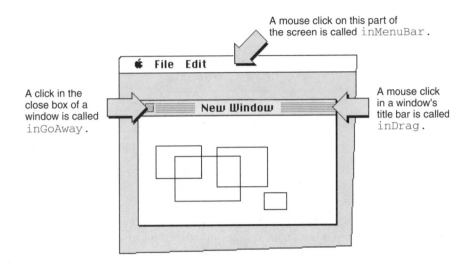

A mouse click on this part of
the screen is called `inMenuBar`.

A click in the
close box of a
window is called
`inGoAway`.

A mouse click
in a window's
title bar is called
`inDrag`.

Which Part of Which Window?

Knowing where a mouse click took place is very useful information that your
program can and will take advantage of. But for some mouse clicks, still more
information is needed. When the user clicks the mouse anywhere in a window,
your program will want to know not only where the click took place, but also in
which window it occurred.

Let's look at the case of a program that has two windows open. That came
about like this:

```
WindowPtr   TheWindow1;
WindowPtr   TheWindow2;
TheWindow1 = GetNewWindow( 128, 0L, (WindowPtr)-1L );
TheWindow2 = GetNewWindow( 129, 0L, (WindowPtr)-1L );
```

To drag one of the windows a user will click the mouse on the window's drag
bar. In the figure below you can see that the cursor is over the drag bar of
TheWindow2.

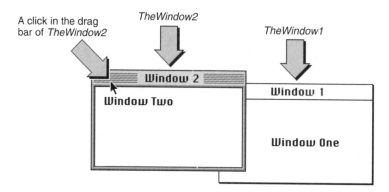

A click in the drag bar of *TheWindow2* tells the program that an *inDrag* part has been clicked on. Your program will then want to start dragging the window as the user moves the mouse. But one important bit of information is missing — which window should be dragged? You know it's the window that *TheWindow2* is pointing to because you've looked at the above figure. But the program isn't reading this book, so it doesn't know. But it can find out.

What's needed is a means to determine both the part that is clicked on, and, if a window is involved, the window in which the click took place. Naturally, the Toolbox offers the answer.

FindWindow is a Toolbox function that gives your program the mouse click information it needs. *FindWindow* isn't psychic though — you've got to help the function out by supplying the location of the mouse click. Thankfully there's no effort needed on your part to come up with this location. In Chapter 16 you learned about the *EventRecord* data type and how a call to *WaitNextEvent* fills a variable of this type with information about an event. One bit of information is the type of event that occurred. Another piece of information filled in for you is where the cursor was when the event occurred. That "where" information is of value to you now. Below is what a typical call to *FindWindow* looks like. For clarity I'll also show the declarations of the variables that I'm using.

```
EventRecord   TheEvent;
WindowPtr     aWindow;
short         ThePart;

ThePart = FindWindow( TheEvent.where, &aWindow );
```

After the call to *FindWindow* is complete, the *short* variable *ThePart* will hold the name of the part that was clicked in. That is, *ThePart* will have a value such as *inDrag* or *inMenuBar*. The last parameter to *FindWindow* will also take on a value it didn't have before the function call. Before calling *FindWindow* you declare a new *WindowPtr* variable — but you don't open a window. Instead, you use this valueless variable as the second parameter to *FindWindow*. If *FindWindow* determines that the mouse click occurred in a window, it will give this variable a value. The value will be a pointer to the clicked-in window — a *WindowPtr*. Here's a breakdown of the call to *FindWindow*:

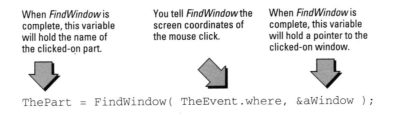

When *FindWindow* is complete, this variable will hold the name of the clicked-on part.

You tell *FindWindow* the screen coordinates of the mouse click.

When *FindWindow* is complete, this variable will hold a pointer to the clicked-on window.

```
ThePart = FindWindow( TheEvent.where, &aWindow );
```

How is it that a variable that is declared to be of type *short* — which is a number — can end up having a value that is a name? That seems to be the case when *ThePart* is declared to be a *short*, and then given a value such as *inDrag* by the *FindWindow* function. The answer lies in the way the Mac keeps track of some names, like *inDrag*, *inGoAway*, and *inMenuBar*. While you see these names as words, the Mac associates a number with each. So when *ThePart* gets a value of *inDrag*, the Mac is secretly doing something like this:

```
ThePart = 4;    /* The Mac views inDrag as the number 4 */
```

Tricky, no? The thing to remember is that the Mac does all this converting of names to numbers behind closed doors — you don't see it and you don't have to worry about it. ▪

After a call to *FindWindow* is complete your program will know:

✔ Which part of the screen, or window, was clicked on.

✔ If a window was clicked on.

✔ Which window, if any, was clicked on.

Variable *ThePart* holds the first two pieces of information. If *ThePart* has a value that pertains to a window — like *inDrag* — then your program knows that a window was clicked on and where in that window the click took place. The third piece of information is held in variable *aWindow*. If the mouse click was in a window, *FindWindow* will give this variable a value — a pointer that tells the Mac which window received the mouse click.

That does it for the theory behind the determination of where a mouse click took place. Now, on to the use of the theory.

Working with Windows Can Be a Drag

Before jumping right into the code used for dragging a window, let's figure out where it should go. Just about everything happens in the event loop, so here's a look at one to refresh your memory:

```
while ( AllDone < 1 )
{
    WaitNextEvent( everyEvent, &TheEvent, 0L, 0L );
    switch ( TheEvent.what )
    {
        case keyDown:
            /* do something */
            break;
        case mouseDown:
            /* do something */
            break;
    }
}
```

Instead of actually doing anything when a key or the mouse button is pressed, I've just stuck a comment in the code. That doesn't make the code very useful, but it makes it nice and short — and easy to look at.

A window gets dragged when the user clicks the mouse button on the drag bar of the window. That tells you the code is going to go under the *case* label *mouseDown*. I'll insert the code now. Take a look at it, then move on to the explanation.

```
while ( AllDone < 1 )
{
    WaitNextEvent( everyEvent, &TheEvent, 0L, 0L );
    switch ( TheEvent.what )
    {
        case keyDown:
            /* do something */
            break;
        case mouseDown:
            ThePart = FindWindow( TheEvent.where, &aWindow );
            switch ( ThePart )
            {
                case inDrag:
                    DragWindow( aWindow, TheEvent.where,
                                &screenBits.bounds );
                    break;
            }
            break;
    }
}
```

The first line of new code is the call to *FindWindow*. Just a few pages back you learned that this Toolbox function will return the part of the screen or window that was clicked on, along with a pointer to the window that was clicked on — if any. The only other code I added was a *switch* statement. The *switch* examines the value of *ThePart*. It will have a value such as *inDrag*, *inGoAway*, or *inMenuBar*. At this time I'm only demonstrating how to respond to a click in the drag region, so that's the only *case* label I've put in the *switch*. A mouse click anywhere else will simply be ignored by the program.

The following figure shows what goes on in the event loop when there's a mouse click on the drag bar of a window. I don't like working in cramped quarters, so I've taken the liberty of inserting a few blank lines — that gives me room to add those fat arrows I like to draw:

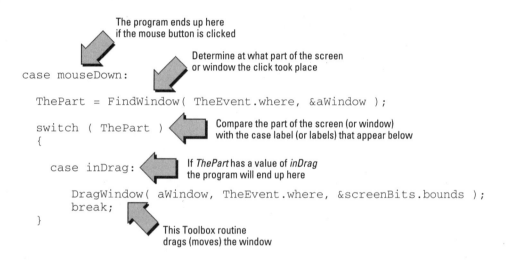

The program ends up here if the mouse button is clicked

Determine at what part of the screen or window the click took place

```
case mouseDown:

    ThePart = FindWindow( TheEvent.where, &aWindow );

    switch ( ThePart )
    {

        case inDrag:

            DragWindow( aWindow, TheEvent.where, &screenBits.bounds );
            break;
    }
```

Compare the part of the screen (or window) with the case label (or labels) that appear below

If *ThePart* has a value of *inDrag* the program will end up here

This Toolbox routine drags (moves) the window

When it comes right down to it, only one line of code actually drags a window. The line is the one with the call to the Toolbox function *DragWindow* in it. When a user moves a window about the screen it is *DragWindow* that's doing all the work.

DragWindow needs three parameters in order to work. The first, the one I called *aWindow*, is the window that is to be dragged. Remember, *aWindow* isn't a window that you opened using *GetNewWindow*. It's a *WindowPtr* variable that you declared with the express purpose of using it in the call to *FindWindow*. When the user clicks on a window — whether there are one, two, or ten windows on the screen, the *FindWindow* function will figure out which one received the mouse click and put a pointer to it in the *aWindow* variable. Now is the time, when a window is being dragged, to use this *WindowPtr* variable.

The second parameter of *DragWindow* is the screen coordinates of the mouse click. That helps *DragWindow* get started as it moves the window. The last parameter is a strange-looking one called *&screenBits.bounds*. The purpose of this parameter is to tell *DragWindow* just how far a window can be dragged. When you set this parameter to *&screenBits.bounds* you're telling the Toolbox that it can feel free to move the window anywhere on the screen — the entire area of the screen is available.

When you call a Toolbox function it typically runs in a blink of the eye. For example, when a program calls *FrameRect* to draw a rectangle the rectangle is drawn almost immediately. *DragWindow* is an interesting function in that it stays running for as long as the user holds the mouse down on a window's drag bar. When the user starts moving a window about the screen, it's the *DragWindow* function that's doing the work. If you were to drag a window around the screen for 10 seconds, that's how long the *DragWindow* function would take to run. ■

Closing a Window

Once you know the procedure for dragging a window, closing one is a breeze. A window gets closed when the user clicks the mouse on the window's close box — or go-away box to some. That means your program must first determine if a *mouseDown* event occurred. That you know how to do. Next, a call to *FindWindow* is in order to see if the mouse click happened *inGoAway* — in the go-away box of the window. That you know how to do. Next, a *case* label is needed inside a *switch* statement. That you know how to do. Lastly, code has to be added to actually close the window. That you *don't* know how to do. But after looking at this one line, you will:

```
DisposeWindow( aWindow );
```

That'll do it. The Toolbox function *DisposeWindow* closes a window. All you have to do is tell *DisposeWindow* which window to close. And that information you already have from the call to *FindWindow*. I've added an *case* label *inGoAway* to the very code I used when I demonstrated how to drag a window. I've put the new code in bold type:

```
while ( AllDone < 1 )
{
   WaitNextEvent( everyEvent, &TheEvent, 0L, 0L );
   switch ( TheEvent.what )
   {
      case mouseDown:
         ThePart = FindWindow( TheEvent.where, &aWindow );
         switch ( ThePart )
         {
            case inDrag:
               DragWindow( aWindow, TheEvent.where,
                           &screenBits.bounds );
               break;
            case inGoAway:
               DisposeWindow( aWindow );
               break;
```

```
        }
        break;
    }
}
```

Example Program: A Window That Works

I'm sure you now have a pretty good idea of how to drag and close a window. Just to reinforce the concepts, here's a complete program listing that does everything you've seen in this chapter.

This program, which I'll call WindowWorks, has only one point that might need explaining. In order to write a program that doesn't run forever, you must always add a line of code somewhere that breaks the program out of the event loop. In my programs that line always looks like this:

```
AllDone = 1;
```

Where you put that line depends on the program you're writing. It makes most sense to use it when the user selects Quit from a menu — but of course my program doesn't have a menu. So I've elected to place this line right after the call to *DisposeWindow*. That means when the user clicks on the window's close box, the window will close and the program will end.

```
main()
{
    WindowPtr    TheWindow;
    EventRecord  TheEvent;
    short        AllDone;
    WindowPtr    aWindow;
    short        ThePart;

    InitGraf( &thePort );
    InitFonts();
    InitWindows();
    InitMenus();
    TEInit();
    InitDialogs( 0L );
    FlushEvents( everyEvent, 0 );
    InitCursor();

    TheWindow = GetNewWindow( 128, 0L, (WindowPtr)-1L );
    SetPort( TheWindow );
    AllDone = 0;
    while ( AllDone < 1 )
    {
        WaitNextEvent( everyEvent, &TheEvent, 0L, 0L );
        switch ( TheEvent.what )
        {
            case mouseDown:
                ThePart = FindWindow( TheEvent.where, &aWindow );
```

continued

```
                              switch ( ThePart )
                              {
                                 case inDrag:
                                    DragWindow( aWindow, TheEvent.where,
                                                 &screenBits.bounds );
                                    break;
                                 case inGoAway:
                                    DisposeWindow( aWindow );
                                    AllDone = 1;
                                    break;
                              }
                              break;
                  }
              }
          }
```

Drop That Menu!

A person can write a lot of source code to show off a lot of Macintosh programming concepts — without ever having to include the code for a menu. That's what I've been doing for seventeen chapters. Now, it's finally time to create a program that's much closer to being a "real" Mac application — one with a menu and menu bar.

The Menu Resources

The short program that I'll show you at the end of this chapter is called MenuDrop. Before looking at menu code, I'll give you a quick peek at the resources that the program will use.

The first thing you might notice about the resource file shown below is that there is no 'WIND' resource. My MenuDrop program doesn't use one — it only displays a single menu in the menu bar.

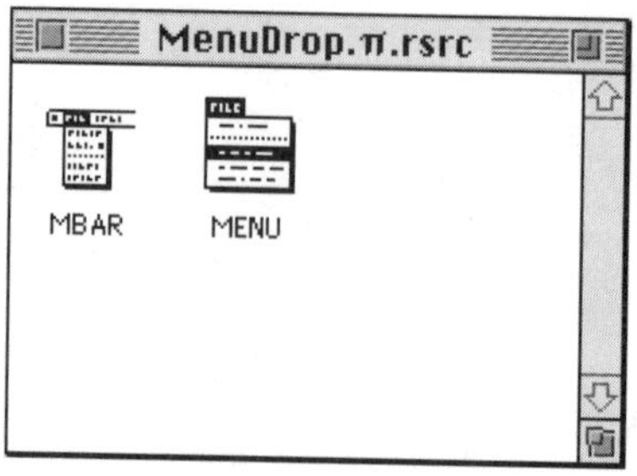

Clicking once on the MENU icon shows the 'MENU' resources in this resource file. There is only one:

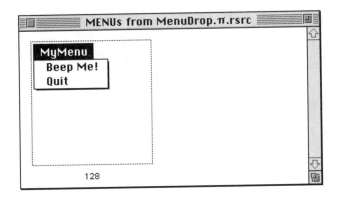

Double-clicking on the menu in the previous figure opens the '*MENU*' editor. Here's what the one '*MENU*' in MenuDrop looks like:

Whether your program will have one menu or ten, it should have a '*MBAR*' resource that lists each one. Here's the '*MBAR*' for MenuDrop:

Displaying the Menu Bar

To get a Mac program to display a window you use two steps:

1. Create a resource ('*WIND*') in a resource file.
2. Use a Toolbox function (*GetNewWindow*) to use the information in the resource and display the window.

Getting a Mac program to display a menu bar with menus requires two similar steps:

1. Create resources ('*MENU*' and '*MBAR*') in a resource file.
2. Use a Toolbox function (*GetNewMBar*) to use the information in the resources and display the menu bar.

Here's a call to *GetNewMBar* — the Toolbox function that takes information from an '*MBAR*' resource and uses it to display a menu:

```
Handle  MenuBarHandle;

MenuBarHandle = GetNewMBar( 128 );
```

The first point worthy of note is the variable declaration. Variable *MenuBarHandle* is a *Handle* type — that's new to you. You might recall from Chapter 14 that a lot of things get stored in the memory of a computer. When that happens your program needs a way of keeping track of *where* in memory something is stored. The data type *Handle* does just that. Thankfully, *how* it keeps track of memory isn't important to you. The bottom line is that a menu bar is the type of thing that the Mac keeps track of using a *Handle*.

GetNewMBar accepts a single parameter — the resource ID of the '*MBAR*' that holds information about the menus that are to appear in the menu bar. If you make one '*MBAR*' resource — as is usually the case — ResEdit automatically assigns it an ID of 128. That's why I've used 128 as the parameter to *GetNewMBar* in my example.

After a call to *GetNewMBar* is complete, the variable *MenuBarHandle* will have a value. That value is used in a second Toolbox call — *SetMenuBar*. Here it is:

```
SetMenuBar( MenuBarHandle );
```

When *GetNewMBar* is called it does a lot of fancy things to get all the information from both the '*MENU*' resources and the '*MBAR*' resource located in your program's resource file. Though it holds on to all this information, it doesn't really *do* much with it. The call to *SetMenuBar* is the thing that establishes that yes, this information should and will be used for the menu bar for this program.

After *GetNewMBar* and *SetMenuBar* you'd think that the menu bar would be there on your screen. Not quite. True, everything is safely stored in memory and ready, but the Toolbox still wants you to make a call to *DrawMenuBar* in order to display the menu bar at the top of the Mac's screen. Here's the call to *DrawMenuBar*, along with the other two Toolbox calls necessary for displaying a menu bar:

```
Handle   MenuBarHandle;

MenuBarHandle = GetNewMBar( 128 );
SetMenuBar( MenuBarHandle );
DrawMenuBar();
```

If I use the above code along with the '*MENU*' and '*MBAR*' resources I created several pages back, I'd have a menu bar that looks like this:

```
 MyMenu
```

You know that my '*MBAR*' holds the ID of one '*MENU*' resource. That '*MENU*' is for a menu that has two items — one called Beep Me! and the other called Quit. So you might be wondering why I didn't show MyMenu dropped down to display these two items. I could have included that in my figure, of course. Heck, I can draw a menu bar and menu in my graphics program any way I want! But I wanted to try to be realistic here. The code that I've shown in this section only *displays* a menu bar and the names of the menus in that bar. It doesn't do anything to make the menu bar *functional*. That is, if you included the code I just showed you in a program, you'd see a menu bar but you wouldn't be able to use it. For that, you need to add code to make the menu usable.

Pulling Down a Menu

In previous pages you learned about the parts of the screen and the parts of the windows on the screen — such as *inDrag*, *inGoAway*, and *inMenuBar*. You also learned that through the use of the Toolbox function *FindWindow* you can find out in which of these parts a mouse click occurs. You also learned that because the moving and closing of a window both involve a click of the mouse, the code that is used to carry out these actions gets added to the event loop — under the *case* label *mouseDown*. All this knowledge will serve to help you in your understanding of how menus work.

The only time your program will pull down a menu is when the user clicks the mouse in the menu bar. So it's important that your program be aware of when this happens. To be sure that it is, you'll make use of the same call to *FindWindow* you used when working with a window. The code below should look familiar — it's from this chapter. I've added a *case* label for *inMenuBar* — but I didn't add any menu-handling code just yet.

```
while ( AllDone < 1 )
{
    WaitNextEvent( everyEvent, &TheEvent, 0L, 0L );
    switch ( TheEvent.what )
    {
        case mouseDown:
            ThePart = FindWindow( TheEvent.where, &aWindow );
            switch ( ThePart )
            {
                case inDrag:
                    DragWindow( aWindow, TheEvent.where,
                                &screenBits.bounds );
                    break;
                case inMenuBar:
                    /* handle a click in the menu */
                    break;
            }
            break;
    }
}
```

If there's a click in the menu bar, *FindWindow* will assign variable *ThePart* a value of *inMenuBar*. Since no window is involved in a menu bar click, variable *aWindow* will be left without a value.

What happens when a mouse click turns out to be in the menu bar? The code under *inMenuBar* runs. I've shown most of that code here:

```
case inMenuBar:
    MenuChoice = MenuSelect( TheEvent.where );
    if ( MenuChoice > 0 )
    {
        TheMenu = HiWord( MenuChoice );
        TheMenuItem = LoWord( MenuChoice );
        switch ( TheMenu )
        {
            /* handle each menu item here */
        }
        HiliteMenu(0);
    }
    break;
```

You'll notice in the above code that rather than handle the selection of each menu item, I've simply inserted a comment. How's that for getting off easy? Actually, I have my reasons for omitting some code. First, I want to keep the code minimal so it's easier to look at and easier to explain. Second, each program handles menu items differently. That is, code for a menu item is dependent on what that menu item is supposed to do. I'll show you the code for my two menu items, Beep Me! and Quit, a little later in this chapter.

On to the explanation. After a click in the menu bar is detected, you'll call the Toolbox function *MenuSelect*. This is one of those Toolbox functions Mac programmers go ga-ga over. Why? 'Cause it's one of those functions that does a lot, and thus saves you a lot of work. Once called, here's what *MenuSelect* does:

✔ Follows the mouse as it moves about in the menu bar.

✔ Shows and hides menus as the mouse moves over them.

✔ Flashes a selected menu item a few times.

✔ When an item is selected, highlights the name of the menu in the menu bar.

✔ Tells your program which menu item was selected — and from which menu.

Wow! Hopefully the Toolbox pays *MenuSelect* at least time and a half! The only things *MenuSelect* needs in order to do all this work are the screen coordinates at which the mouse button was clicked. Just pass *TheEvent.where* as the parameter and *MenuSelect* does the rest.

After dragging the mouse here and there across the menu bar, the user will eventually settle on a menu item and select it. At that time *MenuSelect* will consider its work done. As the Toolbox function ends, it returns a number to your program. This number is a code that represents both the selected menu item and the menu from which the item was selected. Save the number as a *long* variable — I've named mine *MenuChoice*. Here's the call to *MenuSelect*, along with a reminder of how to declare a *long* variable:

```
long  MenuChoice;

MenuChoice = MenuSelect( TheEvent.where );
```

Remember, a *long* is a whole number that can have a value larger than 32,767. And as a further reminder, a *short* and an *integer* are the other two C data types that hold whole numbers. ■

Making the Menu Usable

If I stopped writing code right now, my program would appear to behave much as any Mac program should. If the user clicked on the one menu in my program's menu bar, the menu would drop down. The user could select either item and the menu item would flash a few times and the menu would disappear back into the menu bar. All thanks to a call to *MenuSelect*. What would happen next? Nothing. That's because I haven't written any code to handle the menu item selection.

Any of a thousand different things can happen when a user of a program makes a menu selection — but you decide what, not the Mac. That implies that your program has to become aware of which menu item was selected so that it can respond accordingly. Your program does have that information — kind of. It was returned to variable *MenuChoice* by *MenuSelect*. But the two values — the menu and the menu item — are both bundled into this one number. To break the code and separate them you'll use two Toolbox functions — *HiWord* and

LoWord. Here's how these two functions are used:

```
short   TheMenu;
short   TheMenuItem;

TheMenu = HiWord( MenuChoice );
TheMenuItem = LoWord( MenuChoice );
```

You pass both *HiWord* and *LoWord* the variable that holds the combined menu/menu item value — *MenuChoice*. As each function ends, it returns a new number to your program. *HiWord* returns a number that represents the menu selected, *LoWord* returns a number that represents the menu item selected. Let's use the '*MENU*' resource I developed earlier as an example of what these numbers mean. Here's that resource:

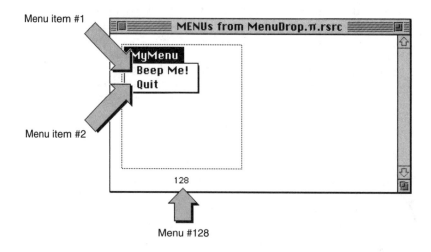

The Mac views a menu by the resource ID of its '*MENU*' resource. It gives each item in a menu a number associated with its order in the menu. The first menu item is 1, the second is 2, and so forth. If a user selected Quit from my example menu, here's what would happen:

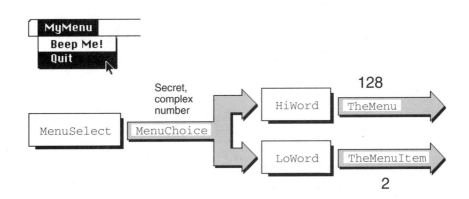

The above figure shows that *MenuSelect* will spit out *MenuChoice* — a number in a form far too complicated for mere mortals to understand. *MenuChoice* is then passed to both *HiWord* and *LoWord*. *HiWord* returns the resource ID of the selected menu — 128 for my example. *LoWord* returns the number of the selected menu item — the second item, or number 2 for my example.

I didn't get the Official Menu Spy Decoder Ring with my Mac, so I'm not exactly sure how *HiWord* and *LoWord* manage to extract both the menu and the menu item from this one number. But from my experience with programming the Mac, they always seem to get it right.

Let's take another look at the *case inMenuBar*, then cover the sections of it that haven't yet been discussed:

```
case inMenuBar:
   MenuChoice = MenuSelect( TheEvent.where );
   if ( MenuChoice > 0 )
   {
      TheMenu = HiWord( MenuChoice );
      TheMenuItem = LoWord( MenuChoice );
      switch ( TheMenu )
      {
         /* handle each menu item here */
      }
      HiliteMenu(0);
   }
   break;
```

Did you ever start to make a menu selection in a program, then change your mind? When a user does that, *MenuSelect* returns a value of 0 to the program — it sets *MenuChoice* to 0. That tells the program that, yes, menus were dropped and looked at but no selection was made. In a case such as this a program won't want to go through the work of deciphering *MenuChoice* with *HiWord* and *LoWord* — there's no menu or menu item numbers embedded in this variable. In fact, since the user decided not to do anything, the program won't want to do anything either. That's the reason for the *if* statement after *MenuSelect*.

If no menu choice is made, *MenuChoice* is 0 and that *if* statement test fails — *MenuChoice* is not greater than 0. That means all the code that handles a menu selection is skipped:

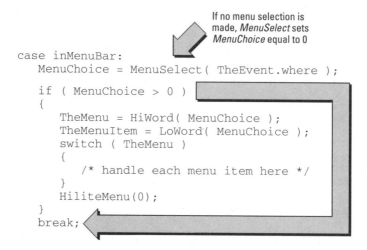

If no menu selection is made, *MenuSelect* sets *MenuChoice* equal to 0

```
case inMenuBar:
   MenuChoice = MenuSelect( TheEvent.where );

   if ( MenuChoice > 0 )
   {
      TheMenu = HiWord( MenuChoice );
      TheMenuItem = LoWord( MenuChoice );
      switch ( TheMenu )
      {
         /* handle each menu item here */
      }
      HiliteMenu(0);
   }
   break;
```

The above figure shows what happens when the user clicks in the menu bar but *doesn't* end up making a menu selection. What happens if the user *does* make a choice? The program enters the *if* loop. *HiWord* and *LoWord* are called to determine the menu and menu item selected. Then a *switch* statement is entered. The code inside the *switch* — which I haven't yet shown — handles whatever tasks are expected of each menu item. Bear with me — I'll cover all that soon enough.

After the *switch* handles the menu selection *HiliteMenu* is called. When a menu selection is made, *MenuSelect* highlights the name of the menu in the menu bar. The name stays highlighted even after the user releases the mouse button:

| MyMenu |

Only after the code that handles a menu selection is complete will the menu name return to its normal condition. *HiliteMenu* is the Toolbox function that does this. Always pass *HiliteMenu* a value of 0 as its one parameter.

Handling a Menu Selection

In the previous section I showed how a menu is made to drop down and how a program can get the number of both the menu item selected and the number of the menu that holds that item. But I stopped short of showing you the details of handling the menu selection. Now I'll fill in the missing code that should be under the *switch* statement. I've put the *switch* in bold type so you can see just where I'm about to add code:

```
case inMenuBar:
   MenuChoice = MenuSelect( TheEvent.where );
   if ( MenuChoice > 0 )
   {
      TheMenu = HiWord( MenuChoice );
      TheMenuItem = LoWord( MenuChoice );
      switch ( TheMenu )
      {
         /* handle each menu item here */
      }
      HiliteMenu(0);
   }
   break;
```

If I had a program with two menus — one with a '*MENU*' resource ID of 128 and one with a '*MENU*' resource ID of 129 — I'd add a *case* label under the *switch* statement for each of them. Under each *case* label I would add more code that handled the tasks necessary for any item selection from that menu. Let's say the '*MENU*' resources for a program I'm writing look like this:

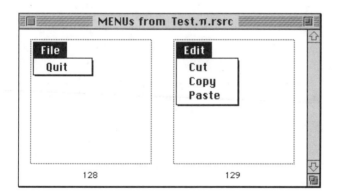

Then my code would look something like this:

```
switch ( TheMenu )
{
   case 128:
      /* handle item 1, Quit,  from menu 128 */
   case 129:
      /* handle item 1, Cut,   from menu 129 */
      /* handle item 2, Copy,  from menu 129 */
      /* handle item 3, Paste, from menu 129 */
}
```

Fortunately — and not by any accident, I might add — the example program I've been working on in this chapter is even easier! Here's the '*MENU*' resource for it:

```
 ≡☐≡≡≡≡≡≡  MENUs from MenuDrop.π.rsrc  ≡≡≡≡≡☐≡

   ┌─────────────────────────────────┐
   │ MyMenu                          │
   │ ┌─────────────┐                 │
   │ │ Beep Me!    │                 │
   │ │ Quit        │                 │
   │ └─────────────┘                 │
   │                                 │
   │                                 │
   │                                 │
   │              128                │
   └─────────────────────────────────┘
```

So the *switch* statement for it — in general terms — will look like this:

```
switch ( TheMenu )
{
   case 128:
      /* handle item 1, Beep Me!, from menu 128 */
      /* handle item 2, Quit,    from menu 128 */
}
```

Now let's get rid of the comments and add the real code. Whenever decisions need to be made — such as which one of several menu items are to be handled — expect to see a *switch* statement. So here once again a *switch* is used.

```
switch ( TheMenu )
{
   case 128:
      switch ( TheMenuItem )
      {
         case 1:
            SysBeep( 1 );
            break;
         case 2:
            AllDone = 1;
            break;
      }
      break;
}
```

The first *switch* uses *TheMenu* to narrow down which menu was selected. In this example there is only one — menu 128. The second *switch* uses *TheMenuItem* to narrow down which menu item was selected. My example has two items — item 1 and item 2. Let's look at how each item is handled.

When the user selects the first item, Beep Me!, the code under the first *case* label runs:

```
case 1:
    SysBeep( 1 );
    break;
```

All this menu item does is sound the Mac's built-in speaker. Usually that means that the speaker will emit a single beep — but other things could happen. If the user has used the Sound control panel to change the system alert sound to something other than a beep, that sound will play once. Or, if the user has the speaker volume set to 0, the menu bar will flash instead. *SysBeep* is the Toolbox function that does the beeping. Just pass *SysBeep* the number 1 and it will give the speaker a beep. While this menu option doesn't do anything terribly exciting, it will at least provide you with verification that the code is working. Every time the user selects this item, the speaker should beep.

Now let's look at how the second menu item, Quit, is handled. Even without the use of menus you know how to end the running of a program. Just set variable *AllDone* to a value of 1 and the event loop will end. So that's exactly what I do:

```
case 2:
    AllDone = 1;
    break;
```

Example Program: A Menu That Drops

Here I'll show the code for a short program that demonstrates how all the menu handling code fits together. The program, which I call MenuDrop, uses all of the menu code that you've seen in this chapter — including the 'MBAR' and 'MENU' resources. A user who runs the program won't see a window, but instead will see one menu in the menu bar:

As described earlier, the first menu item will beep the Mac's speaker and the second menu item will end the program. Here's the complete source code listing for MenuDrop:

```
main()
{                               /* declare the variables       */
    EventRecord   TheEvent;     /* event record for WaitNextEvent */
```

```
short       AllDone;          /* are we done yet? 0=no, 1=yes   */
WindowPtr   aWindow;          /* for use by FindWindow          */
short       ThePart;          /* part code for FindWindow        */
Handle      MenuBarHandle;    /* used during menu bar set up    */
long        MenuChoice;       /* holds selected menu and item   */
short       TheMenu;          /* holds just the selected menu   */
short       TheMenuItem;      /* holds just the selected item   */

InitGraf( &thePort );         /* standard initializations       */
InitFonts();
InitWindows();
InitMenus();
TEInit();
InitDialogs( 0L );
FlushEvents( everyEvent, 0 );
InitCursor();

MenuBarHandle = GetNewMBar( 128 );      /* create the menu bar  */
SetMenuBar( MenuBarHandle );
DrawMenuBar();
AllDone = 0;                            /* we're just starting  */
while ( AllDone < 1 )                   /* loop until user quits */
{
    WaitNextEvent( everyEvent, &TheEvent, 0L, 0L );  /* get event */

    switch ( TheEvent.what )
    {
        case mouseDown:                 /* user clicked the mouse   */
            ThePart = FindWindow( TheEvent.where, &aWindow );
            switch ( ThePart )
            {
                case inMenuBar:         /* handle click in menu bar */
                    MenuChoice = MenuSelect( TheEvent.where );
                    if ( MenuChoice > 0 )
                    {
                        TheMenu = HiWord( MenuChoice );
                        TheMenuItem = LoWord( MenuChoice );
                        switch ( TheMenu )
                        {
                            case 128:
                                switch ( TheMenuItem )
                                {
                                    case 1:
                                        SysBeep( 1 );  /* beep the speaker */
                                        break;
                                    case 2:
                                        AllDone = 1;   /* 1 means quit     */
                                        break;
                                }
                                break;
                        }
                        HiliteMenu(0); /* remove menu bar highlighting */
                    }
                    break;
            }
            break;
    }
}
```

The source code for MenuDrop contains no surprises — you've seen it all before. As a matter of fact, you've seen all the code you need in order to write a complete Macintosh program. And that's exactly what you'll do in the next two chapters.

Chapter 18

Writing a Very Mac-like Program — Part I

• •

In This Chapter

▶ A description of Animator, the example program

▶ Creating a resource file for Animator

▶ Adding the resources to Animator's resource file

▶ Creating the THINK C project for Animator

▶ Adding a library to the project file

▶ Adding the source code file to the project file

• •

*I*n the next two chapters I'll create a Macintosh program from start to finish—without skipping a step. In this chapter I'll first create a resource file to hold the program's resources. The program uses three different resource types, so I'll use ResEdit to create them in my resource file. Then I'll use the THINK Project Manager to create a new project to hold one library and one source code file. In the Project Manager I'll add the library and the source code file. After that, it's time for a short break. After a couple cans of Diet Coke, it's on to Chapter 19 where I'll type in the source code and explain just what the code does. Then I'll compile and run the program to make sure it works. When I'm satisfied that it runs I'll turn it all into a final program. That is, I'll build it into a Mac application that I, or anyone I give it to, can run.

About the Animator Program

In this chapter and the next, I develop a program I've named Animator. While Animator won't win the Most Useful, Exciting, and Intricate Piece of Mac Software award this year, I think you'll find it's just right for you. In less than 100 lines of code the Animator does several of the things you'll want many of your own Mac programs to do. It:

✔ Initializes the Toolbox.

✔ Opens a window.

✔ Allows the user to drag the window.

✔ Allows the user to close the window.

✔ Displays a menu bar with one functional menu.

✔ Draws a moving shape in the window.

What the Animator Does

Running the Animator program displays an empty window and menu bar with one menu in it. If you click on the menu you'll see four items in it:

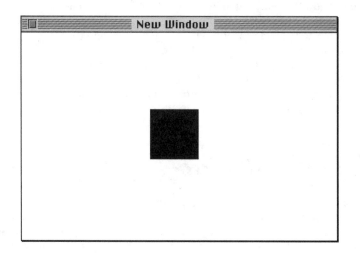

The first menu item simply sounds the Mac's speaker once. You've seen that trick before. The second menu item, Grow Square, draws a very tiny black square in the center of the window, then quickly enlarges it to fill most of the window. While this trick won't rival the special effects of *Star Wars*, it does give you an introduction to simple animation. I've captured the square as it starts to grow — here's a look at it now:

The third menu item, Move Square, creates a small square in the upper left corner of the window. The square immediately and quickly slides diagonally down the window, leaving a path of squares as it goes. Here's what the window looks like after the journey of the square is completed:

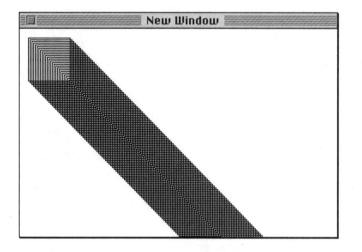

The fourth and final menu item, Quit, does just what you'd think.

What's Needed to Make the Animator

Just about every Mac program consists of a resource file, project file, and source code file. Animator is no exception. In this chapter I'll use ResEdit to create the resource file and the THINK Project Manager to make the project file and source code file. In the next chapter I'll again use the THINK Project Manager to make a fourth file — the Animator application itself.

As always, I'll store all the files associated with my program in one folder. Again, as always, I'll create a folder in the Development folder on my hard disk. I've called my folder the Animator Folder. As I create the files that will be used for my Animator program I'll make sure they end up in the Animator Folder.

When everything is said and done I'll have four files in one folder. Here's what my desktop will look like:

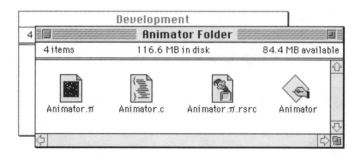

To start things off, double-click on the Development folder and then select New Folder from the File menu. That places a new, untitled folder in the Development folder. Give it the name Animator Folder — that way all of your work will match the figures I use in this and the next chapter.

After you create the new folder it won't match mine. That's because the above figure is a peek at what lies ahead. Instead, your Animator Folder will be empty — but not for long.

Keeping a program's files together is important. That's because the THINK Project Manager will be looking for the source code file and resource file so that they can be included in the project file you're working with.

At some point in your programming you may notice that one of the files appears to be missing from the folder in which you thought it should be. Don't panic! When you initially saved the file you probably saved it into the wrong folder. That means it's on your hard drive somewhere. To find a missing file, select Find from the File menu at the desktop. A dialog box will open up. Enter part or all of the file's name, then click the Find button:

In my example, the Mac will search for any files that have the word "Animator" in them. When it finds the first one, it will open up the folder in which it resides. If that's the file I was missing I'd then simply move it into my Animator Folder. If it's not the file, I can select Find Again from the File menu and the Mac will take another look. Don't give up — eventually the Mac will find that sucker. ■

The Animator's Resource File

I can create the resource file before my other files because I have a pretty good idea of the resources I'll need for the Animator program. Of course I do — I completed and tested the program long before I wrote this chapter! Even if I *really* was creating the program for the first time right here and now, I'd have a good idea of what resources I need.

Creating the Resource File

Begin by running ResEdit. Click the mouse to dismiss the introductory dialog box that appears. A dialog box that lets you create a new resource file appears. Move to the folder that will hold all of this project's files — the Animator Folder. Use the pop-up menu that appears above the scrollable list to move about from folder to folder. You know the Animator Folder is in the Development folder — so look there. Once you get to the Animator Folder you'll see that it's empty. Since you've just recently created this folder, it should be empty. Click the New button now.

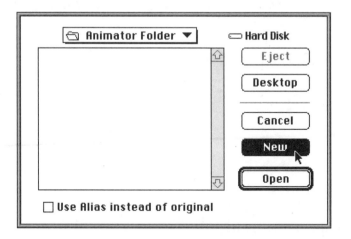

It is very important that the resource file and the project file of a program end up in the same folder. I moved to the Animator Folder because that's where I'll be keeping all my Animator-related files — including the soon-to-be-made Animator project file. ■

In the dialog box that opens, type in the resource file name. Earlier I said that I was going to name my THINK Project file Animator.π. That leaves me with no choice as to the name I'm to give the resource file — Animator.π.rsrc. If you're following along with me, type in that name and click the New button.

```
┌─────────────────────────────────────────────────────┐
│  ┌────────────────────────┐        ▭ Hard Disk        │
│  │ 🗁 Animator Folder ▼ │      ┌───────────────┐     │
│  ├────────────────────┬───┤      │     Eject     │     │
│  │                    │ ⇧ │      └───────────────┘     │
│  │                    │   │      ┌───────────────┐     │
│  │                    │   │      │   Desktop     │     │
│  │                    │   │      └───────────────┘     │
│  │                    │   │      ─────────────────     │
│  │                    │   │      ┌───────────────┐     │
│  │                    │ ⇩ │      │    Cancel     │     │
│  └────────────────────┴───┘      └───────────────┘     │
│  New File Name:                  ┌───────────────┐     │
│  ┌────────────────────────────┐  │      New      │     │
│  │ Animator.π.rsrc            │  └───────────────┘     │
│  └────────────────────────────┘              ▸         │
└─────────────────────────────────────────────────────┘
```

Why don't I have a choice in naming my resource file? In order for the THINK Project Manager to pair a project with a resource file, the resource file must have the same name as the project, followed by ".rsrc" at the end of its name. ▪

After clicking the New button the dialog box will disappear and a new, empty type picker will appear. The resource file is created — and ready for the addition of some resources.

```
┌─────────────────────────────────────┐
│ ▤▤▤▤▤ Animator.π.rsrc ▤▤▤▤▤ 🔲 │
│                                  ⇧ │
│                                    │
│                                    │
│                                    │
│                                    │
│                                    │
│                                  ⇩ │
│                                  🔲 │
└─────────────────────────────────────┘
```

A new program requires a new resource file. Here is a summary of the steps we just went through for creating one:

1. Run ResEdit by double-clicking the ResEdit icon.

2. Click the mouse to dismiss the ResEdit Jack-in-the-Mac introductory screen.

3. In the dialog box that opens, move to the project's folder.

4. Click the New button.

5. In the next dialog box that opens, type in the resource file's name.

6. Click the New button.

Adding the Window Resource

I told you that the Animator program opens a window, so you know a '*WIND*' resource is needed. Select Create New Resource from ResEdit's Resource menu. The Select New Type dialog box will open. Scroll down to WIND, then click once on it. Then click the OK button:

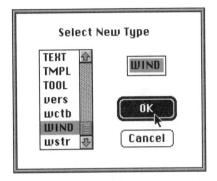

Dismissing the Select New Type dialog box opens a '*WIND*' editor. Mine is shown below. Because the '*WIND*' editor initially displays a rather small window, I changed the size of my '*WIND*' by typing in the numbers shown here in the lower left of the screen:

The only other change I made here was to the window type. I gave the second icon from the left a click in the row of window icons at the top of the editor. That sets up my '*WIND*' for a window that has a title bar and a close box, but no grow box in the lower right corner. When I clicked the close box of the '*WIND*' editor, here's what I saw:

Adding the Menu Resources

From my description of the Animator program at the beginning of this chapter you should have a pretty good idea about what other resources are needed. The Animator has one menu, so it needs one '*MENU*' resource. The menu appears, of course, in the title bar — so I'll also need an '*MBAR*' resource for that. First comes the '*MENU*' resource.

Select Create New Resource from the Resource menu. Scroll down to MENU in the Select New Type dialog box, then click once on it. Follow that with a click on the OK button:

When the '*MENU*' editor opens, type in the menu's title. I called the menu MyMenu. Next, add the four menu items. Select Create New Item from the

Resource menu, then begin typing. For the first item, type in the words Beep Me!. Repeat the process of selecting Create New Item, then typing in a menu item name for each of the remaining menu items. When you're done, your '*MENU*' should look like mine:

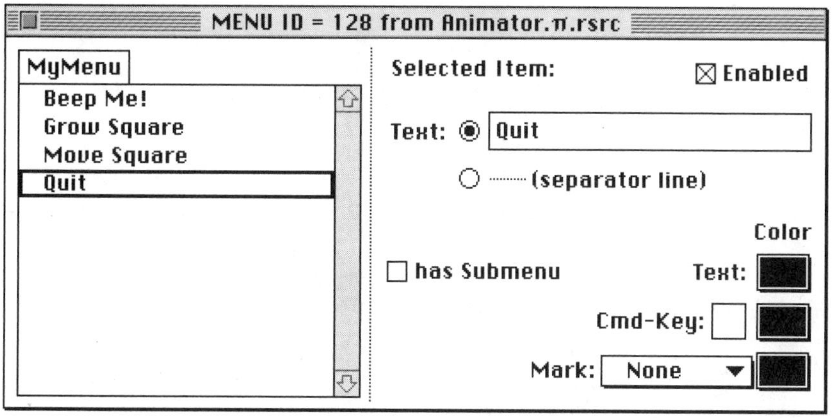

Close the '*MENU*' editor. When you do that, you'll see another view of the '*MENU*' resource. This view gives you a pretty good idea of how the menu will look once it's added to the Animator program.

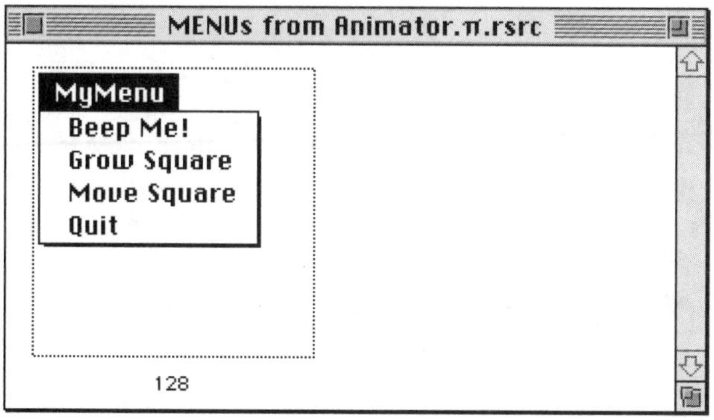

After you're done admiring the new '*MENU*', click the window's close box to bring the type picker to the front. Now there are two different resource types pictured in it:

```
┌─────────────────────────────────┐
│ ▤▤▤▤ Animator.π.rsrc ▤▤▤ ▣ │
├─────────────────────────────────┤
│                              ⬆  │
│  ┌──────┐     ┌──────┐          │
│  │ FILE │     │□=FILE│          │
│  │······│     │      │          │
│  │ ──── │     │      │          │
│  └──────┘     └──────┘          │
│   MENU         WIND             │
│                              ⬇  │
│                              ▢  │
└─────────────────────────────────┘
```

There's one last resource to create. Again select Create New Resource from
the Resource menu. Scroll down to MBAR, click once on it, and then click the
OK button:

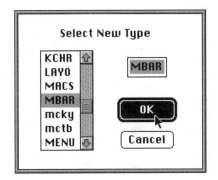

When complete, the Animator program will display a single menu, so the
resource file for Animator has a single '*MENU*' resource. Now is the time to
add it to the list of '*MENU*' resources that the '*MBAR*' keeps. I've added it in the
figure below:

```
┌─────────────────────────────────────────┐
│ ▤▣ MBAR ID = 128 from Animator.π.rsrc ▤ │
├─────────────────────────────────────────┤
│                                      ⬆  │
│  # of menus     1                        │
│                                          │
│  1) *****                                │
│                    ┌─────────┐           │
│  Menu res ID       │ 128     │           │
│                    └─────────┘           │
│  2) *****                                │
│                                      ⬇  │
│                                      ▢  │
└─────────────────────────────────────────┘
```

Did you remember how to add a '*MENU*' to the '*MBAR*' resource? If not, here's a refresher. To add it, first click once on the row of five stars in the '*MBAR*' editor. That will place a rectangle around the stars, like this:

```
┌──────────────────────────────────────────┐
│ ▤▣▤  MBAR ID = 128 from Animator.π.rsrc ▤ │
│                                        ⇧  │
│  # of menus    0                          │
│    ┌──────────────────┐                   │
│    │1) *****          │                   │
│    └──────────────────┘                   │
│                                           │
│                                           │
│                                        ⇩  │
│                                        ▣  │
└──────────────────────────────────────────┘
```

Next, select Insert New Field(s) from the Resource menu. Here's what you'll see:

```
┌──────────────────────────────────────────┐
│ ▤▣▤  MBAR ID = 128 from Animator.π.rsrc ▤ │
│                                        ⇧  │
│  # of menus    1                          │
│    ┌──────────────────┐                   │
│    │1) *****          │                   │
│    └──────────────────┘                   │
│    Menu res ID  ┌─────────────┐           │
│                 └─────────────┘           │
│    2) *****                               │
│                                        ⇩  │
│                                        ▣  │
└──────────────────────────────────────────┘
```

Type the resource ID of the '*MENU*' resource into the edit box that's been added to the '*MBAR*'. This resource file has only one '*MENU*' resource in it (remember that resource numbers start at 128), so the '*MBAR*' is complete. Here's how it looks:

```
┌──────────────────────────────────────────┐
│ ▤▣▤  MBAR ID = 128 from Animator.π.rsrc ▤ │
│                                        ⇧  │
│  # of menus    1                          │
│    ┌──────────────────┐                   │
│    │1) *****          │                   │
│    └──────────────────┘                   │
│    Menu res ID  ┌─────────────┐           │
│                 │ 128         │           │
│                 └─────────────┘           │
│    2) *****                               │
│                                        ⇩  │
│                                        ▣  │
└──────────────────────────────────────────┘
```

Click in the close box of the '*MBAR*' editor and you'll see that the type picker now looks like this:

The resource file for the Animator program is now complete. Select Save from the File menu, then quit ResEdit.

The THINK C Project

The remainder of this chapter will be devoted to the THINK project file that will be used to organize the Animator. I'll start, of course, by creating the project.

Creating the Project File

Start by running the THINK Project Manager. It's in the folder titled Think C 7.0. If you're using version 6.0 of THINK C, then it will of course appear in the folder titled Think C 6.0. Once you're in that folder, double-click on the THINK Project Manager icon. When you do, you'll see a dialog box like this one:

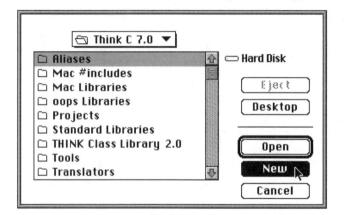

You want to create a new project, so click the New button. Another dialog box will open — it's pictured below. You THINK 7.0 users will first see the New Project dialog box discussed in Chapter 8. Click the check box to uncheck it, and click once on the words "Empty Project". Then click the Create button. Now, whether using THINK 6.0 or THINK 7.0, use the pop-up menu to maneuver your way into the Animator Folder. It's in the Development folder, so move into it first — as I'm doing here:

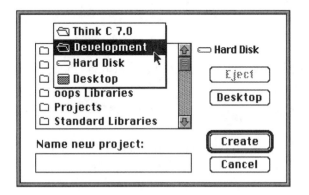

Once I see the Animator Folder in the scrollable list of folders I'll double-click on it. The dialog box will then look like the one pictured below. If you created the resource file — as I did — its name will appear in the list. Type in the name of the project, then click the Create button. Don't forget — because the resource file is named Animator.π.rsrc, the project must be named Animator.π.

After clicking the Create button you'll see a new THINK C project window on the screen. Here's mine:

Animator.π	
Name	**Code**
Totals	578

The project window is empty, which means it must be time to add some files.

Adding the Library

All Mac programs use the MacTraps library. Remember, a library is a collection of code that gets integrated, or merged, with the source code you write. MacTraps is full of useful and necessary things that make your programming job much easier.

Select Add Files from the Source menu. Use the pop-up menu in the dialog that appears to work your way into the Mac Libraries folder. You'll have to use the menu to go into the Think C 7.0 folder — or Think C 6.0 folder for you readers with THINK C 6.0. That's where the Mac Libraries folder lives. Once you're in the correct folder, click on MacTraps, then click the Add button:

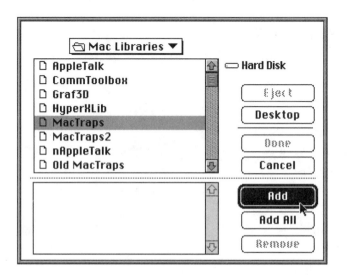

The MacTraps library will move to the list at the bottom of the dialog box. Click the Done button. The Animator's project window will now look like this:

Name	Code
▽ **Segment 2**	4
MacTraps	0
Totals	**582**

Adding the Source Code File

Animator requires a second file — the source code file. That doesn't exist yet, so you'll need to create it by selecting New from the File menu. When you do, an empty window will open. Before working on the code, select Save As from the File menu. When prompted to enter a name, type in "Animator.c" (don't type the quote marks), but don't save the file just yet.

You want to make sure the source code file gets saved to the Animator Folder. If you look at the top of the dialog box you'll see you aren't in the Animator Folder, you're in the Mac Libraries folder. That's because the THINK Project Manager keeps track of the last folder you ventured into. When you added the MacTraps library a moment ago, you were in the Mac Libraries folder. Use the pop-up menu in the dialog box to work your way into the Animator Folder. Then and only then should you click the Save button to save the file.

Though you can give your source code file any name you want, it makes sense to give it a name that associates it with the program you're creating. I've named mine Animator.c. Any name is all right — but make sure it ends with a period followed by the letter "c", as I've done in the above figure. ■

You don't need to type in all the source code before adding the file to your project. In fact, it makes sense to add the file to the project right away so you don't forget. Select Add Files from the Source menu. You'll see the familiar dialog box that I've pictured below. Notice that you'll already be in the Animator Folder — you got there when you saved the source code file. Click the Add button, then the Done button.

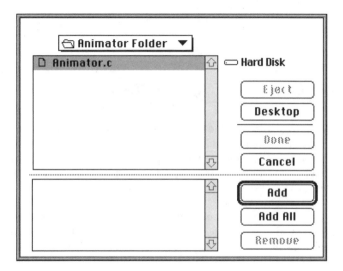

Your project file now looks like the one pictured here:

Now you're just about done. That is, except for that little part about writing the source code. I've saved that for the next chapter. Before moving on to the final steps, take a look at the summary of how I created a project and added the appropriate files to it.

1. Run the THINK Project Manager to create a new project file.

2. Choose Add Files from the Source menu to add the MacTraps library to the project.

3. Choose New from the File menu to create a new, empty source code file.

4. Choose Save As from the File menu to name and save the source code file (make sure to save it in the same folder as your other program files).

5. Choose Add Files from the Source menu to add the new text file to the project.

Chapter 19

Writing a Very Mac-like Program — Part II

*I*n Chapter 18, I — and hopefully you — created a resource file, a project file, and a source code file for a program I call the Animator. In this chapter I'll take a look at what the source code does. After telling you what the program should do, you'll see for yourself by compiling and running the program. When you're satisfied that the Animator works you'll get to turn it into a program. That is, you'll build it into a Mac application that you, I, or anyone else can run.

The Animator Source Code

In Chapter 18 you created a source code file and added it to your project. But you didn't type in any code. Let's take care of that right now.

Nothing to Fear

For the next few pages, I'll present the complete source code listing for the Animator. There's just under 100 lines of code in the listing. Personally, I don't consider that a lot of code. But then, I just read that the software that would run the Star Wars defense system proposed by former President Ronald Reagan would require 100 million lines of code. That should make you feel better about the 100 lines you're about to view. If it doesn't, take a look at this breakdown of the 100 lines of code. It might take away any apprehensions you have.

- ✔ About 20 of those lines are just braces — that leaves about 80 lines.

- ✔ About 10 lines are variable declarations — that leaves about 70 lines.

- ✔ A little less than 10 lines make up the standard Toolbox initialization code that appears in every program — that leaves about 60 lines.

- ✔ You know that *switch* statements group code together and separate those groups with *case* labels and *break* statements. There are a few *switch* statements that have a total of close to 10 *case* labels and 10 *break* statements — one *break* to end each *case*. That's over 20 lines of code, which leaves about 40 lines.

- ✔ In Chapter 17 you saw how to display a menu bar and how to figure out which menu was clicked on. You also saw how to work with a window. There are about 15 lines of code devoted to these two tasks. That leaves about 25 lines.

Twenty-five lines of code? No problem! That's right — after discounting the lines of code that you've had plenty of experience with, there are only about twenty-five lines of code that can't be neatly pegged into a basic programming category. The Animator source code contains very little new code — it just demonstrates how to tie together all the topics I've already covered.

The Code

I'll list all the source code here in a nice, easy-to-look-at, uninterrupted form. Then I'll devote the next section of this chapter to an in-depth description of what's going on. If you've got a few minutes (and the THINK C compiler), go ahead and type the code in now. If you've quit the THINK Project Manager, follow these steps:

1. Run the THINK Project Manager.

2. Open the empty source code file by double-clicking on the Animator.c name in the project window.

3. *Carefully* type in all of the following code:

```
main()
    {                             /* declare the variables         */
        WindowPtr    TheWindow;   /* the window                    */
        EventRecord  TheEvent;    /* event record for WaitNextEvent */
        short        AllDone;     /* are we done yet? 0=no, 1=yes  */
```

```
WindowPtr    aWindow;            /* for use by FindWindow        */
short        ThePart;            /* part code for FindWindow     */
Handle       MenuBarHandle;      /* used during menu bar set up  */
long         MenuChoice;         /* holds selected menu and item */
short        TheMenu;            /* holds just the selected menu */
short        TheMenuItem;        /* holds just the selected item */
Rect         TheRect;            /* used to draw some squares    */
short        count;              /* loop counter                 */

InitGraf( &thePort );            /* standard initializations     */
InitFonts();
InitWindows();
InitMenus();
TEInit();
InitDialogs( 0L );
FlushEvents( everyEvent, 0 );
InitCursor();

MenuBarHandle = GetNewMBar( 128 );      /* create the menu bar   */
SetMenuBar( MenuBarHandle );
DrawMenuBar();
TheWindow = GetNewWindow( 128, 0L, (WindowPtr)-1L );
SetPort( TheWindow );

AllDone = 0;                             /* we're just starting   */
while ( AllDone < 1 )                    /* loop until user quits */
{
   WaitNextEvent( everyEvent, &TheEvent, 0L, 0L );
   switch ( TheEvent.what )
   {
      case mouseDown:                    /* user clicked the mouse   */
         ThePart = FindWindow( TheEvent.where, &aWindow );
         switch ( ThePart )
         {
            case inDrag:                 /* move the window around    */
               DragWindow( aWindow, TheEvent.where,
                           &screenBits.bounds );
               break;
            case inGoAway:
               DisposeWindow( aWindow );  /* close window          */
               AllDone = 1;               /* 1 means quit          */
               break;
            case inMenuBar:              /* handle click in menu bar */
               MenuChoice = MenuSelect( TheEvent.where );
               if ( MenuChoice > 0 )
               {
                  TheMenu = HiWord( MenuChoice );
                  TheMenuItem = LoWord( MenuChoice );
                  switch ( TheMenu )
                  {
                     case 128:
                        switch ( TheMenuItem )
                        {
                           case 1:
                              SysBeep( 1 );  /* beep the speaker */
                              break;
```

continued

```
                                  case 2:
                                     SetRect( &TheRect, 0, 0, 400, 280 );
                                     FillRect( &TheRect, &white );
                                     SetRect( &TheRect, 200, 135, 200, 135 );
                                     count = 0;
                                     while ( count < 120 )
                                     {
                                         FillRect( &TheRect, &black );
                                         InsetRect( &TheRect, -1, -1 );
                                         count++;
                                     }
                                     break;
                                  case 3:
                                     SetRect( &TheRect, 0, 0, 400, 280 );
                                     FillRect( &TheRect, &white );
                                     SetRect( &TheRect, 10, 10, 60, 60 );
                                     count = 0;
                                     while ( count < 280 )
                                     {
                                         FrameRect( &TheRect );
                                         OffsetRect( &TheRect, 2, 2 );
                                         count++;
                                     }
                                     break;
                                  case 4:
                                     AllDone = 1;          /* 1 means quit */
                                     break;
                               }
                               break;
                        }
                        HiliteMenu(0); /* remove menu bar highlighting */
                  }
                  break;
            }
            break;
         }
      }
}
```

Does much of this code look familiar? It should. You've seen some of it in example programs throughout this book — programs such as ExampleOne, WindowWorks, and MenuDrop. You didn't *really* think that every time someone wrote a program they started completely from scratch, did you? Most programmers do like a good challenge, but they don't like repetitively typing in the same code.

When you start a new source code file for a new project, use the Open command from the THINK C File menu and open an existing source code file. Copy any or all of the code and paste it into the source code file of your new project — then modify it. If you've typed in the example programs presented in this book, I hereby grant you permission to copy any of them and modify them. Heck, I didn't invent most of the code anyway. It's similar to Macintosh source code that thousands of other programmers are using! ■

What's Going On in the Code

The Animator ties together all the individual concepts covered in this book — and that makes it worthy of a good long look.

Why "128" ?

It would make the most sense if I described the code starting at the first line and worked my way to the end, don't you agree? That's what I'll do — after a very short diversion.

If you look over the source code for the Animator you'll notice that it contains the number 128 in three separate locations. I've plucked that code out of the listing — here it is:

```
TheWindow = GetNewWindow( 128, 0L, (WindowPtr)-1L );

MenuBarHandle = GetNewMBar( 128 );
switch ( TheMenu )
{
    case 128:
```

Why the number 128? As a reminder of why this number is used, I ran ResEdit and opened the editor for each of the program's three resources. In the figure below I show the title bar from each. Note the ID listed in each title bar.

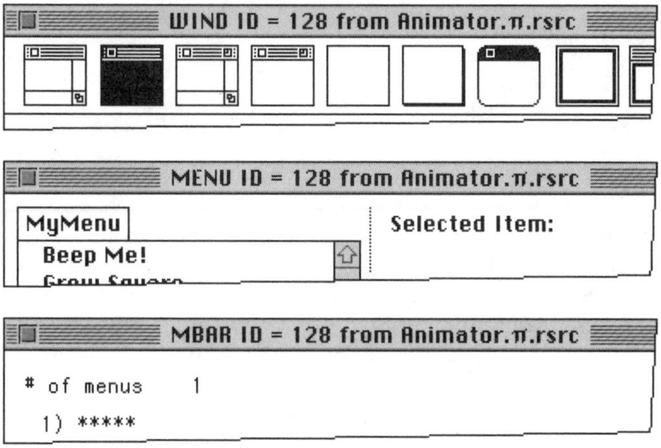

Each resource has an ID of 128. Coincidence? Not at all. When ResEdit creates a new resource, it usually gives it an ID of 128. This isn't true of all resource types, but it is for 'WIND', 'MENU', and 'MBAR' resources. After the first resource of a type is created, the next resource *of that same type* will be given the number 129. If I added a second 'MENU' to my program, ResEdit would give it an ID of 129.

Why the number 128? Why doesn't ResEdit start with number 1? Apple has reserved the numbers up to 127 for its own use. The Macintosh has a set of resources hidden from your view that it uses to display things like the trash can icon and the menu bar you see when you're at the desktop. It is possible to renumber a resource of yours to give it a number less than 128, but Apple insists that you don't.

Variable Declarations

All Mac programs written in C begin with *main( )* and an opening brace. They end with a closing brace. What does that have to do with variable declarations? Nothing, since there's not a whole lot of explaining to accompany the fact that all programs have a *main* function, I didn't think that this concept needed its own section. Now, on to the declarations.

Animator uses 11 variables. I'll very briefly describe each here. I'll give more information about each as I encounter it later in the code. Here are the declarations, followed by the descriptions.

```
WindowPtr    TheWindow;      /* the window                       */
EventRecord  TheEvent;       /* event record for WaitNextEvent */
short        AllDone;        /* are we done yet? 0=no, 1=yes   */
WindowPtr    aWindow;        /* for use by FindWindow          */
short        ThePart;        /* part code for FindWindow        */
Handle       MenuBarHandle;  /* used during menu bar set up    */
long         MenuChoice;     /* holds selected menu and item   */
short        TheMenu;        /* holds just the selected menu   */
short        TheMenuItem;    /* holds just the selected item   */
Rect         TheRect;        /* used to draw some squares      */
short        count;          /* loop counter                    */
```

Animator opens a single window. To keep track of it I've declared a *WindowPtr* variable called *TheWindow*. Like any good Mac program, Animator takes note of events and responds to them. The variable *TheEvent* holds information about the most recent event. Animator is a great program, but users of it will probably want to quit at some point. The variable *AllDone* helps out there.

A click of the mouse button constitutes an event. When that happens, the Animator wants more information about the event. The variable *ThePart* holds the part of the screen at which the mouse click occurred. If the click occurred in a window, variable *aWindow* will hold a *WindowPtr* to that window — useful information later in the program.

The Animator has one menu. The variable *MenuBarHandle* is used in the setup of the menu bar that holds this menu. When the user makes a menu selection, variable *MenuChoice* holds the key to which menu item was selected. As a combined value of menu and menu item, *MenuChoice* is of limited use. So variables *TheMenu* and *TheMenuItem* are used to hold the individual information that is found in a combined form in *MenuChoice*.

What's the Mac without a little bit of drawing going on — right? The Animator use a *Rect* variable called *TheRect* to hold the screen coordinates of a rectangle. That same rectangle variable will be used twice — once to make the rectangle grow and a second time to slide it across the window. Moving things in a window involves looping, and a loop requires a variable to keep track of when the loop should end. That's the purpose of the last variable — a short called *count*.

Toolbox Initialization

You've seen the Toolbox initialization code so many times that I was very tempted to omit this section from the chapter. But for the sake of completeness, here it is:

```
InitGraf( &thePort );     /* standard initializations */
InitFonts();
InitWindows();
InitMenus();
TEInit();
InitDialogs( 0L );
FlushEvents( everyEvent, 0 );
InitCursor();
```

I've said it before, and I'll say it again. To avoid serious problems in your program, include these eight lines of code right after your variable declarations in every program you write. You, and the Toolbox, will be glad you did.

Displaying Windows and Menus

Working with windows and menus is fun — but first you have to get them on the screen. These five lines display one window and a menu bar:

```
MenuBarHandle = GetNewMBar( 128 );
SetMenuBar( MenuBarHandle );
DrawMenuBar();
TheWindow = GetNewWindow( 128, 0L, (WindowPtr)-1L );
SetPort( TheWindow );
```

The first three lines make the Mac aware of a new menu bar, and then display it. The fourth and fifth lines open a new window and tell the Mac that subsequent drawing should take place in it.

The Event Loop

The remainder of the program is the event loop. The variable *AllDone* is set to 0, and then the *while* statement that begins the loop is encountered. *AllDone* is obviously less than 1, so the code under the *while* statement runs. A call to *WaitNextEvent* asks the Toolbox to place information about the most recent event into *TheEvent*. Next, a *switch* statement is used to see if the event is worthy of a response. Animator only cares about one type of event — a click of the mouse button. By excluding all other event types from the *switch* statement, the program effectively filters them out. That is, other events, such as a press of a key, are simply ignored. Here's the event loop code — without the numerous lines that fall under the *case mouseDown*. I've chosen to cover them in separate sections of this chapter.

```
AllDone = 0;
while ( AllDone < 1 )
{
   WaitNextEvent( everyEvent, &TheEvent, 0L, 0L );
   switch ( TheEvent.what )
   {
      case mouseDown:
         /* a bunch of mouse click code here! */
         break;
   }
}
```

Handling a mouseDown Event

If the user clicks the mouse button, *WaitNextEvent* will place a value of *mouseDown* in *TheEvent.what*. The very next line, the *switch* statement, will then match the value of *TheEvent.what* to the *case mouseDown* label, and the code under the *case* will run.

FindWindow determines just where the mouse click occurred. It places a value in variable *ThePart* — a value that represents the part of the screen at which the click took place. A *switch* statement than examines variable *ThePart* and determines which set of code should run to handle the mouse click.

A click in the drag bar of the window results in a call to *DragWindow*. This Toolbox function takes control and handles window movement for you.

A click in the close box of the window brings about a call to *DisposeWindow*. This function disposes of the window — that is, it removes it from the screen. Variable *AllDone* is then set to a value of 1. When the program returns to the top of the event loop, this value of *AllDone* will signal the program to end. Most programs don't end when the user closes a window. But for the simple Animator program, it wouldn't make much sense to continue if the user closes the window. After all, where would drawing then take place?

A click in the menu bar causes the code under *case inMenuBar* to run. I omitted that code here because it represents a significant portion of the program. As such, it gets several pages devoted to it.

```
switch ( TheEvent.what )
{
    case mouseDown:
        ThePart = FindWindow( TheEvent.where, &aWindow );
        switch ( ThePart )
        {
            case inDrag:
                DragWindow( aWindow, TheEvent.where, &screenBits.bounds );
                break;
            case inGoAway:
                DisposeWindow( aWindow );
                AllDone = 1;
                break;
            case inMenuBar:
                /* a bunch of menu-handling code here! */
                break;
        }
        break;
}
```

Handling a Click in the Menu Bar

A mouse click in the menu bar is what causes the real action to take place. When that happens the Toolbox function *MenuSelect* is called to handle the display of the program's one menu. If a menu selection is made, *MenuSelect* places a value in variable *MenuChoice* — a value that represents the menu number and the menu item number. A menu selection *always* gives *MenuChoice* a value greater than 0. That nonzero value is what sends the code into the *if* loop that follows the call to *MenuSelect*.

The Toolbox functions *HiWord* and *LoWord* do the grunt work of separating both the menu number and the menu item number from variable *MenuChoice*. That first bit of information — the menu number — is then used in a *switch* statement to determine which menu to work with. Animator only has one menu — the '*MENU*' resource with ID 128 — but many programs have more than that.

Knowing the menu that houses the selected menu item isn't enough information to determine how to respond to the selection. The program also needs to know which menu item within that menu was selected. The *switch* statement that uses variable *TheMenuItem* handles that. I'll use the next several pages to describe how each menu item is handled. Here I've replaced the code for the menu items with comments in order to give you the overall feel for what's going on.

```
case inMenuBar:
    MenuChoice = MenuSelect( TheEvent.where );
    if ( MenuChoice > 0 )
```

```
{
   TheMenu = HiWord( MenuChoice );
   TheMenuItem = LoWord( MenuChoice );
   switch ( TheMenu )
   {
      case 128:
         switch ( TheMenuItem )
         {
            case 1:
               /* handle Beep Me! item */
               break;
            case 2:
               /* handle Grow Square item */
               break;
            case 3:
               /* handle Move Square item */
               break;
            case 4:
               /* handle Quit item */
               break;
         }
         break;
   }
   HiliteMenu(0);
}
break;
```

Once the menu selection has been handled, *HiliteMenu* is called to return the menu name to its original state. It was highlighted — and left that way — when a menu item was selected.

The Beep Me! Item

I'm devoting a separate section of this chapter to the code that handles each of the four menu items — no matter how few lines of code are necessary to do it! The first menu item, Beep Me!, simply uses the Toolbox function *SysBeep* to play the system alert sound.

```
switch ( TheMenuItem )
{
   case 1:
      SysBeep( 1 );
      break;
   /* other cases go here */
}
```

The Grow Square Item

You know about a couple of the Toolbox functions that work with rectangles. In this chapter you're about to see a few more.

The second menu item, Grow Square, uses a *while* loop to repeatedly draw a square. That wouldn't have the effect of growing the square unless I first enlarged the square a little bit each time the loop ran. That's exactly what the Toolbox function *InsetRect* does. You tell *InsetRect* the rectangle you want to shrink or expand, and by how much, and *InsetRect* does the work. If you pass *InsetRect* positive numbers, the rectangle will get smaller. Negative numbers make the rectangle get larger. Consider this example:

```
SetRect( &TheRect, 150, 50, 200, 100 );
FrameRect( &TheRect );
InsetRect( &TheRect, -60, -30 );
FrameRect( &TheRect );
```

I'll describe what the above code does while you follow along in the figure below. First, a rectangle 50 pixels in width and 50 pixels in height is set and then framed. That's the smaller rectangle in the center of the window in the figure. Next, a call to *InsetRect* is made. The value of -60 means the rectangle should become 60 pixels larger in each of the horizontal directions. The value of -30 means the rectangle should become 30 pixels larger in each of the vertical directions. *InsetRect* changes the size of a rectangle, but it doesn't draw it. So I followed the call to *InsetRect* with another call to *FrameRect*. The result is the larger of the two rectangles in the figure.

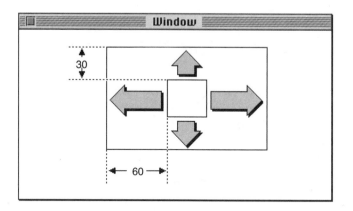

If it seems odd that negative numbers make the rectangle bigger rather than smaller, think of the name of the Toolbox function — *InsetRect*. *InsetRect* is normally used to inset a rectangle — to make a rectangle smaller so that it fits inside another. The parameters to *InsetRect* tell the Toolbox how much smaller to make the rectangle. Since I want the opposite effect, I use negative numbers.

Now, back to the *while* loop. Actually, let's back up a little further. The first thing that happens under the *case* is a call to *SetRect* and *FillRect*. The call to *FillRect* has a parameter of *white*. Look at the size of the rectangle I fill. It just happens to be the size of the window. The result? I'm whiting out, or erasing, anything that was in the window. Why? The user may have already made this menu selection, or another drawing selection, beforehand. I'm getting rid of any leftover drawings. Make a note of this technique for clearing a window:

```
SetRect( &TheRect, 0, 0, 400, 280 );  /* Size of the window */
FillRect( &TheRect, white );          /* White it out      */
```

Now for the drawing. After whiting out the window I again call *SetRect*. This time I create a rectangle that is almost centered in the window. But notice its size:

```
SetRect( &TheRect, 200, 135, 200, 135 );  /* tiny!    */
```

The left and right sides have the same value — 200. And so do the top and bottom sides — 135. That means the rectangle won't even show up when I draw it — but that will soon change. Next comes the *while* loop. I've set variable *count* to a value of 0, and *while* to count < 120, so my loop will run 120 times. Each time through the loop the rectangle will be filled in with black, then made larger by one pixel in each direction. The result? A solid black rectangle will appear to grow from nothing to a size that almost fills the window. Here's the code that makes it all happen.

```
switch ( TheMenuItem )
{
   /* other cases go here */
   case 2:
      SetRect( &TheRect, 0, 0, 400, 280 );
      FillRect( &TheRect, &white );
      SetRect( &TheRect, 200, 135, 200, 135 );
      count = 0;
      while ( count < 120 )
      {
         FillRect( &TheRect, &white );
         InsetRect( &TheRect, -1, -1 );
         count++;
      }
      break;
   /* other cases go here */
}
```

Remember, users of the older THINK C 6.0 should omit the "&" character from in front of the second parameter of all *FillRect* calls:

```
FillRect( &WhiteRect, white );    /* THINK C 6.0 */
FillRect( &WhiteRect, black );
```

THINK C 7.0 users, leave the "&" symbol in place:

```
FillRect( &WhiteRect, &white );   /* THINK C 7.0 */
FillRect( &WhiteRect, &black );
```

The Move Square Item

The third menu item, Move Square, works in a manner very similar to the growing square. First the window is cleared — just in case the big black rectangle is sitting in it. Next, a 50 by 50 pixel square is set up in the upper left corner of the window. Then a *while* loop runs 140 times. Let's take a look at what the *while* loop does.

In each pass through the loop the rectangle is drawn, and then offset. Careful — offset is different than inset. The Toolbox function *OffsetRect* doesn't change the size of a rectangle, it moves it. The amount the rectangle gets moved is specified in the last two parameters. A positive value for the second parameter moves the rectangle to the right, a negative value moves it to the left. A positive value for the third parameter moves the rectangle down, a negative value moves it up. My call to *OffsetRect* moves the rectangle right two pixels and down two pixels. Here's what the window will look like after a few passes through the loop:

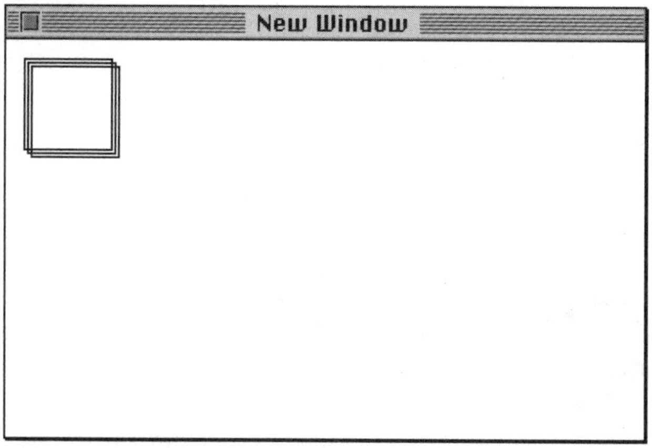

You can see from the above figure that the square will continue to move to the right and down until it goes off the bottom of the window. Here's the code that moves the square.

```
switch ( TheMenuItem )
{
   /* other cases go here */
   case 3:
      SetRect( &TheRect, 0, 0, 400, 280 );
      FillRect( &TheRect, &white );
      SetRect( &TheRect, 10, 10, 60, 60 );
      count = 0;
      while ( count < 140 )
      {
```

```
            FrameRect( &TheRect );
            OffsetRect( &TheRect, 2, 2 );
            count++;
      }
      break;
   /* other cases go here */
}
```

One final reminder:

```
FillRect( &WhiteRect, white );  /* THINK C 6.0 users do it this way  */
FillRect( &WhiteRect, &white ); /* THINK C 7.0 users do it like this */
```

The Quit Item

Here's another simple one — the Quit item. Selecting this fourth menu item simply sets variable *AllDone* to a value of 1. When the program reaches the top of the event loop, the *while* test will fail and the program ends.

```
switch ( TheMenuItem )
{
   /* other cases go here */
   case 4:
      AllDone = 1;
      break;
}
```

Compiling and Running the Animator Program

When you've typed in all the source code for the Animator program, select Save from the File menu. Then it's time to compile it. Choose Compile from the Source menu.

Remember, if the Compile option appears dim, open the source code file — Animator.c — by double-clicking on it in the project window. ■

If the error message window opens, correct the error and try again. If you can't figure out what the error message means, try referring to Appendix C. That appendix lists possible solutions for problems you might encounter while compiling a program.

When your source code compiles successfully, it's time to give it a test run. Select Run from the Project menu.

Selecting Run should start the Animator up. If you forgot to compile, or made a change to the source code since the last compile, the program won't run. Instead, a dialog box that says "Bring the project up to date?" opens. That's just the THINK C way of getting your permission to go ahead with the compile. Click the Update button to let THINK C go ahead and do its thing. ▪

Running the code without the resource file created, or with an incomplete resource file, will crash the Mac. You'll then have to restart your computer and restart THINK C. So don't forget to make, and properly name, that resource file. Without it, and the '*WIND*', '*MENU*', and '*MBAR*' resources it holds, the program can't run. ▪

If everything is okay the Animator will be off and running. Try each of the first three menu items a few times to verify that everything's working. When you're satisfied that the program works, select the fourth menu item, Quit.

Building the Application

Running the Animator was a good way to test it out, but that doesn't cause the THINK Project Manager to turn the code into a Macintosh application. To do that, select Build Application from the Project menu.

THINK C will open a dialog box that lets you name the program. I named the program Animator, but you won't hurt my feelings if you give your version a different name. Here's how the dialog box should look:

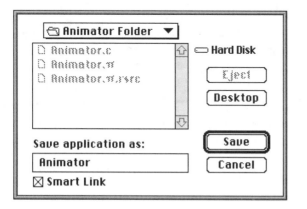

Click the Save button. After a second or two of clicking and clacking, your computer's hard drive will be back to its usual faint hum. The build is complete, and you'll now find that you have a brand new Animator application on your

Mac's desktop. Go ahead and click on the desktop, or quit the THINK Project Manager. When you do, you'll see that your Animator Folder looks like this:

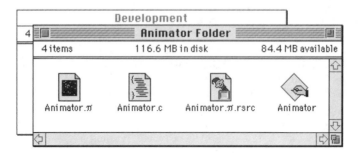

Congratulations! You've just created a Mac program with a window, menu, menu bar, and animation!

Where Do You Go from Here?

That depends.... Did you enjoy programming the Mac? If you did, make sure to read the rest of this book. The next section, The Part of Tens, lists several tips you'll want to follow in future programming endeavors. The appendices are also full of programming code and tips that will make your programs more interesting.

You've seen that programming is fraught with challenges — some of them quite aggravating. But it isn't without its rewards. The satisfaction of overcoming what at first appears to be an insurmountable problem can be a reward in itself. Now that you've gone to the effort of learning to program the Mac, what can you do with what you've learned? You could create a simple game for kids — one that displays faces by drawing shapes. Or, you could write a program that draws graphs and charts. Most important, you can use the knowledge gained in this book to move on to bigger and better things. You are no longer a bewildered novice programmer — you've got a solid foundation in some of the most basic Macintosh programming principles. From here on in, your programs can only get more interesting.

You learned how to draw text and simple graphics to a window. What about more elaborate pictures? You know about windows, but what about dialog boxes? They allow you to let the user make choices and enter numbers for your program to work with. These are just a couple of things to look forward to learning. How do you learn more? From other books, of course. Consider getting one or more of the *Inside Macintosh* books by Apple. Check the computer books section of your local bookstore for other books. Browse the shelves for

Macintosh programming books. Page through them to see what's inside. Also take note of the back cover of each book. Most programming books clearly state what programming level the reader is expected to be at in order to benefit from the book. If you see a book that claims to be for a Macintosh beginner or intermediate programmer — grab it!

Part VI
The Part of Tens

The 5th Wave   By Rich Tennant

IN A STROKE OF SELF RELIANCE, RAY EXTENDS THE POWER ON HIS LAPTOP BY TAPPING INTO THE BATTERY ON HIS SLEEPING NEIGHBORS HEARING AID.

In this part . . .

*J*ust what are the steps to creating a THINK C project? Once a project is created, which Toolbox functions should be used in the source code? And, finally, what are the common programming mistakes that can be — but often aren't — avoided? You'll find the answers to these three questions — in the form of lists — right here.

Each of the three chapters in this part contain short, concise, summaries of what to do — or not do — to create a Mac program. Each chapter has about ten steps, or items, in its list. Why not *exactly* ten — as the title of this part indicates? Sorry, things just don't always work out so evenly. So maybe I took a few liberties when I named the part. But really, now, would you rather it had a more accurate name, like *The Part of Sometimes More, Sometimes Less, But Always Very Close to Ten?*

Chapter 20

Ten Steps to Creating a Mac Program

C reating a new Mac program using THINK C *always* involves the same steps.That's good, because it allows me to create a step-by-step plan that you can follow for every Mac program you write.

Creating a Resource File

You use a resource editor like ResEdit to create a resource file for the program. Remember to give the resource file the same name that the project file will eventually get — then add .rsrc (a period and the letters "rsrc") to the end of the name.

Create a resource for each of the graphical elements your program will use. Then save the file and quit ResEdit. Remember, ResEdit is a resource *editor*. That means that if you forget to include a resource you can always use ResEdit to open the resource file and add more resources.

One last point — don't just leave the resource file hanging around any old place on your Mac's desktop. Create a new folder in the Development folder and keep the resource file there. You'll also want to place the other project-related files in the folder as you create them.

Creating a THINK Project File

The project file is the THINK Project Manager's way of keeping track of all the information about the program you're developing. You'll need a separate project file for each program you write.

When you run the THINK Project Manager you'll see a dialog box that gives you the opportunity to create a new project. Click the New button. In the next dialog box that appears you get to name the project. As you type in a name, make sure it matches the name of the resource file. That is, if your resource file is named MyProg.π.rsrc, name the project MyProg.π. Before clicking the Create button, make sure that the pop-up menu at the top of the dialog box shows that you're in the same folder in which your resource file resides.

Adding the MacTraps Library to the Project

Writing source code can be a tricky business. Fortunately, you have a little help. Much of the code you need for a Mac program is already written for you and is bundled into a library called MacTraps. You'll add this library of code to every Mac project you create.

Select Add Files from the Source menu. Then use the pop-up menu at the top of the dialog box to move into the Mac Libraries folder. You'll have to first move into the Think C 7.0 folder to find it. Or, if you're using THINK C 6.0, move into the Think 6.0 folder. Once there, click on the MacTraps name in the scrollable list, then click the Add button. Dismiss the dialog box by clicking on its Done button.

Creating a New Source Code File

You'll type your source code into a text file that's created in the THINK Project Manager. Select New from the File menu to open an untitled, empty window.

Saving the Source Code File

You can save your source code file at any time, but I suggest that you do so before you even type a line of code. Select Save As from the File menu. Type in a name that is appropriate for the program you're writing. This can be any name you want — but it must end with .c (a period and the letter "c"). Before clicking the Save button, use the pop-up menu at the top of the dialog box to work your way into the folder that holds your resource file and project file.

Adding the Source Code File to the Project

Creating a new source code file isn't enough to make the THINK Project Manager aware of its existence. You've got to add the new file to the project. Don't be concerned with the fact that you don't have any code typed in the new file. As you add source code, the THINK Project Manager will become aware of the changes. Select Add Files from the Source menu — just as you did when you added the MacTraps library. Click on the name of the source code file, then click the Add button. Finish off by clicking the Done button.

Writing the Source Code

Type away! Or, do what most programmers do. Select Open from the File menu and open an existing C source code file — one you created for a different program. Copy part or all of it, then paste it into your new file. Now use the old code as the basis for your new program. Make the necessary changes to turn the old code into new code.

Compiling the Source Code

When you feel satisfied that your source code looks complete, select Compile from the Source menu. Hopefully things will be uneventful. If that's the case, your code was successfully compiled. If a window opens up with an error message, things didn't go quite so smoothly. Take note of the error message and make the necessary corrections to your source code. If you can't figure out the message, try referring to Appendix C. There I list several errors and possible cures that get rid of the pesky messages. Once your corrections are made, try compiling again. Keep trying until you get it right!

Running the Code

When your code has successfully compiled it's time to test it out. Select Run from the Project menu. After just a couple of seconds your program will appear on the screen. Click on menus, move the window — try out all the features you added to the program. When through, quit the program. If you aren't entirely satisfied with the results, or one or more features don't work as you expected, it's time to look over your source code to figure out what went wrong. Make any changes that you want, then compile and run the program again.

Building an Application

Running a program from within the THINK Project Manager gives you a feel for what the program does. But it doesn't create a stand-alone program. To turn your code into a Macintosh application complete with an icon, select Build Application from the Project menu. When you quit the THINK Project Manager you'll see your brand-new program sitting right there in a folder on your desktop.

Chapter 21

Ten Toolbox Functions You Can't Live Without

- -

In This Chapter

▶ Initialization functions

▶ Displaying a window

▶ Activating a window

▶ Displaying a menu bar

▶ Getting event information

▶ Determining the location of a mouse click

▶ Window functions

▶ Menu functions

▶ Graphics functions

- -

*T*he Toolbox is Apple's name for the collection of over 2,000 functions that Mac programmers can use to get their programs to do all sorts of wonderful things. You've seen over two dozen functions scattered throughout this book, and there's still more listed in Appendix B. While you'll find many of the Toolbox functions interesting, there are several that are indispensable — those are the ones I've listed here.

The Toolbox Initialization Functions

The eight functions that are used to initialize the Toolbox are vital to any Mac program. Call them at the start of your program — right after you declare your variables. And call them in the order I've listed here:

```
InitGraf( &thePort );
InitFonts();
InitWindows();
```

```
InitMenus();
TEInit();
InitDialogs( 0L );
FlushEvents( everyEvent, 0 );
InitCursor();
```

Eight functions — that leaves just two more for my list of ten functions you can't live without. Hey, that's no fun! I didn't intend to kill the whole list on boring initialization stuff. So I hope you don't mind if I group all eight of these functions together and only count them as one.

Displaying a Window

Everything that happens in a Mac program happens in a window. So the function that displays a window is one of the most important of all Toolbox functions. Here's a typical call to the function that performs this task, along with the one variable declaration you need to make:

```
WindowPtr  TheWindow;

TheWindow = GetNewWindow( 128, 0L, (WindowPtr)-1L );
```

If your program calls *GetNewWindow,* make sure the resource file for the project has a '*WIND*' resource in it with an ID that matches the first parameter in the call to *GetNewWindow.*

GetNewWindow returns a *WindowPtr* to your program. You can use that *WindowPtr* in other Toolbox calls, including the one I'm about to cover...

Activating a Window

After creating and displaying a window you'll want to draw to it — text, graphics, or both. But before you start whipping out those fancy pictures, make sure to activate the new window with a call to *SetPort*:

```
SetPort( TheWindow );
```

SetPort tells the Mac which window it should draw in. That's always important — especially so if there's more than one window open. To help *SetPort* do its thing you pass it the *WindowPtr* of the window to make it active. Use the *WindowPtr* variable that was returned by the call to *GetNewWindow.*

Displaying a Menu Bar

You'll need to make one variable declaration and three Toolbox calls in order to display a menu bar:

```
Handle  MenuBarHandle;

MenuBarHandle = GetNewMBar( 128 );
SetMenuBar( MenuBarHandle );
DrawMenuBar();
```

Pass *GetNewMBar* the ID of the '*MBAR*' resource that's in the project's resource file. In return, *GetNewMBar* will give your program a *Handle*. That's something that the *SetMenuBar* function needs in order to gather up all the information about the menu bar and the menus in it. Finally, a call to *DrawMenuBar* displays the menu bar on the screen.

Oops, there I've gone and done it again! I'm counting a few functions as one so that I can cram as much important stuff as possible into this Part of Tens chapter. As a matter of fact, don't be surprised if I do this a few more times.

Capturing Events

Capturing events — sounds exciting, doesn't it? Well, it isn't really too thrilling, but it sure is easy — thanks to *WaitNextEvent*. This function looks for an event and, when it notices one, stores all the information about the event in an *EventRecord* variable:

```
EventRecord  TheEvent;

WaitNextEvent( everyEvent, &TheEvent, 0L, 0L );
```

You'll use the information housed in the *EventRecord* at several points in your program. One of those occasions is when the user clicks the mouse button.

Locating a Mouse Click

The user can click the mouse anywhere on the screen. It's up to your program to figure out where the cursor was at the time of the mouse click. Your program needs that information to determine how to respond to the click. To get that information call *FindWindow*:

```
EventRecord  TheEvent;
WindowPtr    aWindow;
short        ThePart

ThePart = FindWindow( TheEvent.where, &aWindow );
```

FindWindow uses information from the *EventRecord* variable, so you'll call the function after *WaitNextEvent*. When completed, *FindWindow* gives your program the screen or window location where the mouse click took place. It stores this information in variable *ThePart*. If the mouse click occurred in a window, *FindWindow* will also provide your program with a *WindowPtr* to the window.

Working with Windows

If *FindWindow* tells your program that a mouse click occurred in the drag bar of a window you should respond by calling *DragWindow*. The *DragWindow* function follows the cursor as the user moves the mouse, and moves the window accordingly.

```
WindowPtr      aWindow;
EventRecord    TheEvent;

DragWindow( aWindow, TheEvent.where, &screenBits.bounds );
```

The first parameter of *DragWindow* tells the Toolbox which window to drag. This variable gets its value from the call to *FindWindow* that was made earlier. The second parameter is the location where the mouse was first clicked. The last parameter tells *DragWindow* to allow the window to be dragged anywhere on the screen.

If *FindWindow* tells your program that a click of the mouse was made in the close box of a window you should call *DisposeWindow* to remove the window. *FindWindow* will notify your program which window needs closing by assigning a value to the *WindowPtr* variable *aWindow*.

```
WindowPtr  aWindow;

DisposeWindow( aWindow );
```

Managing Menus

Displaying a menu is one thing, making it usable is another. When the user clicks the mouse in the menu bar, call *MenuSelect* to take care of the work of dropping menus as the user moves the mouse over them. When the user makes a menu selection, *MenuSelect* is smart enough to know which menu item was selected, and from which menu. It stores this information in variable *MenuChoice*.

```
short  MenuChoice;
MenuChoice = MenuSelect( TheEvent.where );
```

Call the Toolbox functions *HiWord* and *LoWord* to extract the number of the menu and the number of the menu item from *MenuChoice*.

```
TheMenu = HiWord( MenuChoice );
TheMenuItem = LoWord( MenuChoice );
```

The call you made to *MenuSelect* highlighted a menu name in the menu bar. After you've taken care of business, call *HiliteMenu* to return the menu name to it's original state — black text on a white background.

```
HiliteMenu(0);
```

Drawing Text

On a Macintosh, text is said to be drawn, not written. Use the Toolbox function *DrawString* to draw a word or a sentence to a window. Enclose the text in double quotes, and precede the first word of text with the backslash character, "\", and the letter "p".

```
DrawString( "\pDrawing text is easy!" );
```

Where will the text get drawn? I know, wiseguy — in the window. More specifically then, where in the window? That depends on the parameters you pass to the function *MoveTo*. Tell *MoveTo* how many pixels to move in from the left edge of a window and how many pixels to move down from the top. *Then* call *DrawString*:

```
MoveTo( 20, 50 );
DrawString( "\pDrawing text is easy!" );
```

Drawing Shapes

You can use the Toolbox function *FrameRect* to frame a rectangle, or *FillRect* to fill in a rectangle with a pattern. But first tell the Toolbox where the rectangle should go, and how big it should be. Use a call to *SetRect* for this purpose:

```
Rect  TheRect;

SetRect( &TheRect, 0, 0, 400, 280 );
```

Don't mix up the parameters of *SetRect*. Try think of them like this:

```
SetRect( &TheRect, left, top, right, bottom );
```

After setting up the rectangle, call *FrameRect* to draw a black frame around it:

```
FrameRect( &TheRect );
```

If you'd rather fill the rectangle, call *FillRect*. The second parameter tells the Toolbox what pattern to fill the rectangle with. Here's a call that fills the rectangle with a light gray pattern:

```
FillRect( &TheRect, ltGray );    /*Think C 6.0*/

FillRect( &TheRect, &ltGray );   /*Think C 7.0*/
```

You can also use *black*, *white*, *gray*, or *dkGray* to achieve other fill effects.

Chapter 22

The Ten Most Common Mac Programming Mistakes

*I*n programming, making mistakes is commonplace. Everyone who writes programs makes them. While there are easily more than 10 different mistakes a programmer can make, there are about 10 or so slip-ups that just about everyone new to programming the Mac makes.

Forgetting About the Resource File

Don't forget to make a resource file! In your excitement to start writing code, you may jump right in and forget all about resources. Some Toolbox function calls look for a resource. The *GetNewWindow* function is an example:

```
TheWindow = GetNewWindow( 128, 0L, (WindowPtr)-1L );
```

What does the number 128 represent? The ID of a '*WIND*' resource. What happens if you run a program with this *GetNewWindow* line in it and that resource can't be found? You won't get a friendly little reminder to the fact that you forgot to make a resource. Instead, the screen of your Mac will freeze up and an alert like this one will appear:

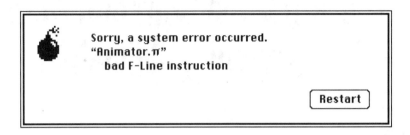

```
   Sorry, a system error occurred.
   "Animator.π"
      bad F-Line instruction

                              [ Restart ]
```

I'm not exactly sure what a "bad F-Line instruction" is, but judging from the fact that there's a little bomb in the corner of the alert, and the Mac freezes up, I can only assume it's not good. What's particularly troubling though is that the error message gives you no clue that the problem is resource-related. You could run the program over and over, bombing each time, and never realize what's going on.

There's actually a few things that can give you an alert like the one pictured above:

- ✔ No resource file.
- ✔ A resource file, but misnamed.
- ✔ A resource file, but in the wrong folder.
- ✔ A resource file, but a resource missing from that file.

The first one is a missing resource file. The next two both fool the THINK Project Manager into thinking there's no resource file — even though you might have made one. The last source of trouble comes when you create and properly name a resource file, but forget to put a needed resource in that file.

There's one other error that involves the resource file. When you create a resource file, you use ResEdit. When you're done, you should save the file and quit ResEdit before using THINK C. Why? It's possible to run THINK C while your resource file is still open in ResEdit. If the resource file is open when you try to Run a project, your Mac will freeze up and you'll have to restart it.

Not Pairing Braces

Every opening brace must have a corresponding closing brace. For example, the code under a loop begins with a brace, so it must end with one as well:

```
while ( count < 10 )
{
   DrawString("\pTest");
   count++;
}
```

What happens if you forget a brace? The THINK C compiler will respond with an error message about an "unexpected end-of-file." The missing brace confuses the compiler, and it can't tell exactly where the code in your source code file ends.

Adding an Extra Semicolon

In C, a semicolon ends just about every line. So when you're typing code it's easy to start sticking semicolons everywhere. That can lead to problems — because the first line of a branch or loop *doesn't* end with a semicolon. Let me put a little emphasis on that:

  ✔ The first line of a branch statement doesn't end with a semicolon.

  ✔ The first line of a loop statement doesn't end with a semicolon.

This is correct:

```
while ( count < 100 )
```

This isn't:

```
while ( count < 100 );
```

Look closely at the above two lines of code. The second *while* statement ends with a semicolon, and that's wrong. In C, declarations, assignments, and Toolbox calls all end with a semicolon:

```
short  dogs;          /*  Declaration   */
dogs = 5;             /*  Assignment    */
MoveTo( 30, 50 );     /*  Toolbox call  */
```

But branches and loops *don't*:

```
while ( count < 100 )  /*  No semicolon  */
switch ( ThePart )     /*  No semicolon  */
```

Adding a semicolon to the end of the first line of a loop or branch won't give you an error message — but it can lead to real confusion. Your code will run, but the results won't be as expected. Adding a semicolon to the first line of a loop will cause the lines below the loop to run only once — regardless of how many times you hoped they would run. For a branch that inadvertently ends with a semicolon, the lines beneath will always run — even if you don't want them to.

Using Incorrect Case

What's wrong with the following declaration?

```
windowPtr  TheWindow;
```

Here's a hint — C is case-sensitive. That means that the proper use of upper-case and lowercase letters is very important. The C data type for a pointer to a window is a *WindowPtr*, not a *windowPtr*. That first letter makes a *big* difference. If you make a mistake of this type the THINK C compiler will display an error message that says a syntax error occurred. A syntax error is basically a typo. That's not real descriptive of what you did wrong. Fortunately the compiler will also tell you at what line number the error occurred. Go to that line and examine the code closely for a spelling error or mistake in capitalization.

Forgetting the "\p" in DrawString

The *DrawString* function is a very handy and easy-to-use Toolbox function — but it does take a little getting used to. There are several mistakes you can make when using it, and most will result in an error message that says something like "argument to function 'DrawString' does not match prototype." Before I show the wrong ways to use DrawString, here's a correct usage for comparison:

```
DrawString( "\pHello, World!" );  /* CORRECT!  */
```

The number one mistake in using *DrawString* comes when a programmer forgets to include \p before the text, like this:

```
DrawString( "Hello, World!" );    /* WRONG! Forgot the \p       */
```

Another common mistake is to forget the quotations before and after the text:

```
DrawString( \pHello, World! );    /* WRONG! Forgot the quotes    */
```

And while you might remember to use quotes, you could mistakenly use the wrong type of quote marks. *DrawString* requires double quotes, not single:

```
DrawString( '\pHello, World!' );  /* WRONG! Used the wrong quotes */
```

Finally, be careful which slash you use. The backslash (\) is the correct one. Here's a look at the incorrect slash being used:

```
DrawString( "/pHello, World!" );  /* WRONG! Used the wrong slash  */
```

Here's a summary of those common *DrawString* mistakes:

```
DrawString( "Hello, World!" );     /* WRONG! Forgot the \p        */
DrawString( \pHello, World! );      /* WRONG! Forgot the quotes    */
DrawString( '\pHello, World!' );    /* WRONG! Used the wrong quotes */
DrawString( "/pHello, World!" );    /* WRONG! Used the wrong slash  */
```

Forgetting the "&" with a Parameter

You'll notice that in many Toolbox calls one of the parameters requires that you include the "&" character before it. I never liked the awkward name of this character — the ampersand — and after working with C I know why. The ampersand can be the cause of a lot of programming headaches. Here's a typical Toolbox call that requires its use:

```
SetRect( &TheRect, 0, 0, 400, 280 );
```

If you try to call *SetRect* without using the ampersand before *TheRect*, you'll get an error message. This message will be much like the one you get when you incorrectly use *DrawString* — something about an argument not matching the prototype. Because many Toolbox functions have parameters that don't require the ampersand, forgetting to include it when required is an easy mistake to make.

There's no set rule I can give you as to when a parameter requires the ampersand. You'll have to make sure you match your source code with that in this book. The good news is that you don't have to page through the entire book to find an example of a call to each function. Before you use a function you can refer to Appendix B. There I list all of the functions used in this book — and a few others. I also give an example call to each, so you can see what the parameters should be. For now, here's a look at the functions I've used in this book that require an ampersand before one or more of the parameters:

- ✔ *InitGraf*
- ✔ *WaitNextEvent*
- ✔ *DragWindow*
- ✔ *FindWindow*
- ✔ *SetRect*
- ✔ *FillRect*
- ✔ *InsetRect*
- ✔ *OffsetRect*

Besides the problem of forgetting to add an "&" before certain parameters, there's the confusion brought on by the different versions of the THINK C compiler. For "fill" routines like *FillRect*, the second parameter doesn't have an "&" in version 6.0, but does in version 7.0. Here's how *FillRect* is used in THINK C 6.0:

```
FillRect( &TheRect, white );    /*  THINK C 6.0  */
```

Now, here's how *FillRect* is used in THINK C 7.0:

```
FillRect( &TheRect, &white );   /*  THINK C 7.0  */
```

Forgetting to Increment a Loop Counter

How many times will the following loop run? Three times? Four times?

```
count = 0;
while ( count < 4 )
{
    DrawString( "\pHello!" );
}
```

How many times? That depends on when you turn your computer off — 'cause that's the only thing that will stop this loop from running! Nowhere in the loop does variable *count* ever get incremented. That means that *count* will always have a value of 0, and 0 is always less than 4. That's called an infinite loop. I'll rewrite the loop — this time with *count* properly incremented:

```
count = 0;
while ( count < 4 )
{
    DrawString( "\pHello!" );
    count++;
}
```

Forgetting to Give a Variable an Initial Value

When you declare a variable, it doesn't have a value. Actually, it might have a value, but you can't be sure of what that value is:

```
short  AllDone;    /* Variable AllDone = ?? */
```

Only after you use a variable in an assignment statement can you be sure of its value:

```
AllDone = 0;       /* Variable AllDone has a value of zero */
```

Using a variable in a branch statement or loop statement before giving it a value can lead to unexpected results. Let's look at a little bit of the code from my Animator program. This code appears right at the start of the program's event loop:

```
AllDone = 0;
while ( AllDone < 1 )
{
    WaitNextEvent( everyEvent, &TheEvent, 0L, 0L );
    /* rest of program here */
```

What would happen if I omitted the line that assigns *AllDone* a value of 0? Variable *AllDone* could then easily have a value *other* than 0. If that's the case, what will happen when the program reaches the next line of code — the *while* statement? *AllDone* might not be less than 1, the loop won't run, and the Animator program will end. And that's not good.

Forgetting a break in a switch Statement

A *switch* statement places code in groups, and lets your program select which group to run. Each group of code starts with a *case* label and ends with a *break* statement. Here's an example:

```
switch ( BooksWritten )
{
    case 1:
        DrawString("\pYour first book!");
        break;
    case 2:
        DrawString("\pYour second book!");
        break;
}
```

If *BooksWritten* has a value of 1, the code under the first *case* label will run. If *BooksWritten* has a value of 2, the code under the second *case* label runs. Now, look at the same example without a *break* statement after the code under the first *case* label:

```
switch ( BooksWritten )
{
    case 1:
        DrawString("\pYour first book!");   /* forgot a break */
    case 2:
        DrawString("\pYour second book!");
        break;
}
```

Now what happens if *BooksWritten* has a value of 1? The code under both *case* labels will run! The *break* statement is the signal to the *switch* to stop running. Without a *break*, the determined *switch* just plods on to the next line of code — the *case* 2 label, and then the code under it.

Part VII
Appendices

The 5th Wave
By Rich Tennant

"YEAH, I USED TO WORK ON REFRIGERATORS, WASHING MACHINES, STUFF LIKE THAT- HOW'D YOU GUESS?"

In This Part . . .

*J*ust when you think you've got this C stuff under control, you realize you don't remember how to write an if-else branch. Or you forgot just what it is that goes between the parentheses that follow a call to the Toolbox function GetNewMBar. Appendix A is a reference to the C language, so it will quickly answer questions like the second. Don't you just hate it when you try to compile a program using THINK C, and that error message window pops open at the bottom of the screen? What, it hasn't happened to you? Keep programming – it will! When it does, refer to Appendix C for solutions to your compiling dilemmas. Finally, if you come across an odd-looking word that has something to do with Mac programming – and you can't remember just where you first saw it – thumb through Appendix D, the glossary.

Appendix A
C Language Reference

- -

*E*ntire books have been written on the C language — so how did I manage to cover it all in just a few pages of an appendix? By not covering it all, of course. But I do summarize all of the features you've been exposed to in this book, plus a few additional choice tidbits of C not covered previously.

Variables

A variable holds a value. What kind of value? That depends on the type of the variable. Variable types are covered in detail a little later in this appendix.

Declaring Variables

A variable must be declared so that the compiler becomes aware of it. The format of a variable declaration is always the same — regardless of the type of variable. First list the data type, then the variable name. Follow that with a semi-colon. Here's an example that declares a variable named *tickets* to be of the *short* data type:

```
short  tickets;
```

Variable Names

Give your variables names that are descriptive of the type of information they will hold. Almost any name will work, but you do have to keep a couple of restrictions in mind:

- ✔ Use only letters, digits, and the underscore character in a variable name.
- ✔ The first character of the name must be a letter or underscore — not a digit.

The following are examples of valid variable names:

```
testScore
TestScore
test_score
count1
```

The variables in this next list are invalid names:

```
1count         /* Can't start a variable name with a digit  */
$money         /* Can't use symbols such as the $ character */
money$         /* Can't use symbols such as the $ character */
GrandTotal!    /* Can't use symbols such as the ! character */
```

Assigning a Variable a Value

When you declare a variable, it has no value. Well, it might have some random value — but probably not the value you want it to have. To give a variable a value, first specify the variable you're working with. Follow that name with the equal sign, then the value you want to assign. End it all with a semicolon. Here I declare a *short* variable named *Total*, then give it a value of 25:

```
short  Total;
Total = 25;
```

Data Types

When you declare a variable you state the type of data that variable will hold, along with the name of the variable.

Number Types

If you want a variable to hold a whole number, you have three options. The *int* data type holds numbers as high in value as 32,767. So does the *short* data type. Though the *int* and the *short* data types are just about one and the same, I recommend you use the *short* type. In the Macintosh world, the *short* data type is becoming much more popular than the *int* data type. I'm not sure why the *short* is so trendy, but I want to be hip — so I use it.

For numbers larger than 32,767, use the *long* data type — it holds whole numbers as large as 2 billion.

If the number you want to use is greater than 2 billion, or it contains a decimal point, use the *float* data type. Some people call this type of number a real number, but C requires that you use the word *float*.

Here's an example of a declaration and assignment of each of the four data types mentioned in this section:

```
int    Students;
short  Teachers;
long   population;
float  BigPopulation;

Students = 44;
Teachers = 2;
population = 285500;
BigPopulation = 5000600300.0;
```

Window Types

Variables don't always hold numbers — so some data types hold other information. The *WindowPtr* data type is an example. If you call a Toolbox function that works with a window, you have to let the Toolbox know which window you're referring to. When a window is created, your program gets something called a pointer to the window — a *WindowPtr*. Think of this *WindowPtr* as a reference to one particular window.

Here's the declaration of a window pointer variable, and its use in two Toolbox functions:

```
WindowPtr  TheWindow;

TheWindow = GetNewWindow( 128, 0L, (WindowPtr)-1L );
SetPort( TheWindow );
```

Menu Types

When you display a menu bar in your program, you have to help the Toolbox out by providing it with a *Handle* to the menu bar. The *Handle* has many purposes, but in this book you've only seen it used with the menu bar. The *Handle* helps the Toolbox "get a handle" on the information that describes the menu bar. Here's how I used the *Handle* data type in this book:

```
Handle  MenuBarHandle;

MenuBarHandle = GetNewMBar( 128 );
```

Operators

A surgeon who operates on you makes changes inside you. A computer program that operates on variables makes changes inside them, too. In C, the symbols that are used to perform different mathematical and comparative operations are called operators.

Math Operators

C has a symbol, or operator, for each of the four major mathematical operations: addition, subtraction, multiplication, and division. Intuitively enough, the plus sign is used for addition and the minus sign is used for subtraction. For multiplication, place an asterisk between two variables or numbers. For division, use the slash symbol. Here are several examples:

```
short   score1;
short   score2;
short   total;

score1 = 30;
score2 = 10;

total = score1 + score2;   /* total = 30 plus 10        =  40   */
total = score1 - score2;   /* total = 30 minus 10       =  20   */
total = score1 * score2;   /* total = 30 times 10       = 300   */
total = score1 / score2;   /* total = 30 divided by 10 =   3   */
```

You can use operators on any combination of variables and/or numbers, as shown in these examples:

```
short   score1;
short   score2;
short   total;

score1 = 25;
score2 = 5;

total = score1 + score2 + 10;   /* total = 25 + 5 + 10    =  40  */
total = score1 - score2 + 10;   /* total = 25 - 5 + 10    =  30  */
total = score1 / 5;             /* total = 25 / 5         =   5  */
total = 50 + (score1 * score2); /* total = 50 + (25 * 5) = 175  */
```

I've thrown a new twist into that last example — a pair of parentheses. If you have more than one operation on one line of code, you can tell the computer which operation to perform first by setting it off in parentheses. In the last example above, variable *score1* will be multiplied by variable *score2* first. Then 50 will be added to that result.

In programming, the situation often arises where you'll want to increment the value of a variable by one. The increment operator — two plus signs in a row — does that. Here a variable named *index* is first given a value of 5, then incremented to 6:

```
short index;

index = 5;    /* index now equals 5  */
index++;      /* index now equals 6  */
```

Adding one to the value of a variable is called *incrementing* the variable. Subtracting one from a variable is called *decrementing* the variable. The C language provides a means to easily do that. Use the decrement operator — two minus signs in a row. Here's an example:

```
short index;

index = 5;    /* index now equals 5  */
index--;      /* index now equals 4  */
```

Comparative Operators

Programmers often test the value of a variable by comparing it to the value of another variable or to a number. Tests like this are most often done to determine if a loop should run another time. To make this test use one of the comparative operators. The less-than operator checks to see if the value to the left of it is less than the value to the right — as in this example:

```
while ( count < 5 )    /* Is count less than 5 ?    */
```

The greater-than operator is used to see if the value to the left of it is greater than the value to the right:

```
while ( count > 0 )    /* Is count greater than 0 ?  */
```

Assignment Operator

Every time you assign a variable a value you're using an operator — the assignment operator. That's what C calls the equal sign. In this example variable *NumberOfWins* is given a value of 7 through the use of the assignment operator:

```
short   NumberOfWins;

NumberOfWins = 7;
```

Looping Statements

By setting up a loop you can make any section of source code run more than once. And by changing a single number in the loop you can have that section of code run two, ten, or 10,000 times. Now that's power!

The while Statement

A *while* loop, or *while* statement, begins with the word *while* followed by a test in parentheses. The test determines how many times the code under the *while* will run. The test compares a variable with a value. The test is performed after each running of the code beneath the *while*. When the test condition is not met, the test is said to have failed, and the code under the *while* will no longer run. The following *while* loop writes the word "Warning!" three times:

```
short   count;

count = 0;

while ( count < 3 )
{
    DrawString( "\pWarning!" );
    count++;
}
```

Make sure you don't place a semicolon at the end of the line of code that contains the word *while*. ■

Here's a *while* loop that adds the numbers one through five together. Examine the code carefully until you feel confident that the loop will add the numbers 1, 2, 3, 4, and 5 together to get a total of 15:

```
short   total;
short   count;

total = 0;
count = 1;

while ( count < 6 )
{
    total = total + count;   /* total equals its own value, plus count */
    count++;
}
```

Branching Statements

A loop runs the same code more than once. A branch runs code only once — but it allows the program to select the code from more than one grouping.

The switch Statement

A *switch* branching statement begins with the word "switch" followed by a variable between parentheses. Underneath the *switch* are groups of code. Each group begins with the word *case* and ends with the word *break*. The *switch* statement works by making a comparison between the value of the variable between the parentheses on the *switch* line and each of the values associated with the *case* labels. Here's an example that gives a response based on the number of computers the user has:

```
short   NumberOfComputers;

switch ( NumberOfComputers )
{
   case 0:
      DrawString( "\pUsing someone else's, eh?" );
      break;
   case 1:
      DrawString( "\pSometimes one is one too many!" );
      break;
   case 2:
      DrawString( "\pLove chaos, huh?" );
      break;
}
```

Don't inadvertently add a semicolon to the end of the line of code that contains the word *switch*. ■

In many situations you'll be interested in just a few of many possible numbers, but you'll still want to acknowledge the other possibilities. C provides a "catch-all" provision you can add to the *switch* branch — the *default* statement. After you've added all the *case* labels you need, add the word "default." Then add the code you want to run in the instances when none of the *cases* is met. In the example below, my code will let the user know that he or she won if their number is 7 or 11. Any number other than those two numbers will result in the message "Sorry, try again!" being written.

```
short   DiceTotal;

switch ( DiceTotal )
{
   case 7:
      DrawString( "\p7 is a winner!" );
      break;
   case 11:
      DrawString( "\p11 is a winner!" );
      break;
   default:
      DrawString( "\pSorry, try again!" );
      break;
}
```

The if Statement

The *switch* branch is used when you want your program to be able to choose from two or more possibilities. For situations where you only want your program to run a section of code or not run it, use the *if* branch instead. Here's an example:

```
short  Dollars;
if ( Dollars < 10 )
{
   MoveTo( 30, 50 );
   DrawString( "\pSorry, you need at least $10 to play bingo." );
}
```

The *if* branch uses a test condition to determine if the code under the *if* should run or not run. In the above example the *if* examines the value of the variable *Dollars* to see if it is less than 10. If it is, then the two lines of code between the braces will run. If *Dollars* isn't less than 10, the lines will be skipped — no message will be written.

Notice that there is no semicolon at the end of the line that includes the word *if*. ■

Toolbox Functions

See Appendix B!

Appendix B

Toolbox Reference

· ·

*A*fter typing in all the programs listed in this book, you'll be pretty proficient at using Toolbox functions. But there will still be times when you can't remember the exact spelling of one, or how many parameters get passed to it. Look here for information of this type.

This appendix lists all the Toolbox functions you've encountered in this book. While I didn't cover all of the Toolbox functions — after all, there are over two *thousand* — I did throw in a few bonus ones not mentioned previously. And free of charge, yet!

Initialization

When a program runs, the Toolbox needs a little information about it. This is called Toolbox initialization. Fortunately, the Toolbox is capable of initializing itself. Every program you write should include these eight Toolbox initialization calls:

InitGraf
InitFonts
InitWindows
InitMenus
TEInit
InitDialogs
FlushEvents
InitCursor

By calling these eight functions, in the above order, the Toolbox will be initialized. Call the functions just after declaring your program's variables. The parameters for each call are listed below.

```
InitGraf( &thePort );
InitFonts();
InitWindows();
InitMenus();
TEInit();
InitDialogs( 0L );
FlushEvents( everyEvent, 0 );
InitCursor();
```

Events

An action such as a mouse click is called an event. The Macintosh stores information about events as they occur. The Toolbox can help you get information about events so that your program can respond appropriately to them.

Getting Event Information

WaitNextEvent Your program can get information for the most recent event by calling *WaitNextEvent*. The first parameter to *WaitNextEvent* tells your program to keep a watch for every type of event. Always use *everyEvent*. The second parameter is an *EventRecord* variable that holds the information about the event. This parameter *must* be preceded by an ampersand character. The third and fourth parameters are used when other programs are running concurrently with yours and for special cursor-handling work. Always set them to 0L. That is, the number zero followed by an uppercase letter "L".

```
EventRecord  TheEvent;

WaitNextEvent( everyEvent, &TheEvent, 0L, 0L );
```

Windows

Macintosh means windows. Not much happens on the screen without at least one window present. The Toolbox does much of the work of displaying, moving, and closing windows.

Opening and Displaying a Window

GetNewWindow To open and display a new window, call *GetNewWindow*. The traits of the window — its type, size, and initial screen location — are found in a 'WIND' resource. The first parameter to *GetNewWindow* is the resource ID of this 'WIND' resource. The second and third parameters are used for window memory storage and positioning — always use the two values shown in the next example.

After opening the window, *GetNewWindow* returns a *WindowPtr* to your program. This *WindowPtr* variable can then be used in future Toolbox calls such as *SetPort* and *DisposeWindow*.

```
WindowPtr  TheWindow;

TheWindow = GetNewWindow( 128, 0L, (WindowPtr)-1L );
```

Closing a Window

DisposeWindow To remove a window from the screen, call *DisposeWindow*. To let the Toolbox know which window to close, pass the *WindowPtr* variable that was returned to your program by *GetNewWindow*.

```
WindowPtr  TheWindow;

TheWindow = GetNewWindow( 128, 0L, (WindowPtr)-1L ); /* Open... */
DisposeWindow( TheWindow );                          /* ...close */
```

Moving a Window

DragWindow Call *DragWindow* when your program receives a *mouseDown* event in a window's drag bar. *DragWindow* will do all of the work of moving the window about the screen as the user drags the mouse. The first parameter to *DragWindow* is a *WindowPtr* to the window to drag. Use a call to *FindWindow* to get this value. The second parameter is the screen coordinates where the mouse click took place. The third parameter tells the Toolbox what part of the screen it can use to drag the window. Passing a value of *&screenBits.bounds* tells the Toolbox to use the entire screen. Don't forget to precede this third parameter with an ampersand.

```
EventRecord  TheEvent;
WindowPtr    aWindow;

DragWindow( aWindow, TheEvent.where, &screenBits.bounds );
```

Responding to the Mouse Button

When the user clicks the mouse button, your program will want to know where. Did the user have the cursor positioned over a window? Over the menu bar? This information is vital if you want your program to respond in an appropriate and logical manner. The Toolbox gives you this information in one easy-to-use function call.

Determining What Was Clicked On

FindWindow When a *mouseDown* event happens, respond by calling *FindWindow* to determine in what part of the screen or window the mouse click occurred. The first parameter to *FindWindow* holds the screen coordinates where the mouse button was pressed. The second parameter is a pointer to the window that was clicked in — if one was. The second parameter is not the pointer that was returned by the Toolbox in a call to *GetNewWindow*. Instead, it is a different *WindowPtr* variable created just for this purpose. It gets its value from *FindWindow*. This second parameter *must* be preceded by an ampersand character.

After the call to *FindWindow* is complete, variable *ThePart* will hold a value that represents the part of the screen or window that was clicked on.

```
EventRecord   TheEvent;
WindowPtr     aWindow;
short         ThePart;

ThePart = FindWindow( TheEvent.where, &aWindow );
```

Menus

What's a Mac program without at least one menu? The Toolbox will help you set up a menu bar and handle a user's menu selection.

Displaying Menus and the Menu Bar

GetNewMBar To let your program know which '*MBAR*' resource it should use as the basis for a menu bar, call *GetNewMBar*. Pass this function the resource ID of the '*MBAR*' that's in your program's resource file. In return, *GetNewMBar* will provide your program with a *Handle* that you'll use in a call to *SetMenuBar*.

```
Handle  MenuBarHandle;

MenuBarHandle = GetNewMBar( 128 );
```

SetMenuBar To help your program set up the menu bar with the appropriate menus, call *SetMenuBar*. Pass the *Handle* obtained from the preceding call to *GetNewMBar* as the only parameter.

```
Handle  MenuBarHandle;

SetMenuBar( MenuBarHandle );
```

DrawMenuBar Neither *GetNewMBar* or *SetMenuBar* actually display the menu bar on the screen. To do this, call *DrawMenuBar*. This function requires no parameters — but you still need to include a pair of parentheses after the function name.

```
DrawMenuBar();
```

Responding to a Mouse Click in the Menu Bar

MenuSelect In response to a click in the menu bar, call *MenuSelect*. This function does the work of tracking the mouse as the user moves it about the menu bar. *MenuSelect* will display and hide menus as the user moves over their names in the menu bar. The only parameter *MenuSelect* requires is the screen coordinates where the mouse button was first pressed in the menu bar. When the user makes a menu selection, *MenuSelect* returns information about the selected item in the *long* variable *MenuChoice*. Use the Toolbox functions *HiWord* and *LoWord* to extract information from this variable.

```
EventRecord   TheEvent;
long          MenuChoice;

MenuChoice = MenuSelect( TheEvent.where );
```

HiliteMenu When a menu selection is made *MenuSelect* highlights the name of the menu in the menu bar. When your program has finished handling the menu item, call *HiliteMenu* to return the menu name to its original state of black text on a white background.

```
HiliteMenu(0)
```

Determining Which Menu Item Was Selected

HiWord *MenuSelect* returns a number that represents both the menu and the menu item. This information is stored in the *long* variable *MenuChoice*. To extract just the number of the menu from this variable, call *HiWord*. Pass *MenuChoice* as the only parameter. When the function is complete, *HiWord* returns the resource ID of the '*MENU*' resource from which the menu selection was made.

```
long  MenuChoice;
short TheMenu;

TheMenu = HiWord( MenuChoice );
```

LoWord As mentioned in the description of *HiWord*, *MenuSelect* returns a number that represents both the menu and the menu item. To extract just the number of the menu item from this variable, call *LoWord*. Pass *MenuChoice* as the sole parameter. When the function is complete, *LoWord* returns a number that tells your program which menu item was selected. The first menu item is number 1, the second item is number 2, and so forth.

```
long  MenuChoice;
short TheMenuItem;

TheMenuItem = LoWord( MenuChoice );
```

Drawing with QuickDraw

Programming is like life — there are chores that have to be taken care of, but there's also time for fun. Drawing is the fun part. QuickDraw is the name of the set of Toolbox functions that performs text, line, and shape drawing in the windows of your programs.

Ports

SetPort Every window has a port, and all drawing takes place in the port. After using the Toolbox function *GetNewWindow* to create and display a window, make its port the current, or active, port. Make a call to *SetPort* to do this. Pass *SetPort* one parameter — the *WindowPtr* of the window to draw to.

```
WindowPtr  TheWindow;

TheWindow = GetNewWindow( 128, 0L, (WindowPtr)-1L );
SetPort( TheWindow );
```

Moving to a Location

MoveTo The *MoveTo* function moves, without drawing, to a location in a window. The first parameter is the pixel distance in from the left of the window, the second parameter is the pixel distance down from the top of the window.

```
MoveTo( 20, 50 );        /* Move 20 pixels in, 50 pixels down */
DrawString( "\pText" );  /* Draw some text                    */
```

Line Thickness

PenSize Here's a bonus function not mentioned elsewhere in the book! Normally, all lines are drawn with a thickness of one pixel. You can make fatter lines by first calling *PenSize*. Pass *PenSize* the pixel width and pixel height in which all subsequent lines should be drawn.

```
PenSize( 3, 3 );    /* Following line will be 3 pixels thick */
Line( 50, 100 );
PenSize( 1, 1 );    /* Return to normal thickness of 1 pixel */
```

Line Drawing

Line Unsurprisingly, the *Line* function draws a line. The first parameter tells how many pixels to the right the line should go, and the second parameter tells how many pixels down the line should go. The starting point of the line is determined by a call to *MoveTo*.

```
MoveTo( 20, 50 );   /* Move 20 pixels in, 50 pixels down     */
Line( 200, 10 );    /* Draw a line 200 pixels across, 10 down */
```

Shape Drawing

SetRect Before a rectangle can be drawn, its boundaries must be established. *SetRect* sets up the coordinates of the *Rect* variable named as the first parameter. *SetRect* does not draw a rectangle — use *FrameRect* or *FillRect* to do that. The first parameter to *SetRect must* be preceded by an ampersand character. The last four parameters are the pixel coordinates of the rectangle. The ordering of the last parameters is the left, top, right, and bottom of the rectangle.

```
Rect   TheRect;

SetRect( &TheRect, 20, 40, 300, 150 );
FrameRect( &TheRect );
MoveTo( 20, 50 );   /* Move 20 pixels in, 50 pixels down     */
```

FrameRect After setting the boundaries of a rectangle using *SetRect*, that same same rectangle can now be framed using a call to *FrameRect*. Pass *FrameRect* a *Rect* variable as the only parameter. The parameter *must* be preceded by an ampersand character.

```
Rect   TheRect;

SetRect( &TheRect, 10, 10, 100, 100 );
FrameRect( &TheRect );
```

FillRect After setting the boundaries of a rectangle using *SetRect*, that same rectangle can now be filled with a pattern using a call to *FillRect*. Pass *FillRect* a *Rect* variable as the first parameter. The first parameter *must* be preceded by an ampersand character. The second parameter to *FillRect* is the pattern that the Toolbox will use to fill in the rectangle. The available patterns are:

```
white, ltGray, gray, dkGray, black
```

Patterns must use capitalization as shown above.

```
Rect   TheRect;

SetRect( &TheRect, 10, 10, 100, 100 );
```

continued

```
FillRect( &TheRect, &white );     /* white rectangle       */
FillRect( &TheRect, &ltGray );    /* light gray rectangle */
FillRect( &TheRect, &gray );      /* gray rectangle        */
FillRect( &TheRect, &dkGray );    /* dark gray rectangle  */
FillRect( &TheRect, &black );     /* black rectangle       */
```

THINK C 7.0 users write *FillRect* using a "&" symbol before the fill shade:

```
FillRect( &WhiteRect, &white );   /* THINK C 7.0 */
```

Users of THINK C 6.0 don't:

```
FillRect( &WhiteRect, white );    /* THINK C 6.0 */
```

FrameOval You had to have known that rectangles aren't the only shape you can draw! To draw an oval, first set up a rectangle using *SetRect*. Follow the call to *SetRect* with a call to *FrameOval*. This function will draw the frame of an oval, neatly inscribed just within the boundaries established by *SetRect*. The one and only parameter to *FrameOval* is a *Rect* variable that *must* be preceded by an ampersand.

```
Rect   TheRect;

SetRect( &TheRect, 20, 20, 80, 100 );
FrameOval( &TheRect );
```

FillOval *FillOval* works just like *FillRect* — but it of course fills in an oval. After setting the boundaries of a rectangle using *SetRect*, call *FillOval* to fill an oval that fits into the rectangle with a pattern. Pass *FillOval* a *Rect* variable as the first parameter. The first parameter *must* be preceded by an ampersand character. The second parameter is the pattern that the Toolbox will use to fill in the oval. The available patterns are the same ones used by *FillRect*:

```
white, ltGray, gray, dkGray, black
```

Use the capitalization shown above for all patterns.

```
Rect   TheRect;

SetRect( &TheRect, 100, 100, 150, 150 );
FillOval( &TheRect, &ltGray );
```

The same caution that was stated for *FillRect* applies to *FillOval*. THINK C 7.0 users write *FillOval* using a "&" symbol before the fill shade:

```
FillOval( &TheRect, &white );   /* THINK C 7.0 */
```

Users of THINK C 6.0 don't:

```
FillOval( &TheRect, white );    /* THINK C 6.0 */
```

Text Drawing

TextSize Here's another function not covered in the book. You can change the size at which text is drawn using *TextSize*. Pass in the new size as the only parameter. Text size is given in *points*. A point isn't exactly equal to a pixel, but it's fairly close. The most popular size for text is 12 points.

```
TextSize( 24 );             /* Set to write double-sized text    */
DrawString( "\pTest24" );   /* This will appear in 24 point size */
TextSize( 12 );             /* Set to write normal-sized text    */
DrawString( "\pTest12" );   /* This will appear in 12 point size */
```

DrawString On a Macintosh, text is drawn — not written. To write a letter, word, or sentence, use *DrawString*. The only parameter *DrawString* needs is the text to draw. Always enclose the text in double quotes, and precede the text with "\p". Where the text appears is dependent on the previous call to *MoveTo*.

```
MoveTo( 35, 60 );             /* Here's where text will start */
DrawString( "\pTest text" );  /* Draw some text              */
```

Appendix C
If Something Should Go Wrong...

With the crystal-clear explanations and examples presented in this book, how could anything possibly go wrong in your programming endeavors? I'm sure it won't, but you might still want to browse through this appendix just for fun!

If you run into difficulty while trying to write a program, first look under one of the three main headings in this appendix:

- ✔ Errors While Trying to Compile.
- ✔ Errors While Trying To Run.
- ✔ Errors While Running.

Once you're at one of these three main headings, narrow your search by looking at the section's subheadings — they list the THINK C error message or some other descriptive information about various problems you might encounter.

Errors While Trying to Compile

Compilers are sticklers for detail, and are quick to complain when they find something out of place. The THINK C compiler is no exception. When you select Compile from the Source menu you might end up seeing an error message in the Compile Errors window. If that happens, look through the headings of this section to find the error message — and the means to correct the mistake.

The Compile Menu Item is Dim

You can't compile your source code if the menu item can't be selected! The THINK Project Manager doesn't know what to compile if your source code isn't open. If your source code file has been added to the project file, that's great. But now you have to open it by double-clicking on the file's name in the project window. Do that, then click the Source menu to see that the Compile option is now enabled.

Syntax Error

When THINK C encounters a word it doesn't recognize it calls it a *syntax error*. Here's what you'll see in the Compile Error window:

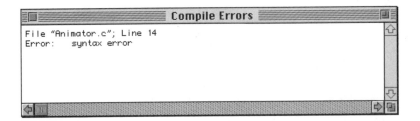

There are a few things that cause the THINK C compiler to issue an error of this type:

- A C word that is misspelled.
- A C word that uses incorrect uppercase or lowercase.
- A word that is not part of the C language.

Below are three declarations of a *float* variable named *GrandTotal*. Each is incorrect.

```
floot   GrandTotal;   /* Misspelled "float"                    */
Float   GrandTotal;   /* Incorrectly used uppercase letter "f" */
real    GrandTotal;   /* "real" isn't a C language word        */
```

Unexpected End-Of-File Error

Always remember the age-old words of the wise man, "For every opening brace there must be a closing brace." If you get an error message like the one pictured here, then your braces don't match up:

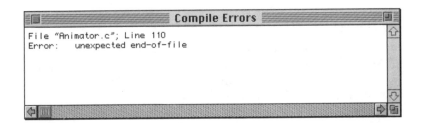

By omitting a brace you've confused the THINK C compiler — it can't figure out just where your source code ends. Double-click on the error message to move to the location of the error in your source code. Once there, hunt for a missing brace — most likely a closing one. Here's an example:

```
while ( count < 10 )
{
   DrawString( "\pTest " );
   count++;
MoveTo( 20, 40 );               /* should be a brace before this line */
DrawString( "\pEnd test" );
```

Argument Does Not Match Error

Many Toolbox functions require one or more parameters to be passed to them. Parameters are also called *arguments*. If the Compile Errors window shows an error message with the word "argument" in it — like the one below — then you'll need to take a close look at a function call.

Some people feel an appendix is no place for a quiz, but I think that any page of a book is fair game. So here goes. What is wrong with the arguments in each of these three Toolbox calls?

```
DrawString( "What, this isn't correct?" );
FrameRect( TheRect );
TheWindow = GetNewWindow( 128, 0L, -1L );
```

Each of the above calls would result in an error message that says something about an argument not matching the prototype. For the call to *DrawString*, I forgot to lead of the text with "\p". For *FrameRect* I forgot to precede *TheRect* with the ampersand — the "&" symbol. Finally, in the call to *GetNewWindow* I got the last parameter wrong. Here's a corrected version of each:

```
DrawString( "\pWhat, this isn't correct?" );
FrameRect( &TheRect );
TheWindow = GetNewWindow( 128, 0L, (WindowPtr)-1L );
```

If you get an error message that says "second argument to function 'FillRect' does not match prototype," then you have to check which version of THINK C you're using. Version 7.0 users write a call to FillRect like this:

```
FillRect( &TheRect, &white );    /* THINK C 7.0 */
```

Users of the older THINK C 6.0 must omit the "&" symbol before the fill shade, like this:

```
FillRect( &TheRect, white );    /* THINK C 6.0 */
```

Errors While Trying to Run

After successfully compiling your source code you'll want to test it out by selecting Run from the Project menu. That runs your code without building an application. That is, if all goes well. If it doesn't, check out the problems and solutions listed in this section.

First Off, Are You in the Right Section?

If you select Run from the Project menu you might see this dialog box:

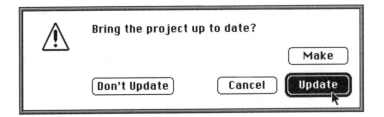

If you do, then that means that the THINK Project Manager is going to compile your code before running it. If that results in the Compile Errors window opening, then your mistake involves something the compiler didn't like. Check under the first section in this appendix, Errors While Trying to Compile — not here. This section is for the times when the code gets compiled successfully but something goes wrong as the THINK Project Manager tries to run the code. In those instances you won't see the Compile Errors window.

Nothing Seems to Happen

If you select Run from the Project menu and nothing happens, you may have forgotten to include the Toolbox initialization calls. If that's the case, the THINK Project Manager menu bar might flash once, and that's it. Don't forget to include these eight lines in every program:

```
InitGraf( &thePort );
InitFonts();
InitWindows();
InitMenus();
TEInit();
InitDialogs( 0L );
FlushEvents( everyEvent, 0 );
InitCursor();
```

The Program Runs, Then Quits Immediately

What went wrong if you select Run from the Project menu and you see your program's menu bar for a moment, and then your program ends? You probably forgot to give variable *AllDone* a value, or you gave it the wrong value. That would mean your event loop got skipped and your program assumed it was time to pack up and leave. Here's the part of your source code to examine:

```
AllDone = 0;    /* Must give AllDone a value of 0 here */

while ( AllDone < 1 )
{
   WaitNextEvent( everyEvent, &TheEvent, 0L, 0L );

   /* rest of program here */
```

Link Failed Error

When you run your code, two things might happen. First, if the source code has been changed since the last time you compiled, THINK C will compile it again. Second, THINK C will link the code. That just means that your source code is merged with whatever code is in the MacTraps library. If all goes well, your program will run on the screen. If all *doesn't* go well, you might see the following message on your screen:

link failed

A "link failed" error means the THINK Project Manager couldn't find some code it needs to complete the program. If this error occurs, THINK C will also open an error message window to let you know what code it couldn't find. Here's the most commonly seen message:

```
Link Errors
undefined: main
```

There are a couple of potential causes for this. The most common is that you forgot to add the source code file to the project. The project window should show that two files are in the project — the MacTraps library and your source code file. If the source code file isn't listed, select Add Files from the Source menu and add it now. Then try to run the code again.

A second possible cause of the above error is a simple spelling error on your part. All programs must contain the *main* function. The word "main" must be spelled correctly, it must appear in all lowercase letters, and it must be followed by a pair of parentheses:

```
main()    /*  CORRECT!  */
```

If you do something like the following, the THINK Project Manager will assume your *main* function is missing — even if all the source code for *main* appears in your program:

```
Main()    /*  WRONG!    */
```

If your source code has the word "main" spelled incorrectly or in the wrong case, retype it and then run the code again.

What if the error message window has something other than "undefined: main" as the message? If there are different undefined words, then you probably forgot to add the MacTraps library to the project. If that's the case, the error message window might have these or other undefined words listed:

```
┌──────────────────────── Link Errors ────────────────────────┐
│ undefined: black                                             │
│ undefined: screenBits                                        │
│ undefined: white                                             │
│ undefined: thePort                                           │
│                                                              │
└──────────────────────────────────────────────────────────────┘
```

Make sure the project window lists both the MacTraps library and the source
code file. If either one is missing, select Add Files from the Source menu and
add the missing file. Then try to run the code again.

A Bomb and a Frozen Mac

The scariest error of all is one that posts an alert with a bomb in it and a cryptic
message — like this:

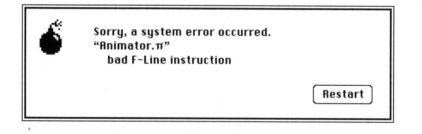

Even worse than the scary-looking alert is the fact that your Mac is frozen. The
only way to return it to a healthy condition is to restart it.

An alert like the one shown here is usually the result of a missing resource. For
example, the Mac gets hopelessly confused if your program attempts to display
a menu bar and there is no '*MBAR*' resource in the resource file.

There are a few different mistakes you could have made to end up in this pre-
dicament. Though they all sound a little different from one another, the net
result is that the Mac can't find one or more resources. If you encounter this
error, check all of the following:

✔ Did you forgot to make a resource file?

✔ Did you misname your resource file?

✔ Did you forget to add one or more resources to your resource file?

Here's the solution to each of the above pitfalls:

- ✔ Make a resource file!
- ✔ Give the resource file the same name as the project, followed by ".rsrc".
- ✔ Verify that the resource file has the '*WIND*', '*MENU*', and '*MBAR*' resources it needs.

Duplicate Resource Error

To make a project aware of source code you use the Add Files menu option to add the MacTraps library and your source code file to the project. Doesn't it then seem a little surprising that you don't have to add the resource file to the project? Many people think so — and they then go ahead and use the Add Files command to add their resource file to the project. If you do that, you'll see the following error message when you try to run the program:

> duplicate resource 'WIND',128

You get this error because the THINK Project Manager is clever enough to add the resource file to the project — without your help. When you add it, the Project Manager then has two copies of it. It then feels there are two copies of each resource. That's a no-no. Having two resources of the same type with the same ID is not allowed — and the THINK Project Manager will let you know it.

Errors While Running

So your program compiled and is running — great news! But wait a minute — you say it's not doing something that it should be doing? Check this section for answers to problems of this nature.

Things Aren't Getting Drawn in the Window

If your program is supposed to be drawing text or graphics to a window, but it's not, you might have omitted the call to *SetPort*. Make sure the call appears after the call to *GetNewWindow* — like this:

```
TheWindow = GetNewWindow( 128, 0L, (WindowPtr)-1L );
SetPort( TheWindow );
```

A Rectangle That Should Be There, Ain't

When drawing a rectangle, don't forget to first set up the coordinates for the rectangle. Without a call to *SetRect*, a call to *FrameRect* or *FillRect* won't work.

So you insist that you *did* call *SetRect*, but the rectangle still hasn't appeared? Double-check the order of the coordinates you passed to *SetRect*. Here's how *SetRect* views the four numbers you give it:

```
SetRect( &TheRect, left, top, right, bottom );
```

What do you suppose would be the result of this code:

```
SetRect( &TheRect, 10, 100, 50, 20 );
FrameRect( &TheRect );
```

Absolutely nothing! Why? Because the fourth number, 20, is less than the second number, 100. That means that you want the bottom of the rectangle to appear *above* the top of it — and that's something *SetRect* can't do.

The Mac Isn't Beeping When It Should

The Toolbox function *SysBeep* plays the system's alert sound on your Mac's internal speaker. In order for *SysBeep* to work properly, the Mac's sound must be turned on. If it's not, the menu bar might flash instead. To remedy this, select Control Panels from the Apple menu. Then double-click on the Sound control panel. Move the slider upward to turn the volume of your Mac up. Close the Sound control panel and try running your program again.

Appendix D

Glossary

argument: The same as a parameter — a variable or value passed to a function.

branch: Source code that allows a program to follow just one of two or more paths. The *switch* and the *if* statements are examples of C branches.

Central Processing Unit (CPU): The computer chip that serves as the "brains" of a computer.

comparative operator: A symbol that is used to compare the value on the operator's left side with the value on its right side. The less-than operator (<) is an example.

compiler: The software program that turns source code into code that a computer can understand.

coordinate system: The means of identifying every pixel on a monitor.

counter: A variable used to control the number of times a loop runs.

decrement: To decrease the value of a variable by one. The decrement operator is the "--" symbol (two minus signs).

desktop: The (usually) gray area of the screen that holds icons such as folders and the trash can.

dialog box: A special type of window that contains items — such as buttons — that allow a program user to communicate with the program.

event: Each action a program user takes is an event. A click of the mouse or a press of a key are each events. The C data type that holds information about an event is an *EventRecord*.

event loop: A section of source code that repeatedly watches and responds to events as they occur. The event loop runs until the program ends.

floating-point number: A number that has a decimal point. The numbers 5.24, 9200.0, and -72.3 are examples. The C data type for a floating-point number is the *float* type.

function: A section of source code that serves a specific task. That is, it has a single function to perform.

graphical user interface (GUI): The user interface of a computer helps the user communicate with the computer. When the user interface contains graphical elements such as icons, menus, and windows, it is said to be a graphical user interface.

icon: A small image that represents something. The trash can on the desktop is an example.

increment: To increase the value of a variable by one. The increment operator is the "++" symbol.

initialization: To give something a value for the first time. The group of functions that give the Toolbox some initial values at the start of a program are called Toolbox initialization functions.

integer: A whole number — a number with no decimal point. The numbers 7, 8214, and -42 are examples. The C data type for an integer is the *int* type.

loop: A section of source code that repeats itself. The *while* and the *for* statements are C loops.

memory: The chips in a computer that are used to store a program.

menu: A part of the graphical user interface that allows the computer user to make selections from a list of choices.

menu bar: A collection of menus, located at the top of the screen.

MBAR: A type of resource that represents a menu bar.

MENU: A type of resource that represents a single menu.

operating system: Software that controls the very basic activities of a computer, such as copying files.

operator: A symbol that is used to perform an operation on variables or values. An example is the addition operator (+), used to add two variables or values together.

parameter: A variable or value passed to a function.

part code: An integer that represents a part of the Macintosh screen or a part of a window. Used to determine where the mouse was when the mouse button was clicked by the user.

pixel: The smallest dot on the screen. There are approximately 70 pixels in a one-inch line.

pop-up menu: A menu that doesn't appear in the menu bar. Usually found in a dialog box.

port: The means of identifying which window should be used to draw to.

project file: A THINK C file that holds information about the contents of a project. The project file holds the name of the source code file and library used to create a single program.

RAM: Random Access Memory. A type of memory chip that holds a program as it runs.

rectangle: A commonly and easily drawn graphics shape. The C data type that holds information about a rectangle is the _Rect_ type.

resource: Information that defines one part of the graphical user interface, such as a menu or window. Resources are used in conjunction with source code.

ROM: Read Only Memory. A type of memory chip that holds information added by the computer manufacturer. The Macintosh ROM holds the Toolbox functions.

routines: Another word for functions.

short: A C data type that holds a whole number. The numbers 4, 991, and -56 are examples.

source code: A series of statements, or instructions, written in a computer language such as C.

string: A letter, word, or group of words. In C, a string is preceded by the "\p" characters and enclosed in quotes, as shown here: "\pExample string".

Toolbox function: A function written by Apple and stored in the ROM chips in the Macintosh.

type: Every variable has a type — a category that defines what kind of data the variable can hold.

variable: Something used to store a value. A variable has a name by which you refer to it.

WIND: A type of resource that represents a window.

window: The object that is used to display text and graphics. A window can usually be opened, moved, and closed by the user.

Index

IDG BOOKS WORLDWIDE REGISTRATION CARD

RETURN THIS REGISTRATION CARD FOR FREE CATALOG

Title of this book: **MAC PROGRAMMING FOR DUMMIES**

My overall rating of this book: ❑ Very good [1] ❑ Good [2] ❑ Satisfactory [3] ❑ Fair [4] ❑ Poor [5]

How I first heard about this book:

❑ Found in bookstore; name: [6] _____   ❑ Book review: [7]

❑ Advertisement: [8]   ❑ Catalog: [9]

❑ Word of mouth; heard about book from friend, co-worker, etc.: [10]   ❑ Other: [11]

What I liked most about this book:

_____
_____
_____

What I would change, add, delete, etc., in future editions of this book:

_____
_____
_____

Other comments:

_____
_____

Number of computer books I purchase in a year: ❑ 1 [12]   ❑ 2-5 [13]   ❑ 6-10 [14]   ❑ More than 10 [15]

I would characterize my computer skills as: ❑ Beginner [16] ❑ Intermediate [17] ❑ Advanced [18] ❑ Professional [19]

I use ❑ DOS [20] ❑ Windows [21] ❑ OS/2 [22] ❑ Unix [23] ❑ Macintosh [24] ❑ Other: [25] _____
(please specify)

I would be interested in new books on the following subjects:
(please check all that apply, and use the spaces provided to identify specific software)

❑ Word processing: [26]   ❑ Spreadsheets: [27]

❑ Data bases: [28]   ❑ Desktop publishing: [29]

❑ File Utilities: [30]   ❑ Money management: [31]

❑ Networking: [32]   ❑ Programming languages: [33]

❑ Other: [34]

I use a PC at (please check all that apply): ❑ home [35] ❑ work [36] ❑ school [37] ❑ other: [38] _____

The disks I prefer to use are ❑ 5.25 [39] ❑ 3.5 [40] ❑ other: [41] _____

I have a CD ROM: ❑ yes [42]   ❑ no [43]

I plan to buy or upgrade computer hardware this year: ❑ yes [44]   ❑ no [45]

I plan to buy or upgrade computer software this year: ❑ yes [46]   ❑ no [47]

Name: _____   Business title: [48] _____   Type of Business: [49] _____

Address (❑ home [50] ❑ work [51] /Company name: _____)

Street/Suite# _____

City [52] /State [53] /Zipcode [54]: _____   Country [55] _____

❑ **I liked this book!** You may quote me by name in future
IDG Books Worldwide promotional materials.

My daytime phone number is _____

IDG BOOKS

THE WORLD OF
COMPUTER
KNOWLEDGE

❏ YES!

Please keep me informed about IDG's World of Computer Knowledge
Send me the latest IDG Books catalog.